UNLOCKING *the* GATES

UNLOCKING *the* GATES

· ·

HOW AND WHY LEADING UNIVERSITIES ARE
OPENING UP ACCESS TO THEIR COURSES

TAYLOR WALSH

IN CONJUNCTION WITH ITHAKA S+R

PRINCETON UNIVERSITY PRESS

PRINCETON AND OXFORD

Copyright © 2011 by Princeton University Press

Published by Princeton University Press, 41 William Street,
Princeton, New Jersey 08540
In the United Kingdom: Princeton University Press, 6 Oxford Street,
Woodstock, Oxfordshire OX20 1TW
press.princeton.edu

Jacket photograph: Intersession, Harold Helm Auditorium (McCosh 50 lecture hall),
Princeton University. Photo by John V. Brennan.

Library of Congress Cataloging-in-Publication Data

Walsh, Taylor.
   Unlocking the gates : how and why leading universities are opening
up access to their courses / Taylor Walsh.
      p.   cm.
   Includes bibliographical references and index.
   ISBN 978-0-691-14874-8 (hardcover : alk. paper)
      1. Private universities and colleges—United States—Data processing.
2. Internet in education—United States.   3. University extension—United
States.   4. Education, Higher—Effect of technological innovations on—
United States.   I. Title.
   LB2395.7.W35 2011
   378.1758—dc22   2010029017

British Library Cataloging-in-Publication Data is available

This book has been composed in Sabon and Scala Sans LF by
Princeton Editorial Associates Inc., Scottsdale, Arizona.

Printed on acid-free paper. ∞
Printed in the United States of America

10 9 8 7 6 5 4 3 2 1

CONTENTS

FOREWORD

The seven case studies of "online courseware" initiatives presented in *Unlocking the Gates* are instructive in a number of ways. At the most basic level, the rich detail provided by Taylor Walsh (on the basis of numerous interviews she conducted with the key participants, as well as her close examination of memos, reports, reviews, and other written materials) allows the reader to understand the thinking that went into the Fathom and AllLearn experiments, MIT's bold creation of OpenCourseWare (OCW), Carnegie Mellon's Open Learning Initiative (OLI), Open Yale Courses (OYC), webcast.berkeley, and India's National Programme on Technology Enhanced Learning (NPTEL). Considered together, these seven initiatives illustrate the many different options open to universities that wish to undertake online courseware projects, which differ from the by-now standard distance education models.[1] This compilation of case studies demonstrates that there are multiple choices to be made in determining

---

[1]Online courses in higher education typically take the form of credit-bearing distance education for enrolled students—some of whom take a mix of online and traditional on-campus courses, while others complete entire degree programs online. According to a 2009 report on online education in the United States commissioned by the Sloan Consortium, "over 4.6 million students were taking at least one online course during the fall 2008 term," placing the rate of higher education students who take at least one of their courses online at more than one in four (Allen, Elaine, and Jeff Seaman, "Learning on Demand: Online Education in the United States, 2009," report supported by the Sloan Consortium and the Babson Survey Research Group, January 2010, 1). Colleges and universities can also use a growing number of specialized "course modules" provided by for-profit companies such as Statistics.com—in effect, outsourcing some of their teaching. See Kolowich, Steve, "The Specialists," *Inside Higher Ed,* April 5, 2010.

how much to invest in online courseware, what subjects to present, what audience to target, and what objectives—educational or reputational—to pursue. There is nothing approaching a single model, and comparing such different projects teaches a variety of lessons.

There was a time, not all that long ago, when some in higher education believed that digital technologies offered a ripe opportunity to advance the educational mission of the institution ready to venture into this terrain and, simultaneously, to make money that the institution could use for purposes of all kinds. That assumption proved to be incorrect, and it is perhaps the major lesson to be learned from Columbia's ill-fated effort to sell content through Fathom to a broad public and from the ultimately unsuccessful effort of Oxford, Princeton, Stanford, and Yale to market courseware to a primarily alumni constituency via a consortial entity called AllLearn. It is of course easier to understand what happened with hindsight than it was to anticipate problems at the start of these ambitious ventures; but the skeptic would have been right to warn against relying on untested assumptions when placing bets as big as the one Columbia placed on Fathom.

The MIT OCW saga is the best known of these initiatives. The leadership at MIT also flirted with a for-profit model but concluded, following a careful study of different options that included advice from outside consultants, that there was no likelihood of a vibrant market for what MIT wanted to provide: online access to comprehensive course materials, but with *no "tutoring" in using them and no "credentialing."* These two "no's" are extremely important. Studies of online courses that involve continuing interactions with faculty have warned for years that providing such interactions can be demanding and expensive.[2] We also know that it is the certificate or degree associated with completing a course of study that, in the minds of many, is what is really valuable (and thus marketable). Yet highly selective colleges and universities such

---

[2] I discussed some of these issues, and other questions related to digitization and commercialization, in the Romanes Lecture that I gave at the University of Oxford in 2000 (Bowen, William G., "At a Slight Angle to the Universe: The University in a Digitized, Commercialized Age," http://www.mellon.org/news_publications/publications/romanes.pdf/view).

as MIT have never seriously considered going down this "credentialing" path. The reasons are both understandable and straightforward. Universities such as MIT believe that the educational value that they offer to their carefully chosen students derives in large part from the on-campus and in-person setting in which teaching and research take place. They do not want to undercut this value proposition by giving "MIT credit" for a very different online offering that, in their view, would not be of "MIT quality." Presenting some of their own on-campus courses in a strictly online mode could also compromise their ability to compete with other elite universities for the very best students—many of whom expect face-to-face contact with professors and regular in-class interactions with talented peers.

Charles Vest, MIT's exceedingly able president at the time the OCW initiative was launched, was both clear and eloquent in stating that making the outlines of MIT courses available for free, worldwide, was in his mind a direct extension of MIT's basic educational mission and justifiable on those grounds alone. Vest also understood that a highly visible—and highly accessible—OCW would strengthen MIT's already stellar international reputation. In addition, MIT has found that its own student community benefits from easy online access to course syllabi, lecture notes, and other teaching materials which serve to enhance, not replace, traditional modes of instruction.

Yale's more targeted effort to produce truly high-quality versions of some of its most popular courses, with the "look and feel" of being in the Yale classroom, is said to have been well received by Yale's alumni and, like MIT OCW, has received significant positive attention from the press. Yale believes that it has gotten good value from its investment in OYC. Benefits do not have to be financial to be consequential.

Webcast.berkeley is intended primarily to serve instructional purposes on the home campus. This is an instance of a large public university investing its own resources in the creation of relatively low-tech online instructional materials. The contrast with the elegance of OYC is striking. Severe resource constraints have clearly shaped Berkeley's approach and led it to pioneer in the development of low-cost instructional materials that are helpful to students who cannot attend a lecture at the time it is given or simply value the convenience of studying the material online at whatever time and place suit them.

India's NPTEL represents yet another model that is suited to local circumstances. The Indian government has already begun investing heavily in online teaching because of its need to take fuller advantage of valuable teaching resources concentrated in elite institutes. The burgeoning demand for higher education in India argues strongly in favor of making fuller use of the country's top academic talent—of extending the reach of these faculty in cost-effective ways. It seems likely that other countries facing comparable needs to augment their teaching resources will experiment with similar models. Active government sponsorship of NPTEL addresses directly the considerable upfront investments in online resources that are required and also provides a valuable imprimatur.

One project studied by Walsh, Carnegie Mellon's OLI, is so different from the others in certain key respects that I discuss it at greater length. As Walsh explains in detail in Chapter 4, Carnegie Mellon used generous support from the William and Flora Hewlett Foundation to construct entirely new online introductory courses in fields such as statistics. What is distinctive about the OLI approach is that it does not simply mimic traditional classroom methods of teaching; rather, it uses embedded cognitive tutors, interactive techniques, and rapid feedback to create a rich learning environment that takes full advantage of the features of the online medium. And there is some evidence that students who use this sophisticated form of online teaching in basic courses such as introductory statistics have learning outcomes at least as good as—and sometimes better than—those of comparable students taught in the traditional way.

The potential ramifications of the OLI approach should be thought about in the context of the current financial constraints that are afflicting higher education. In contemplating the long-run uses of various types of sophisticated online courseware, such as the OLI courses, it is essential to recognize the dramatic changes in the economic landscape that have occurred between the time when the initiatives Walsh has studied were first undertaken (in the late 1990s through 2006) and today. As William E. Kirwan, chancellor of the University of Maryland, observed,

> We are in a period of fiscal *famine*, experiencing unprecedented resource trauma that threatens the ability of many, if not most of our institutions to carry out their core missions. . . . I never thought I would see the day when our best endowed private universities would have to borrow money to meet annual operating expenses, lay off staff and close programs. Nor could I have imagined public universities furloughing Nobel Prize winners and other distinguished faculty. The breadth and depth of the fiscal carnage are both stunning and debilitating.

Kirwan then goes on to call attention to "the dim prospects for recovery in the foreseeable future."[3] In the case of the state university systems in particular, where there may be the best opportunity to make use of new online courseware, I am every bit as pessimistic as Kirwan. I am skeptical that these state systems will ever again enjoy the level of general support from state governments for teaching programs that they have known in the past. The fiscal realities of the states (including deep-seated opposition to new taxes), combined with the pressures for more spending on programs of other kinds (including prisons and health care), make it very unlikely that state appropriations for teaching programs will recover. Moreover, we should not forget that, as three experienced University of Michigan administrators have pointed out, "State support of public universities, on a per student basis, has been declining for over two decades; it was at the lowest level in 25 years even before the current economic crisis, which has caused state after state to further reduce appropriations for higher education, with cuts ranging as high as 20 percent to 30 percent."[4]

[3]Kirwan, William E., "The Research University of the Future," speech delivered March 22, 2010, before the AAU Government Relations Professionals, www.aau.edu/WorkArea/showcontent.aspx?id=10590.

[4]Courant, Paul, James Duderstadt, and Edie Goldenberg, "Needed: A National Strategy to Preserve Public Research Universities," *Chronicle of Higher Education,* online edition, January 3, 2010, http://chronicle.com/article/A-Plan-to-Save-Americas/63358/. For a vivid account of the situation in the state of Nevada, see Hebel, Sara, "State Cuts Are Pushing Public Colleges into Peril," *Chronicle of Higher Education,* online edition, March 14, 2010.

One obvious implication of this dire situation is that it is going to be exceedingly difficult for educational institutions—private as well as public—to experiment with the creation of new online courseware initiatives or even to continue to subsidize the costs of current initiatives *unless there are compelling reasons for making such investments.* As Walsh points out, to date all of the U.S. initiatives have been funded either internally or by foundations pursuing philanthropic aims (with the Hewlett Foundation having been by far the most important grant maker in this field). Questions of sustainability have been regularly raised but rarely answered.

At the same time, I think that present and prospective economic realities dictate that there be a serious rethinking of the way some forms of instruction are provided, especially in those parts of the public sector that have been hurt the most by funding cuts. It is in this context that Carnegie Mellon's OLI is especially interesting—not so much for its near-term impact on teaching in the "parent sector" in which it was born (the world of the elite private research university) as for its potential impact in the much larger and much needier public sector.

The OLI is exciting precisely because it may offer the possibility of achieving real productivity gains by substituting well-designed online instruction for the labor-intensive ways in which we still teach many basic courses, including some that lend themselves to less labor-intensive teaching methods.[5] I am well aware that in

---

She writes: "As the chancellor of Nevada's higher-education system faced yet another round of budget cuts last month, he said that he had no reason to make misleading claims that 'the sky is falling' on public colleges in his state. The truth, he said, is that it is. . . . Weeks later state lawmakers approved a 6.9 percent mid-year cut for higher education, a reduction that came on top of a 24 percent cut in state funds the system had already been dealt in last year's budget session. As a result, Nevada universities are preparing to close colleges, departments, and programs; demoralized professors are fleeing the state; and thousands of students are being shut out of classes at community colleges. The prospect of shutting down an entire institution remains a 'distinct possibility' for the future, the chancellor says."

[5]In my view, Carnegie Mellon was wise to focus its efforts on courses like introductory statistics, in which there are more or less standard notions of core content and at least something approaching "a single right answer" to many questions. It is far from clear to me that the OLI approach would be as useful in teaching subjects that generally require much more nuanced discussion, such as literature, ethics, and international politics.

some quarters speaking of "productivity gains" is close to blasphemy. But we have to get over that mindset: we just can't afford to continue doing business as usual. We have to find ways to do more with less. Resources saved in this way could be redeployed to teach more students or, conceivably, to teach advanced students more effectively.

Some readers may know that I am a co-author (with William J. Baumol) of an explanation for rising costs in higher education that has stood the test of time. Writing initially about the performing arts, Baumol and I argued that the costs of labor-intensive activities such as performances by string quartets and standard classroom teaching would inevitably rise faster than costs in general—i.e., faster than the general inflation rate. This phenomenon is sometimes called "the cost disease," and its presence in higher education, going back a century or more, is well documented.[6] Now, more than 40 years after we first articulated the economic basis for the cost disease, I am wondering if the time is finally at hand when new methods of using online teaching technologies in basic introductory courses might change things. I have been on record for some time as being skeptical about the likely effects on productivity in higher education of various new technologies.[7] But the evidence that Walsh presents about the work at Carnegie Mellon has caused me to rethink my position. This could turn out to be the time when a modest number of large investments aimed at developing online courses in applicable subjects (those in which there is more or less a single right answer to basic questions) could have a large impact. I agree with Bill Gates that developing a small number of really well-designed online courses is preferable to having a large number of less-effective offerings.[8] There should be opportunities here to take advantage of substantial economies of scale, even though creating mechanisms for assembling the needed capital could prove challenging.

[6]Bowen, William G., "The Economics of the Major Private Universities," Carnegie Commission on the Future of Higher Education, Berkeley, Calif., 1968.

[7]Bowen, "At a Slight Angle to the Universe."

[8]Gates, Bill, "2010 Annual Letter from Bill Gates," http://www.gatesfoundation.org/annual-letter/2010/Pages/bill-gates-annual-letter.aspx.

If these optimistic ruminations prove to have merit—and that is what we must find out through further research—it might be possible to save significant amounts of resources while actually improving outcomes. I don't know if this is only wishful thinking, but I am increasingly convinced that the fiscal realities of our time obligate us to at least examine carefully new ideas for providing instruction. And the examination needs to be rigorous. Walsh is clear in noting that careful evaluation of the actual impact of most of these projects has been difficult and limited. Of course, the market itself rendered a verdict on Fathom and AllLearn. The OLI initiative is intriguing in part because it lends itself to standard statistical assessments of outcomes—of what was achieved, and at what cost.

Additionally, a word should be said about the likelihood that various online learning projects will have different impacts within the various sectors of higher education. I think we need to be realistic in the assumptions we make about what is likely to happen in different settings. Institutions like Yale and MIT may be willing and able to continue to support initiatives that are important to them in terms of their missions and their reputations. But few other institutions will be in a position to make such investments, especially in the present financial climate. Universities such as Carnegie Mellon, with great faculty strength in cognitive science and a track record of pioneering work in instructional technologies, should be encouraged to continue to create innovative online teaching environments—and ways need to be found for the educational community at large to help underwrite their work. It is unlikely, however, that the highly selective private colleges and universities (including Carnegie Mellon itself) will be the consumers of such courseware, at least in the near term. As already explained, these universities specialize in an educational model that puts a high premium on direct faculty-student interaction, even in beginning courses. Over time, even the most selective institutions may also find ways (and I suspect that they will) to use online courseware to enhance their educational offerings. Students who enroll at these universities will, increasingly, come to college expecting to find much instructional material available electronically, and colleges and universities would be unwise to ignore this appetite for online resources.

Today the greatest opportunity to use approaches such as the OLI to improve educational outcomes and reduce costs seems to me to exist within the public sector—in both community colleges and BA-granting institutions. The economic need to conserve resources is greatest here, and the scale of the institutions meshes well with this approach. The most courageous of the state systems will have an opportunity (as Nancy Zimpher, chancellor of SUNY, has suggested) to re-imagine the faculty role in undergraduate education. They will do this by providing more opportunities for the ablest teachers to have an even greater impact on education than they do today, especially at advanced levels. In time, some of these public institutions, hard pressed as they are today to meet escalating demands on them, could be models for cost-effective modes of teaching basic courses that at least some of today's "richer" institutions will want to emulate.

Countries such as India are at still another place along this instructional continuum. They have an especially pressing need for new methods of delivering content to rapidly increasing student populations. Many of their elite institutions have the research and intellectual capacity to invent or to adapt new teaching technologies, and centralized funding will enable them to invest collectively and for the long run. Government sponsorship may also reduce the risk that internal disagreements—i.e., faculty opposition—will threaten the success of a project. It may be in countries such as India that online courseware will have its greatest impact in the next decade.

A final point, perhaps obvious in what has already been said, is that a hundred flowers should be allowed to bloom. Each institution has its own peculiarities and its own history. What makes sense for University A today may never make sense for University B, or may make sense for University B only ten years from now. This variety of experiences, and of time horizons, should be considered a good thing, not a cause for either envy or boasting.

Unlocking the Gates is a splendid introduction to a fascinating and fast-changing world. Unless I am badly mistaken, over time all sectors of higher education will be affected in one way or another by what are truly transformational changes in the way knowledge is created and disseminated. Now that increasing numbers of universities, including some of the most prestigious, are using technology to let the world into their precincts, it will never again be possible to lock the gates.

William G. Bowen

The world's great universities are defined by walls. Physical walls demarcate the space of the campus and distinguish it from its surroundings, but less visible barriers also block entry to those outside. Tens of thousands of students apply to each of the most selective U.S. universities every year, yet only a small fraction are admitted through the gates. Since the formation of the modern university nearly two centuries ago, this fact has troubled many, prompting reform efforts on a number of fronts. Advocates have fought to eliminate impediments to higher education on the basis of class, gender, religion, and race—with impressive success. Yet significant barriers remain, especially to the top-tier universities.

The internet may prove to be the most powerful tool yet in the struggle for greater access to higher education. Digital technology and the networked environment offer transformative possibilities for how information is delivered, who can view it, and at what cost. Not only has the quantity of scholarly materials available online exploded over the past two decades, but hundreds of online programs and courses—even entire online-only universities—have offered new forms of access to education around the world. Technology has presented institutions of higher learning with the opportunity to revamp their practice. But across the higher-education spectrum, the rate of change has been decidedly uneven, ranging from enthusiastic overhauls to cautious, incremental adjustments. While the most elite universities have implemented a wealth of digital technologies to enhance, for example, administrative and communications-related functions affecting enrolled students' daily lives, in few cases have they applied that technology to more radical ends, such as expanding the audiences their core undergraduate programs can reach.

Unlocking the Gates examines one small but important set of experiments in such expansion: projects initiated by elite universities to share online course materials with the public and unlock their gates to the world. Collectively dubbed "online courseware" for the purposes of this book, the initiatives profiled here involve converting traditional course content, originally developed for enrolled students, into web-based versions available to a mass audience. Although relatively limited in number, these experiments have been closely watched. The stature and prestige of the universities involved ensured that the outcomes, whether positive or negative, would have repercussions across higher education. The few highly selective institutions currently pursuing online courseware may prove to be outliers; perhaps most universities in the very top tier will never drastically alter the audiences their teaching materials reach in light of technological advances. But, as this book shows, the online courseware initiatives undertaken by some of the world's best universities may be harbingers of major changes to come.

Out of a complex mix of motives and goals, these universities have elected to give away portions of their core intellectual assets to learners beyond their traditional student populations. In one sense, online courseware radically expands access to education, as it exposes the university's course content to audiences no longer limited by geography, age, or prior qualifications; anyone with a computer and internet access is welcome. But unlike longer-standing efforts to broaden educational access through admissions measures like need-based aid or affirmative action, online courseware has offered only limited exposure to and participation in the traditional university experience. Barriers to content may be lowered, but other key aspects of a university education—peer and faculty interactions, advising, grading, and (perhaps most significantly) the granting of credit and awarding of degrees—often remain available exclusively to enrolled students. Why would a university choose to give (or sell) its course materials to the general public? What are the implications of those decisions? And how might these first forays into online courseware shed light on greater changes to come for the selective university in the twenty-first century?

Scope and Organization

Unlocking the Gates is organized as a series of case studies that illustrate the histories of individual online courseware projects. These particular initiatives were selected from numerous examples of related projects to convey the variety of approaches that participating universities have taken to online courseware.

Case studies of two now-defunct initiatives—Fathom, a Columbia University–led for-profit endeavor, and AllLearn, a consortial effort on the part of Oxford, Princeton, Stanford, and Yale to sell courseware primarily to their alumni—point to challenges faced by revenue-generating projects and provide crucial context for the subsequent development of open and free programs. The story of MIT OpenCourseWare (OCW)—the first and most prominent of such open initiatives, and the only one to provide course materials (e.g., syllabi, homework assignments, lecture notes) from virtually every course taught there—describes many foundational principles of the field. A chapter on Carnegie Mellon's Open Learning Initiative (OLI) highlights a unique effort to incorporate the university's expertise in the science of learning into a fully interactive online environment, open to the public and geared toward achieving measurable learning outcomes. Open Yale Courses (OYC) and webcast.berkeley offer two distinct approaches to video-based lecture capture, providing recorded lectures so that remote users can glimpse the traditional classroom experience at these universities. Finally, a chapter on India's National Programme on Technology Enhanced Learning (NPTEL) provides an international perspective, describing a partnership between government and higher education to address challenges of national importance. Three of the seven programs profiled here in depth—MIT OCW, the OLI, and OYC—were funded primarily by the William and Flora Hewlett Foundation, which also supported much of the research for this book.

Collectively the case studies included here represent a range of funding models (foundation-, government-, and self-funded) and hail from geographically diverse—though all highly selective—public and private parent institutions. They demonstrate that online courseware is not a monolithic concept; there are as many ways to design and operate an online courseware project as there are universities doing so. And as the following chapters will demonstrate, online courseware projects respond to and fuel specific institutional goals: each initiative is shaped by the circumstances of its host institution—the strategic opportunities the parent university is choosing to pursue, its particular strengths and weaknesses, and its resource base all influence its online courseware offerings.

The case studies describe each initiative's beginnings, unique objectives, business model, course offerings, relationship with its host institution(s) and funder(s), efforts at self-evaluation, and plans for financial sustainability. An introductory chapter sets the context in which these initiatives emerged, and the concluding chapter analyzes them in relation to one another and draws a set of findings from the facts laid out in the case studies. The conclusion also addresses some of the broader questions these initiatives raise for the higher-education sector, including: How can universities distinguish themselves in competition for reputation, students, and faculty as their research and teaching outputs become more widely available online? How will the open-access trends sweeping the online world affect the business model and societal role of the elite university, traditionally sealed off to the vast majority of the public? Can selective higher-education institutions maintain the essential strategies that have sustained them for centuries while redefining access to the knowledge they produce via new technologies? An epilogue explores the potential effects of these online courseware experiments on higher education, even at the most selective institutions.

A Note on Methodology

Research for this book began in June 2008 and concluded in April 2010; it relied primarily on information gathered from interviews and primary and secondary documents.

The research started with a landscape review of the online courseware field aimed at selecting exemplary projects as subjects for the case studies at the core of the book. Several initiatives at selective universities were chosen from an array of existing projects to convey the variability of online courseware, as well as to highlight points of comparison and contrast between programs.

Extensive literature reviews of media coverage and other secondary literature were undertaken at an early stage of the research. Archival materials and other primary sources, provided by the projects themselves as well as by funders, were consulted whenever possible. The volume of preserved and available documents varied widely from one initiative to the next. For instance, MIT OCW has kept an extensive, if uncatalogued, archive of documents related to the project's history, but it has not been possible to locate any original records of Fathom and AllLearn, perhaps due to their independent status as organizations separate from the universities that created them. Budget figures and usage statistics cited here are self-reported, although Google Analytics data were consulted for the projects that have subscribed to that tool and were willing to grant access to the data.

Naturally investigations of these online resources relied on extensive consultation of each project's website. Researching Fathom and AllLearn, initiatives that were shuttered several years ago and no longer have live websites, required the use of the Internet Archive. However, this useful but imperfect tool does not preserve all of these websites' former functionality, limiting the ability to fully recreate the user experience in those cases.

Over 80 individuals were interviewed in the course of researching this book. For each project profiled, interviews were conducted with project directors and other key staffers, associated faculty members, and senior university administrators (including current and former presidents and provosts), almost always in conjunction with site visits to relevant campuses. Program staff at key foundations were also interviewed. Whenever possible, interviews were conducted in person by the author, and they often included follow-up communication in the form of brief phone calls or email messages. A full list of on-the-record interviews is included after the reference list at the back of the book.

Prior to publication, project leaders from each initiative profiled here were given the opportunity to review the relevant chapter to provide any needed corrections or further explanation. Editing of the manuscript concluded in July 2010.

Acknowledgments

This book has been enabled in every way by the support of the William and Flora Hewlett Foundation. In addition to providing funding that allowed me to explore the online courseware space full time, the Foundation's leadership and the staff of the education program—whose efforts in the area of Open Educational Resources have been nothing short of pioneering—were unfailingly generous with their broad and deep knowledge of this field. Specific thanks are due to Paul Brest, Marshall "Mike" Smith, Catherine Casserly, Victor Vuchic, Jennie Fong, Phoenix Wang, Kathy Nicholson, and Sally Tracy. The transparency that Hewlett demonstrated by permitting unfettered access to Foundation records, as well as its encouragement of a dispassionate and objective study of a field it has seeded, truly embraced the spirit of openness that it encourages in its grantees.

Creating an account of such recent history is impossible without the cooperation of those who were there. In writing this book I have had the privilege of meeting and interviewing many of the principal figures in the field. These leaders in higher education shared their time, insights, and candid recollections to help me piece together an oral history of online courseware's development. Special thanks are also due to each of the project leaders, who, in addition to providing archival materials and relevant usage data, often served as gracious hosts during my visits to their respective campuses. In this regard, I am particularly grateful to Mangala Sunder Krishnan of IIT Madras for his assistance in planning a productive research trip to India in the spring of 2009.

This project found its first champions in Roger Schonfeld, Ithaka S+R's manager of research, and Kevin Guthrie, president of ITHAKA. I am indebted to them for having the idea to take on such a study in the first place, for trusting me to adapt and execute their concept, and, above all, for their constant counsel and guidance. Schonfeld in particular has shepherded this project from inception to completion and has served as my primary interlocutor on the analysis that follows. In offering incisive, always constructive feedback that proved essential in shaping the direction of this book, Guthrie was joined by Laura Brown, ITHAKA's executive vice president of strategy and research.

Since commencing this project in June 2008, I have had the privilege of belonging to a truly gifted team of strategic thinkers who work daily to help the academic community transform scholarly communications. In addition to Brown and Schonfeld, I am deeply indebted to the other members of the Ithaka S+R team. Particular thanks are due to Ross Housewright, who was frequently the first reader of these pages, and to Sabrina Manville, Nancy Maron, and Kirby Smith for their prescient editorial comments on issues large and small. Kate Wittenberg's willingness to share her considerable expertise in the publication process, as well as Tom Nygren's assistance in framing this book's prefatory section, were an enormous help. The provocative questions posed by members of S+R, also including Jennifer Kim and Matthew Loy, were powerful drivers in shaping my thinking on this subject matter and its presentation, and their readiness to turn a sharp editorial eye on the manuscript has improved the present volume immensely. Perhaps most of all, I am thankful for my colleagues' friendship and encouragement; they have both kept me on track and provided welcome distraction throughout the long process of bringing this book to publication.

Beyond S+R, I have benefited from the help of ITHAKA's finance and legal teams in some of the administrative tasks related to this project. Marita LaMonica and Heidi McGregor, of ITHAKA's marketing and communications group, deserve special mention for their welcome contributions. The research assistance provided by Mellon Foundation librarians Lisa Bonifacic and Ellen Nasto, as well as S+R intern Julia TerMaat, was nothing short of heroic. And day-to-day office life was enlivened considerably by Bernadette Aquart and Deborah Longino. The collegial atmosphere bred at ITHAKA was the ideal environment in which to research and write one's first book, and I will always be grateful to those who made it so.

Several outside readers—Henry Bienen, Saul Fisher, Ira Fuchs, Dan Greenstein, Diane Harley, Clifford Lynch, Christopher Mackie, and Jo Ellen Parker—generously read the manuscript in full at an early stage and provided invaluable suggestions. The productive feedback from these experts in their fields was a major contribution to this book's final state.

I have been aided at all stages of this project by the wise counsel of William G. Bowen, whose gracious offer to write the foreword was only the most obvious of his many kindnesses toward me over the past several years.

I am grateful to everyone at Princeton University Press who endeavored to help bring this book to fruition, with particular thanks owed to my editor, Peter Dougherty, who both instantly "got" what I was trying to do and pushed me to think about the topic in new ways. His very patient assistant Christopher Chung, Terri O'Prey and Dimitri Karetnikov of the Press's editing and production team, and the meticulous Peter Strupp and the staff of Princeton Editorial Associates, Inc., have also been a pleasure to work with.

The final word of thanks is, of course, for my family: Richard, Candice, and Logan Walsh, and Sam Ryan. Their love, support, and much-needed good humor have enabled everything else.

I could never have written this book without the participation and assistance of so many. But reliant as I have been on the helpful contributions of others, responsibility for any shortcomings or errors rests solely with me.

1

INTRODUCTION:
CONTEXT AND BACKGROUND

The term "online courseware"—used throughout this book to refer to initiatives in which traditional degree-granting institutions convert course materials, originally designed for their own undergraduates, into non-credit-bearing online versions for the general public—is perhaps best defined in relation to better-established forms of university teaching: traditional undergraduate education and credit-bearing distance education.

The traditional undergraduate experience, at the core of modern higher education, can be divided into pedagogical and residential components. The basic unit of the pedagogical component is the course, which is taught in person to enrolled students in lecture or seminar format and is supplemented by features like peer interaction, discussion sessions with teaching assistants, hands-on labs, and independent work. Students may ask questions of their professors during class or office hours, receive feedback on their performance, and earn credits; if they complete all required coursework satisfactorily, the university eventually grants them degrees. The residential component of the traditional undergraduate experience includes a leafy campus, dormitory living, a host of extracurricular activities, participation in collegiate traditions, amenities like increasingly lavish student centers and gymnasiums, and constant opportunities for peer interaction in a diverse environment.[1] Of course, beyond those activities that directly contribute to the undergraduate experience, universities

---

[1] Although they may lack dormitories, commuter institutions retain other aspects of this experience through the on-campus interactions afforded their students.

also do much more. In *The Idea of the University: A Reexamination,* Jaroslav Pelikan notes that the university is defined not only by the "extension of knowledge through undergraduate and graduate teaching," but also by its "advancement of knowledge through research . . . training that involves both knowledge and professional skill in the professional programs or schools of the university; preservation of knowledge in libraries, galleries, and museums; and diffusion of knowledge through scholarly publications. A university may do many other things, and all of them do."[2] These additional elements of the university enterprise are beyond the scope of this book, but they are vital aspects of higher education's overall contribution to society.

The online environment has provided a means for universities to expand their teaching activities beyond the walls of the classroom, allowing course content and pedagogical practices developed on campus to serve a broader group of students than the physical campus can support. Such external course dissemination efforts have most commonly taken the form of online degree programs, a type of distance education in which the university provides educational materials, along with some level of instruction and credentialing, in exchange for student tuition or fees. In other words, the pedagogical component of the traditional university experience is unbundled from the residential component, and the medium in which courses are delivered changes. This distance education model has been embraced by for-profit institutions, such as the University of Phoenix, as well as by traditional university systems, as in the University of Maryland's University College and Penn State's Global Campus, which offer online degree programs in addition to on-campus instruction.[3] In their capacity to serve a larger and

[2]Pelikan, Jaroslav, *The Idea of the University: A Reexamination,* New Haven: Yale University Press, 1992, 76. Emphasizing the importance of the research function performed by the United States' premier universities, Jonathan Cole writes that "although the transmission of knowledge is a core mission of our universities, it is not what makes them the best institutions of higher learning in the world. We are the greatest because our finest universities are able to produce . . . the most important fundamental knowledge and practical research discoveries" (Cole, Jonathan R., *The Great American University: Its Rise to Preeminence, Its Indispensable National Role, Why It Must Be Protected,* New York: PublicAffairs, 2009, 5).

[3]Some of the most selective institutions also offer online courses for credit. In that sector, though, such distance education programs have largely been confined to professional masters

geographically disparate student body, these credit-bearing online degree programs function much like correspondence courses did historically, albeit with significant technological upgrades.[4]

But in recent years, an additional set of initiatives have emerged that, despite sharing some features with distance education efforts, do not securely belong in this existing category. Online courseware further unbundles the pedagogical components of the university. Not only is the professor-created content offered without credit attached to it, but online courseware providers also typically strip away many of the interactions characteristic of traditional teaching—interactions which distance credit-bearing education efforts try to retain in some form.[5] MIT's OpenCourseWare (OCW) is explicit about this distinction, describing its courseware initiative as providing course *materials,* rather than complete online courses. The audience for these materials is also radically different—no longer restricted to a finite and well-understood enrolled student population, online courseware is offered to the general public.

---

degrees or schools of continuing education and do not affect core undergraduate course offerings. The sociologist Martin Trow hints at why this might be, writing that "the non-credit learning of universal-access education is made to order for 'anywhere, anytime'; this is what the correspondence wings of the university's extension school have been doing for a very long time. . . . extension does not deal internally with a powerful academic senate; the administrators own the curriculum as well as the budget, and that makes innovation a good deal easier than in the rest of the university" (Trow, Martin, "The Development of Information Technology in American Higher Education," *Daedalus* 126, no. 4 [Fall 1997], 297).

[4] Outside the United States, such activities have been going on for decades in the form of open universities, distance education–based institutions with few or no entry requirements that are designed to provide broad access to education. The first of such institutions, the United Kingdom's Open University, was founded in the 1960s, and similar institutions have since been created all over the world.

[5] The concept of such unbundling assisted by information technology extends beyond the specific instance of online courseware: as the higher education researchers William Massy and Robert Zemsky have written, "traditionally, higher education institutions have combined several functions in their faculty. Faculty are architects as they design learning programs; navigators as they help advise students in their course of study; instructors when they lecture; mentors when they help students form a sense of connectedness to the world; and evaluators and certifiers as they decide to grant students grades or degrees. IT will allow educational providers to separate some key functions traditionally bundled together" (Massy, William F., and Robert Zemsky, "Using Information Technology to Enhance Academic Productivity," white paper prepared by Educom's National Learning Infrastructure Initiative [NLII], http://net.educause.edu/ir/library/html/nli0004.html, 4). One program that does attempt to replicate instruction at a distance, the Open Learning Initiative, is the subject of this book's fourth chapter.

Each of these offerings—traditional classroom teaching, distance education over the internet, and online courseware—has a corresponding value proposition. The traditional undergraduate experience allows students to learn, network with faculty and peers,[6] experience personal growth,[7] and, perhaps most importantly, receive credentials certifying their achievements. In "Universities in the Digital Age," John Seely Brown and Paul Duguid ask what "are higher education's 'core competencies'? What do its accredited institutions do that other institutions don't? Why are individuals, families, states, and government agencies willing to invest so much in it? What is it they want—and the system offers —that's so valuable? The easiest answer . . . is that it offers degrees."[8] Distance education offers a slightly different, yet no less clear, value proposition: much of the networking and the residential experience may be absent, but online degree programs still allow students to learn and earn credits. What the student gives the university (tuition dollars) and what the university provides to the student in exchange (instruction, credentialing) is well understood.

But in the shift to online courseware, in which course materials are offered for enrichment only, the nature of the exchange becomes far more subtle—and complex. Many of these initiatives do not generate revenue for the universities, and none offers credit to the users. Online courseware requires no formal transaction, no rela-

---

[6]Not only can a strong peer group facilitate students' social development and lifelong network of contacts, it can even push individuals to perform better academically. Based on their empirical research, Gordon C. Winston and David J. Zimmerman found that "peer effects exist—students' characteristics and behavior do, indeed, influence other students' behavior. . . . strong students tend to increase peers' academic performance, and weak students tend to reduce it" (Winston, Gordon C., and David J. Zimmerman, "Peer Effects in Higher Education," in *College Choices: The Economics of Where to Go, When to Go, and How to Pay for It*, ed. Caroline M. Hoxby, Chicago: University of Chicago Press, 2004, 418).

[7]As Stanford University President Gerhard Casper has noted, "universities, especially the American college, also perform the function of furthering the process of coming of age, of growing up. . . . The rite of passage is one reason, anthropologically speaking, Americans go to college" (Casper, Gerhard, "Come the Millennium, Where the University?" address to the annual meeting of the American Educational Research Association, San Francisco, April 18, 1995, http://www.stanford.edu/dept/pres-provost/president/speeches/950418millennium.html, 6).

[8]Brown, John Seely, and Paul Duguid, "Universities in the Digital Age," *Change* 28, no. 4 (August 1996), 12.

tionship between the institution and its students. Neither group owes anything to the other: students (users) are under no obligation to give online courseware their full attention or to demonstrate any mastery over the material, and the professors and institutions that create the materials do not have to provide their audience with support in using them.

As Table 1.1 illustrates, online courseware projects therefore mark a significant shift in most components of a university course. The offerings, the audience, and the value proposition inherent in online courseware can differ dramatically from their counterparts in traditional or distance education, raising the question of why some selective institutions are pursuing initiatives in this terrain. As this book shows, the internet has provided institutions of higher education with an extraordinary opportunity to share a key asset—their courses—with the public, a service which by all accounts has been an end unto itself. But online courseware has also enabled universities to use courses to accomplish other things—strategic objectives that may have little to do with teaching and learning.

Of course, universities have always been interested in activities like outreach, marketing, attracting attention from outside academia, distinguishing themselves from competitors, alumni relations, and appealing to government and other funders. These institutions have historically engaged the public in a variety of ways—on-campus events, summer programs for high school students, faculty-led educational trips for alumni, continuing education courses for local adults—all of which in some way expose external constituencies to the life of the university. In addition, students in far-flung locales have long benefited from the intellectual output of faculty at the country's most elite institutions through the textbooks those faculty have authored, which have enormous reach beyond the gates of a professor's home institution.[9] The internet has affected and will continue to affect each of these activities, allowing uni-

---

[9]Former MIT President Charles Vest shared an anecdote about studying from an MIT professor's textbook as a student in West Virginia (interview with Charles Vest, 9/30/08). That experience would later contribute to Vest's enthusiasm for the OpenCourseWare concept.

TABLE 1.1
Characteristics of University Teaching

Traditional Degree Programs	Online Degree Programs	Online Courseware
Course materials	Course materials	Course materials
In-person	Online	Online
Enrolled students	Enrolled students	Non-enrolled students
Credit-bearing	Credit-bearing	Non-credit-bearing
Instruction	Instruction	? Instruction
Fee-based	Fee-based	? Fee-based

versities to potentially reach wider audiences by migrating them to digital formats.

But the internet, perhaps for the first time, has allowed universities to use *courses* as a means of furthering these other aims—all of which are far afield from the original goals and value propositions of the traditional university course. Unlike other opportunities for community engagement, online courseware allows those outside the gates to see the day-to-day actual classroom teaching that goes on at top institutions.[10]

The Context in Which Online Courseware Originated

As the following chapters make clear, universities that take on online courseware projects do so for their own reasons, often with

---

[10]As the following chapters show, those teaching activities are conveyed through online courseware with varying degrees of precision, depending on the approach taken. Many MIT OCW courses contain each semester's syllabi, homework assignments, and lecture notes, but often in a text-based format that is not so different from a textbook. In contrast, programs like Open Yale Courses provide full audio and video records of lectures as they were delivered to actual Yale students, with the goal of making the home user feel as if he or she were present in that classroom. The Open Learning Initiative (OLI) utilizes the content developed in Carnegie Mellon courses but asks that faculty re-imagine their teaching approaches to optimize the online versions for remote delivery, in an attempt to ensure that, through an interactive online learning environment, students using the OLI course can really learn to the extent that their enrolled counterparts have. In this sense, the OLI is less about replicating the day-to-

institution-specific goals in mind or particular desired impacts. But a set of external forces has helped to shape opportunities available to universities in this space, and other key developments in both higher education and the online environment provide crucial context for understanding institutional decision making in the case studies that follow. Online courseware projects represent a response by elite institutions to profound changes afoot within and outside the academy, and they must be considered within the context of broader issues like access to higher education, the changing nature of the commercial internet, the commercialization and globalization of the selective university, and the wider range of experiments in teaching with technology and developing digital content referred to as Open Educational Resources.

Divergent Trends in Access to Higher Education

The online courseware concept emerged in the mid- to late 1990s and gained momentum following MIT's historic announcement in 2001 of its plan to make versions of all of its courses available online for free. This period has been marked by several divergent trends in terms of selectivity in higher education. There is great demand for higher education in the United States, the bulk of which is met by less-selective institutions like community colleges, non-flagship state institutions, and burgeoning for-profit colleges.[11] At the same time, the elite tier of institutions accepts an ever-shrinking percentage of those who want to attend, with 90 percent of Ivy League applicants rejected in 2007.[12] As economist Caroline Hox-

---

day teaching that occurs in Carnegie Mellon classrooms and more about helping end users achieve the level of learning that traditional students have realized.

[11] A recent Pew Research Center study based on census data confirms that more college-age Americans than ever—around 40 percent—were enrolled in some form of higher education in October 2008. Nearly all of the growth over years past came from a spike in community college enrollments, while enrollments at four-year institutions remained essentially flat (Taylor, Paul, Richard Fry, Wendy Wang, Daniel Dockterman, and Gabriel Velasco, "College Enrollment Hits All-Time High, Fueled by Community College Surge," Pew Research Center, October 29, 2009, http://pewsocialtrends.org/assets/pdf/college-enrollment.pdf).

[12] Bianco, Anthony, and Sonal Rupani, "The Dangerous Wealth of the Ivy League," *Business Week*, online edition, December 3, 2007. The article also reported that "the Ivies have steadily raised the list price they charge their traditional clientele: the wealthy and the well-

by's recent research shows, the top 10 percent of American colleges have become dramatically more selective, and "by 2007, the most selective colleges were up against the ceiling of selectivity," drawing their average students from the 98th percentile nationally.[13]

A parallel trend is the rising cost of higher education, particularly at top-tier colleges and universities: tuition at these selective institutions has increased much faster than the rate of inflation, consuming ever-higher percentages of family income (although record numbers of students are receiving financial aid to defray or even cover the costs of their education).[14] Increased prices charged to students and families are directly related to escalating costs within the university, which, as a labor-intensive public service, is subject to the "cost disease."[15] Endowments can be a means of compensating for rising costs, but endowment windfalls are often reinvested in new initiatives rather than in holding the list price of tuition steady. And prior to the global financial crisis of mid-2008—in which university endowments, like nearly all investments, decreased considerably—this increase in the costs of elite university education came at the same time that these institutions became considerably wealthier.[16] The combination of heftier edu-

---

born. Tuition, room and board, and fees now run an average of $45,000 a year, which, the schools are quick to point out, covers only one-half to two-thirds of operating costs. But even at those prices, demand, in the form of undergraduate applications, continues to soar."

[13]Hoxby, Caroline M., "The Changing Selectivity of American Colleges," National Bureau of Economic Research Working Paper 15446, 2009, http://www.nber.org/papers/w15446, 5.

[14]On climbing costs, see Ehrenberg, Ronald G., *Tuition Rising: Why College Costs So Much,* Cambridge, Mass.: Harvard University Press, 2000, 8. But Hoxby notes that "even though tuition has been rising rapidly at the most selective schools, the *deal* students get there has arguably improved greatly": the top tier of colleges are the most costly, but they also have significantly higher subsidies per student (Hoxby, "Changing Selectivity," 2).

[15]Baumol, William J., and William G. Bowen, "On the Performing Arts: The Anatomy of Their Economic Problems," *American Economic Review* 55, no. 1–2 (March 1, 1965).

[16]Regarding the decrease in the value of endowments, see Zezima, Katie, "Data Show College Endowments Loss Is Worst Drop since '70s," *New York Times,* online edition, January 26, 2009. Ehrenberg says of the most selective institutions that "As their endowment levels have increased, so too have the levels of tuition that they charge undergraduate students," and that many American families "are angry that the institutions have the audacity to increase their tuition at all, given that the institutions are becoming increasingly wealthy" (Ehrenberg, *Tuition Rising,* 4).

cation price tags coupled with rising endowments at elite private institutions has been the subject of considerable scrutiny in Washington. In recent years, Congress has held hearings on the finances of universities in light of their tax-exempt status.[17]

In short, over the past several decades, the most elite sector of higher education has become more selective—and expensive—than ever. But this tendency of the wealthiest institutions to become more rarefied is not the story for most of higher education, as the vast majority of students attend less-selective institutions that, as Hoxby demonstrates, operate differently.[18] In *Shakespeare, Einstein, and the Bottom Line,* David L. Kirp writes that "even as higher education has become more stratified at the top, it has also become more widely available. . . . on the lower rungs of the academic ladder, where what matters are money and enrollment figures, not prestige. Less selective and non-selective schools—four out of five American college students attend such institutions—vie to fill classroom seats," with for-profit, nonselective public, and community colleges trying innovative methods, either to further their missions or to increase their market share.[19] Online education has been an increasingly common strategy to make education more accessible to a growing and ever more diverse range of students in the less-selective tier. This shift has been felt across higher education; a 2008 Sloan Consortium report on online education

[17]Senator Charles Grassley, the ranking Republican on the Senate Finance Committee, who has had a sustained commitment to the issue of college endowment spending, told the *New York Times* in 2008 that "Tuition has gone up, college presidents' salaries have gone up, and endowments continue to go up and up. . . . We need to start seeing tuition relief for families go up just as fast" (quoted in Arenson, Karen W., "Senate Looking at Endowments as Tuition Rises," *New York Times,* online edition, January 25, 2008). Issues of college costs and rising tuition (among others) were also taken up by former Secretary of Education Margaret Spellings' Commission on the Future of Higher Education, beginning in 2005.

[18]Hoxby's major finding was that despite the outsized attention paid to the mounting selectivity of the nation's most prestigious institutions, "Rising selectivity is by no means a pervasive phenomenon. Only the top ten percent of colleges are substantially more selective now than they were in 1962. Moreover, at least 50 percent of colleges are substantially *less* selective now than they were in 1962" (Hoxby, "Changing Selectivity," 1).

[19]Kirp, David L., *Shakespeare, Einstein, and the Bottom Line: The Marketing of Higher Education,* Cambridge, Mass.: Harvard University Press, 2003, 5.

found that online enrollments have grown much faster than over-all higher-education enrollments in the United States.[20]

The commercial institutions have perhaps entered this space most eagerly. Entirely online branches of for-profit institutions have sprung up, with great commercial success: while the most prestigious universities have shied away from pursuing distance degree programs for their core undergraduate curricula, the University of Phoenix has seen its enrollments rise from 100,000 in 2000 to over 450,000 in 2010.[21] Some large public institutions like the University of Massachusetts have completely reinvented their educational and business models by developing online-only or hybrid degree programs for undergraduates.[22] Competition from for-profits offering online courses has recently driven smaller community colleges and regional public universities to create similar options to better serve local students.[23] The 2008 Sloan report states that "Both public universities and two-year colleges did agree that online courses were 'critical' to their long-term strategies, while [private] baccalaureate institutions generally refrained from ascribing them such dramatic importance."[24]

But the most elite universities—including the parent institutions of the initiatives profiled here—have not felt this same pressure to use the internet to expand enrollments in their core undergradu-

[20]Brooks, Margaret, "The Excellent Inevitability of Online Courses," *Chronicle of Higher Education,* online edition, May 21, 2009.

[21]http://30years.phoenix.edu/timeline.asp and "Apollo Group, Inc. Reports Fiscal 2010 First Quarter Results," press release, http://phx.corporate-ir.net/phoenix.zhtml?c=79624&p=irol-newsArticle&ID=1372667&highlight=. And as Anya Kamenetz points out in *DIY U,* "the best for-profits are aggressively focused on innovating in the use of technology to create economies of scale and improve convenience" (Kamenetz, Anya, *DIY U: Edupunks, Edupreneurs, and the Coming Transformation of Higher Education,* New York: Chelsea Green, 2010, 71).

[22]UMassOnline offers 22 different online bachelors degree options, and no distinction is made in transcripts or degrees between online and campus-based credits earned ("About UMassOnline," http://www.umassonline.net/AboutUs.html).

[23]See Parry, Marc, "They Thought Globally, but Now Colleges Push Online Courses Locally," Wired Campus blog (*Chronicle of Higher Education*), June 29, 2009, http://chronicle.com/blogPost/They-Thought-Globally-but-Now/7253/.

[24]Kolowich, Steve, "Recession May Drive More Adult Students to Take Online Classes," *Chronicle of Higher Education,* online edition, January 16, 2009, referring to Allen, I. Elaine, and Jeff Seaman, "Staying the Course: Online Education in the United States, 2008," report supported by the Sloan Consortium and the Babson Survey Research Group, November 2008, http://www.sloan-c.org/publications/survey/staying_course, 2.

ate degree programs. As a result of disproportionate growth on the part of less-selective institutions over the past several decades, elite universities have seen their "market share" drop considerably. In other industries, this would be highly problematic, and businesses would attempt to grow their product lines to keep pace with demand. But the selective tier of higher education is atypical, in that serving lower proportions of interested students only makes these institutions more desirable.[25] Against the backdrop of declining admissions rates and vast growth and innovation on the part of less-selective competitors, some elite universities have begun to explore online courseware initiatives, thus tentatively building a teaching presence on the web. These projects are highly visible means of making university materials available to a broader audience than would otherwise be possible—a benefit offered to society in an era in which wealthy parent universities that spend so much to educate so few have faced pushback from the public. As Dr. Ramamurti Shankar, a participating professor in Open Yale Courses, told the *Philadelphia Inquirer,* "we can't admit everybody to Yale, but we can give this to everybody absolutely for free."[26] At the same time, by offering course content—but not the university credit that has typically accompanied it—to nonmatriculated students, these elite institutions maintain a key barrier to entry that keeps their exclusivity intact.

The Development of the Commercial Internet

As this book's first chapters describe, changes in online courseware models are indicative of an overall shift on the part of numerous businesses from charging for online content to offering it for free. The dot-com boom that reached full strength around 1998

---

[25]Kirp writes that "in the realm of commerce, when demand exceeds supply, firms are supposed to expand or else jack up their prices, a practice that encourages new entrants. But that isn't how higher education operates. . . . The very idea of expansion is anathema to the elite. . . . Instead, these schools set ever-higher standards for admission. The most selective reject seven out of eight applicants, almost all of whom are qualified" (Kirp, *Shakespeare, Einstein, and the Bottom Line,* 2).

[26]Quoted in Snyder, Susan, "Number of Free, Noncredit Courses on Web Increasing," *Philadelphia Inquirer,* online edition, January 12, 2010.

was marked by a fervent belief in the vast revenues available in online-enabled markets.[27] The wild early success of some much-publicized internet start-ups, the availability of venture capital for nascent online endeavors, and the "brazen self-confidence of dot-com entrepreneurs" all helped to create a shared sense of the commercial potential that the internet held for virtually any business.[28]

Selective institutions' early forays into online courseware launched at the height of the dot-com boom (including, among numerous others, Fathom.com, profiled in Chapter 2) were very much influenced by this culture. Both Fathom and AllLearn (also profiled in Chapter 2) attempted to set up a form of e-commerce that would monetize courseware, but they found that charging fees for access to content failed to bring in sufficient revenue. Based in part on the well-publicized difficulties of Fathom, AllLearn, and their peers, online courseware projects conceived after the dot-com crash in 2000 and 2001 opted instead to make courseware available for free.[29] Initiatives like MIT OCW and subsequent efforts received generous startup funding from foundations, allowing them to create online content—and in doing so, to enhance the online presence of their parent universities—without requiring that the money follow. The past decade has seen tremendous experimentation with mechanisms for generating online revenue, including "freemium"

[27]In *dot.con: The Greatest Story Ever Sold,* John Cassidy offers a concise description of the first several decades of internet business models, describing how what began as a free resource was progressively commercialized, resulting in the dot-com bubble of the 1990s and then its inevitable decline. Of the early history of the internet, Cassidy writes that "Anyone who wanted access to the NSFNET, the Internet's backbone, had to abide by an 'Acceptable Use Policy,' which restricted it to 'research and education.' . . . by and large, the Internet remained commerce-free—often militantly so." "Not until the early 1990s, when millions of people around the world were already using the network to communicate with each other, did the private sector show much of an interest. When Wall Street and corporate America did discover the Internet, they adopted it with the zeal of converts, and the bubble started to inflate. Once that happened, the process was self-reinforcing, with everyone involved trapped in the peculiar competitive logic of a speculative boom" (Cassidy, John, *dot.con: The Greatest Story Ever Sold,* New York: HarperCollins, 2002, 22, 7).

[28]McCarthy, Ellen, "U-Md. Professor Archives History of Dot-Com Bombs," *Washington Post,* online edition, October 28, 2004.

[29]In *Free: The Future of the Radical Price,* Chris Anderson writes that "A decade and a half into the great online experiment, free has become the default, and pay walls the route to obscurity" (Anderson, Chris, *Free: The Future of a Radical Price,* New York: Hyperion, 2009, 12–13).

models or those based on advertising revenues.[30] But the extant projects profiled here have relied on foundation, institutional, or government support for the majority of their funding.

The freely available "open" courseware projects that have come to dominate this field resonate conceptually with a broader movement that encourages the open sharing of information online and the removal of barriers to accessing that information. Rooted partly in and extending the thinking behind the free software movement, proponents generally protest against what they consider artificial limitations—legal or otherwise—on end users' ability to share and modify content, suggesting that the internet enables creative and productive reuse by the average user (often described as "remix culture").[31] The free and open programs in the case studies that

[30]The freemium approach was first defined as "Give your service away for free, possibly ad supported but maybe not, acquire a lot of customers very efficiently through word of mouth, referral networks, organic search marketing, etc., then offer premium priced value added services or an enhanced version of your service to your customer base" (Wilson, Fred, "My Favorite Business Model," *A VC*, March 2006, http://www.avc.com/a_vc/2006/03/ my_favorite_bus.html). Such changes have already had major impacts on the functioning of multiple industries, including newspapers and music. The newspaper industry has attempted both models for online content (ad-supported and keeping some content behind a pay wall) with very limited success thus far. (For a brief summary of the problems facing the newspaper industry in the online environment, see Shirky, Clay, "Newspapers and Thinking the Unthinkable," blog post, March 13, 2009, http://www.shirky.com/weblog/2009/03/newspapers-and-thinking-the-unthinkable/.) In the music industry, technological change has disrupted long-standing business models, as music is increasingly disseminated through sources like iTunes that enable unbundling of content (selling individual songs rather than complete albums) and may in some cases disintermediate traditional gatekeepers like record labels.

[31]The free software movement, which formalizes long-standing practices of sharing code freely between early software programmers, has grown out of the philosophies of Richard M. Stallman, as demonstrated in his work with the GNU Project and Free Software Foundation. Stallman casts the free sharing of software as a moral imperative, insisting that all users must share the "freedoms" to run, modify, and distribute software, in original or modified form (Stallman, Richard, "About the GNU Project," http://www.gnu.org/gnu/thegnuproject.html). Perhaps the most visible manifestation of the movement's objection to limits on the rights of end users is the Free Software Foundation's "Defective by Design" effort, which protests the application of digital rights management—or, as they title it, "digital restrictions management"—claiming that it takes control away from the end user (Brown, Peter, "What Is DRM? Digital Restrictions Management," http://www.defectivebydesign.org/what_is_drm). Regarding remix culture, see *Remix: Making Art and Commerce Thrive in the Hybrid Economy*, New York: Penguin Press, 2008, as well as other writings of Lawrence Lessig. In addition to Lessig, this cause has been championed by the group Students for Free Culture (http://freeculture .org/). The Creative Commons movement, which allows users to easily license materials for such reuse, also provides a backbone for this culture of sharing (http://creativecommons.org).

follow also mirror a long-standing practice of sharing information within academic communities, with scholars prioritizing impact on their fields over revenue from their intellectual products. In recent years, this value system has led many to advocate for open access to scholarly publications, a change aimed primarily at increasing the speed of publication and reducing the price of scholarly communications.[32] Given the radical new ability to copy, modify, and distribute content far more simply and at lower cost in digital form,[33] an ideology of free sharing and reuse of information online has been embraced by many—and is perhaps at work in the Hewlett Foundation–supported examples of "open" courseware projects in the case studies that follow.

Commercialization and Globalization of Higher Education

In addition to these sweeping trends, online courseware touches on a variety of perennial issues in higher education, one of which is the concern over mounting commercialization of the university. The digital age offers universities unparalleled opportunity to share their resources and knowledge outputs with the world. But, as William G. Bowen, then-president of the Andrew W. Mellon Foundation and president emeritus of Princeton University, stated in his 2000 Romanes lecture, these opportunities "have to be balanced against the associated temptations and risks, many of which

---

[32]This movement is predicated on the convergence of "an old tradition . . . the willingness of scientists and scholars to publish the fruits of their research in scholarly journals without payment, for the sake of inquiry and knowledge" and "a new technology . . . the internet" (Budapest Open Access Initiative, http://www.soros.org/openaccess/read.shtml). Peter Suber refers to the movement around open access as "the campaign for OA" and writes that, in the case of scholarly journal content, open access allows content creators to "take advantage of the internet as a powerful new technology for sharing knowledge instantly, with a worldwide audience, at zero marginal cost, in a digital form amenable to unlimited processing" (Suber, Peter, "Open Access Overview: Focusing on Open Access to Peer-Reviewed Research Articles and Their Pre-prints," last revised June 19, 2007, http://www.earlham.edu/~peters/fos/overview.htm).

[33]"The physical capital costs of information production have declined dramatically with the introduction of cheap processor-based computer networks" (Benkler, Yochai, "Coase's Penguin, or, Linux and *The Nature of the Firm*," *Yale Law Journal* 112, no. 3 [December 2002], http://www.yalelawjournal.org/images/pdfs/354.pdf).

have a commercial dimension."[34] One such risk was that market forces might encourage universities to focus on activities with the best chances of achieving financial success, perhaps diverting attention or resources from pursuits related to their core missions.[35] These comments came at a moment when nearly every highly selective university felt that it had to stake out a position in the online space—to either become a leader on the internet or risk being left behind. Bowen's warning implied that such digital endeavors might generate powerful conflicting interests that would upend the centuries-old values of the university itself. Early fee-based initiatives like Fathom, along with a slew of contemporaries, exemplify the university's application of its courses toward commercial ends. MIT OCW (and implicitly all the subsequent open initiatives) was a direct reaction to that trend and has taken on a somewhat politicized anticommercial stance.

Over the past several decades, numerous commentators have remarked upon—indeed, expressed anxiety over—the intensifying commercial pressures on higher education and the degree to which universities have come to resemble businesses. The influence of commercialism on higher education is not new, but as Kirp writes, "what *is* new, and troubling, is the raw power that money directly exerts over so many aspects of higher education."[36] Universities' desires to distinguish themselves in a competitive marketplace by luring the best faculty and students have led them to develop active marketing departments and increased the attention paid to issues of presentation.[37] MIT OCW and others may have rejected

---

[34]Bowen, "At a Slight Angle to the Universe," 11.

[35]Bowen's speech summarized the thoughts of many observers of higher education at the time. As Casper said, "in addition to the 'information industry' a 'knowledge industry' will develop—is indeed lurking around the corner. For better or for worse, knowledge will be commercialized at an ever increasing rate" (Casper, "Come the Millennium," 3). And according to Martin Trow, "commercial markets have already moved into the university's research laboratories . . . blurring the distinction between pure and applied research and between research and development. I believe we are seeing a similar movement of market forces into the instructional life of the university" (Trow, "Development of Information Technology," 312).

[36]Kirp, *Shakespeare, Einstein, and the Bottom Line*, 3.

[37]"Investment in marketing efforts and more generally in the presentation of the institu-

the commercialism typified by Fathom, but the extant online course-ware projects still can serve a marketing function aimed at burnishing the university's brand. As Kirp suggests, attention-grabbing acts of altruism like MIT OCW allow the institution to promote "its reputation by giving everything away" through the "symbolic capital" of such a gesture, and subsequent chapters show that MIT is not alone in deriving branding benefits from online course-ware.[38] Maintaining and bolstering their public reputations has always been a priority for universities, and recent trends toward placing greater importance on such activities are not inherently negative; however, there is some concern that an outsized focus on branding activities may distract from mission-related pursuits.[39]

Online courseware initiatives also developed in parallel with universities' aggressive efforts to extend their geographic reach. Echoing a sentiment expressed by so many others at the time, former University of California President Richard C. Atkinson said in 2001, "our rapidly expanding ability to share information and ideas is leading to what can be called the globalization of the university."[40] Whether through redoubled efforts to attract international students or through "a kind of educational gold rush" to establish branch campuses in far-flung and potentially lucrative global locales (including China, Singapore, and the wealthy Persian Gulf countries of Qatar and the United Arab Emirates), universities are attempting to expand their presence and raise their profiles overseas, increasing their exposure in other regions to tap new markets.[41] By showcasing

---

tion has, we believe, grown markedly in recent years, especially among the more prestigious private universities" (McPherson, Michael S., and Gordon C. Winston, "The Economics of Cost, Price, and Quality in U.S. Higher Education," in *Paying the Piper: Productivity, Incentives, and Financing in U.S. Higher Education,* Ann Arbor: University of Michigan Press, 1993, 84).

[38]Kirp, *Shakespeare, Einstein, and the Bottom Line,* 169, 182.

[39]"'How "businesslike" should universities be?' Underlying the concerns expressed by many (including the use of marketplace language such as 'brands,' which has worrying symbolic overtones for some faculty) is the fundamental risk of 'mission drift'" (Bowen, "At a Slight Angle to the Universe," 33).

[40]Atkinson, Richard C., "The Globalization of the University," speech delivered at Nagasaki University of Foreign Studies, Japan, May 26, 2001, http://ucop.edu/pres/speeches/japanspc.htm.

[41]Universities are becoming increasingly dependent on tuition from overseas. Inter-

the university's core teaching activities in a readily accessible digital format, online courseware positions participating institutions to reach a world audience.

Past Experiments in Teaching with Technology

Experimenting with online courseware is one of many ways in which elite universities have incorporated technology into the patterns and structures of university life. Email has become the default medium for communications within the university, digital library systems have supplanted card catalogues, and technology has grown increasingly integrated into all aspects of the teaching process. Professors routinely use course management systems like Blackboard and Sakai to organize their instructional materials; students choose their classes via internet-based course enrollment programs; and instructors in all subjects incorporate PowerPoint into their lectures while students take notes on laptops.

In addition to these subtle integrations of technology into the structures of teaching, many universities have also been using technology to more fundamentally reshape the teaching process itself, seeking to improve learning outcomes or cut costs. Examples of coordinated efforts to redesign courses by incorporating technol-

---

national students pay more than their U.S. counterparts (in the case of public universities) and often do not receive the same financial aid benefits, thus subsidizing need-blind financial aid for American students. Oregon State University's vice president for finance and administration told the *Chronicle* in 2008 that "Full-paying international students enhance our ability to deliver services to all of the students here" (Moser, Katie, "New Model for Recruitment of Foreign Students Sparks Debate," *Chronicle of Higher Education,* online edition, June 27, 2008, http://chronicle.com/article/New-Model-for-Recruitment-of/10321/). A study conducted by the Institute of International Education found that "In all, the 623,805 international students who studied here in 2007–8, an increase of 7 percent from a year earlier, contributed an estimated $15 billion to the U.S. economy" (McMurtrie, Beth, "Foreign Students Pour Back into the U.S.," *Chronicle of Higher Education* online edition, November 21, 2008). According to the "Open Doors 2009 Report on International Educational Exchange," even during a global recession in 2008–9, the number of international students in the United States was at an all-time high ("International Student and Total U.S. Enrollment," in Institute of International Education, "Open Doors 2009 Report on International Educational Exchange," http://opendoors.iienetwork. org/?p=150810). On the "educational gold rush," see Lewin, Tamar, "U.S. Universities Rush to Set Up Outposts Abroad," *New York Times,* online edition, February 10, 2008.

ogy are legion; for instance, in 1993 the Alfred P. Sloan Foundation began working to encourage the proliferation of quality online elements into the mainstream of higher education through its Asynchronous Learning Network (ALN).[42] The Mellon Foundation's Cost-Effective Uses of Technology in Teaching (CEUTT) program funded controlled experiments at 25 institutions between 1996 and 2001, aimed at collecting data on learning improvements and cost savings accrued through the incorporation of technology into undergraduate courses.[43] In a similar vein, the Pew Charitable Trusts invested $8.8 million in its Program on Course Redesign (PCR), which from 1999 to 2002 funded 30 institutions' experiments on the potential gains—both pedagogical and economic—that technology in teaching could bring to universities.[44] Thus online courseware projects emerged in an environment of widespread experimentation with the use of networked technologies in the undergraduate classroom, often involving prestigious participants and high-profile funders.[45]

These earlier experiments in the use of technology have certainly influenced how universities operate internally and educate their own students. But while the activities outlined here were aimed mostly inward, the series of open courseware projects described elsewhere in this book have sought not only to put undergraduate course content online, but to do so in a branded, public-facing way that extends beyond the gates of the university, sharing components of elite higher education with the world.

---

[42]"Coming to Terms: ALN," *Sloan-C View: Perspectives in Quality Online Education 2,* no. 4 (June 2003), 3, http://www.aln.org/publications/view/v2n4/pdf/v2n4.pdf.

[43]Fisher, Saul, "Teaching and Technology: Promising Directions for Research on Online Learning and Distance Education in the Selective Institutions," Andrew W. Mellon Foundation, http://cshe.berkeley.edu/research/ebusiness/papers/teaching_and_technology.pdf.

[44]Twigg, Carol A., "Improving Learning and Reducing Costs: New Models for Online Learning," *Educause Review* 38, no. 5 (September–October 2003), 30. This program was enacted by the National Center for Academic Transformation, led by Carol Twigg.

[45]As subsequent chapters describe in more detail, Berkeley participated in the CEUTT program, conducting a controlled experiment on one of its webcast courses, and Carnegie Mellon's participation in the Pew PCR laid some of the technical foundation for what later became an Open Learning Initiative course.

The Open Educational Resources Movement

The set of projects profiled here can also be understood in the context of the broader Open Educational Resources (OER) movement. As previously described, this book's primary intention is to analyze elite universities' uses of the internet to publish core undergraduate course materials, in a variety of ways and for a variety of purposes. Initiatives like Fathom and AllLearn, the subjects of Chapter 2, charged fees to users for many of their materials, thus limiting access to paying customers. But the other courseware projects profiled here provide their content free of charge, often using licenses that allow end users to edit and reuse that content in diverse ways. These *open* courseware projects—the three initiatives funded by the Hewlett Foundation in addition to webcast .berkeley, a member of the OpenCourseWare Consortium (described in detail in Chapter 3)—also fall under the umbrella of the more expansive OER movement. These initiatives include "free tools and content" available on the web that "can include full courses, textbooks, streaming videos, exams, software, and any other materials or techniques supporting learning."[46]

Though conceptually related to the long-standing open-source software movement, the term "Open Educational Resources" was coined in 2002 at the United Nations Educational, Scientific and Cultural Organization (UNESCO) Forum on the Impact of Open Courseware for Higher Education in Developing Countries, which was "convened to consider the potential, for developing countries, of the Massachusetts Institute of Technology (MIT) initiative to put course materials online for open access."[47] Also in 2002, the Hewlett Foundation launched what would become known as the OER division of its education program, with the goal of using "information technology to help equalize the distribution of high-

---

[46]William and Flora Hewlett Foundation, "Education: Open Educational Resources," http://www.hewlett.org/oer. NPTEL also offers online courseware free of charge, but its content does not currently carry an open license.

[47]D'Antoni, Susan, "Introduction," in *Open Educational Resources: Conversations in Cyberspace*, ed S. D'Antoni and C. Savage, Paris: UNESCO, 2009, 17.

quality knowledge and educational opportunities for individuals, faculty, and institutions within the United States and throughout the world."[48] Pioneered in many ways by the Hewlett Foundation's early and ongoing efforts, this promising field has grown tremendously over the past decade, attracting the attention of additional foundations (among them the Carnegie Foundation for the Advancement of Teaching, the Bill and Melinda Gates Foundation, the Lumina Foundation, the Shuttleworth Foundation, and the Soros Foundation's Open Society Institute) and governments around the world in support of creating and sharing high-quality educational materials.

OER includes diverse open materials created by a range of producers and intended for varying uses. Open digital textbooks (from producers like Flat World Knowledge and Rice University's Connexions project, to name just two) aim to provide students with course texts that are not only free but also more interactive, granular, and customizable than traditional textbooks through the remix and reuse options afforded by their open licenses.[49] (This sector of the OER community also seeks to solve a daunting problem facing education: the sharp increase in textbook costs, which have risen to the point where students are resorting to renting or pirating textbooks they cannot afford to buy.)[50] In addition to the core content itself, the OER movement also encompasses resources to find OER (like OER Commons, OCW Finder, DiscoverEd, and

[48]Atkins, Daniel E., John Seely Brown, and Allen L. Hammond, "A Review of the Open Educational Resources (OER) Movement: Achievements, Challenges, and New Opportunities," report to the William and Flora Hewlett Foundation, February 2007, 2.

[49]See, respectively, http://www.flatworldknowledge.com/ and http://cnx.org/.

[50]According to a General Accounting Office study, the "cost of the average college textbook increased 186 percent between 1986 and 2004" (Kingsbury, Alex, and Lindsey Galloway, "Textbooks Enter the Digital Era," *U.S. News and World Report,* online edition, October 8, 2006). In a 2007 paper detailing the proceedings of a conference on open textbooks, Gary Matkin and Jia Frydenberg write that "The average cost of textbooks per year at one California community college is over $900—about 75 percent of community college tuition!" (Frydenberg, Jia, and Gary Matkin, "Open Textbooks: Why? What? How? When?" University of California, Irvine, Distance Learning Center, October 2007, 8). On rentals, see Lewin, Tamar, "Textbook Publisher to Rent to College Students," *New York Times,* online edition, August 13, 2009. On textbook piracy, see Stross, Randall, "First It Was Song Downloads. Now It's Organic Chemistry," *New York Times,* online edition, July 27, 2008.

World Lecture Hall), portals to post updates and discuss them (such as OER Blogs), and the licensing infrastructure that makes all this sharing possible (Creative Commons).[51]

Open courseware and open textbooks are being created all over the world by institutions in all sectors, including K-12 schools, universities like Michigan State, and community colleges like California's Foothill De Anza.[52] As evidenced by the membership in the OCW Consortium, much of the activity in this space is in the developing world, with numerous initiatives coming from Asia and South America.[53]

While there are instances of overlap between the OER field and the cases examined here, this book does not attempt to cover the OER movement or to offer an assessment of its progress or potential. Rather, by zeroing in on a few exemplary courseware projects (most of which are also examples of OER—although others, like Fathom and AllLearn, are not), *Unlocking the Gates* aims to understand what sharing undergraduate curricular materials with the general public has meant for some of the elite institutions currently engaged in these projects.

· · · · · · · · · · · · · · · ·

[51]See, respectively, http://www.oercommons.org/oer, http://www.ocwfinder.org/, http://discovered.creativecommons.org/search/, http://wlh.webhost.utexas.edu/, http://oerblogs.org/, and http://creativecommons.org/education?utm_source=ccorg&utm_medium=ccedu.

[52]Curriki, a website promoting the sharing and collaboration of free and open-source curricular materials for K-12 education, can be found on the web at http://www.curriki.org/xwiki/bin/view/Main/WebHome. Another source of mostly K-12 open course materials is the National Repository of Online Courses, http://www.montereyinstitute.org/nroc/. For Michigan State and Foothill De Anza, see, respectively, http://www.msuglobal.com/ocw and http://sofia.fhda.edu/gallery/.

[53]http://www.ocwconsortium.org/members/consortium-members.html. The NPTEL effort profiled in Chapter 7 is not a member of the OCW Consortium; its content is openly and freely available over the internet, but it does not carry an open license allowing for derivative versions, one of the criteria for membership in the Consortium. Yet it is exemplary of a strong localized open courseware presence throughout Asia, with similar efforts taking root in China, Japan, South Korea, and Vietnam. Widespread international support for free and open courseware content generated around the world is evident in UNESCO's support of OER (see the project on Open Educational Resources by UNESCO's International Institute for Educational Planning: http://www.unesco.org/iiep/virtualuniversity/forumshome.php?queryforums_id=3) and the Cape Town Open Education Declaration, a virtual document with over 2,000 signers that calls OER "a wise investment in teaching and learning for the 21st century" ("The Cape Town Open Education Declaration: Unlocking the Promise of Open Educational Resources," http://www.capetowndeclaration.org/read-the-declaration).

Universities' willingness to share their course content, traditionally reserved for only a limited number of students, represents a laudable contribution to society. Through online courseware projects, some of the most selective institutions have exposed their intellectual capital in an unprecedented way. But—often with good reason—they have done so while protecting the substantial part of their value proposition derived from their residential experience, interactions between students and faculty, and, of course, their prestigious degrees. In other words, these institutions have struck a careful balance between altruism and self-interest and have often, as we will see, garnered other ancillary benefits along the way. The online courseware projects at elite institutions reveal an industry in transition—selective universities making tentative adjustments in response to the networked environment, while fundamentally adhering to the model that has defined them for centuries. But these first steps by early adopters may lay important groundwork for a shift in the way that even the most elite institutions pursue their educational missions.

2

EARLY EXPERIMENTS: FATHOM AND ALLLEARN

In the late 1990s, leaders in higher education—as in many sectors of the economy—were deeply interested in the internet's power to fundamentally transform all aspects of doing business. Universities were eager to harness the networked environment to their advantage, and were particularly intrigued by the internet's potential to transform education. Fathom, an online effort led by Columbia University, and AllLearn, a concurrent initiative of Oxford, Princeton, Stanford, and Yale, were two of a group of similar projects conceived in the late 1990s and launched around 2000, including California Virtual University, eCornell, NYUonline, UNext, and Virtual Temple.[1] Speculation was rampant that education would be the next "killer application" for the internet, and a number of higher education institutions were eager to explore the possibilities: a November 2000 article on online learning initiatives quotes a dean at the Wharton School as saying that "at least 75 percent of universities of any significance are looking at this, or dabbling with it to some extent."[2] Fathom and AllLearn reflect the dot-com era's confidence in the enormous moneymaking

---

[1]Fathom and AllLearn were unique among these in that they dealt with the liberal arts core of their host universities by publishing content related to undergraduate courses or developed by popular undergraduate faculty, rather than zeroing in on preprofessional or certain graduate programs, as UNext or NYUOnline did with business curricula.

[2]Cisco Systems chair John Chambers gave the "killer application" quote to *New York Times* columnist Thomas Friedman (Friedman, Thomas L., "Foreign Affairs: Next, It's E-ducation," *New York Times*, online edition, November 17, 1999). For the comment from the Wharton dean, see Singer, Karen, "Distance-Learning Ventures Propel Top Universities into For-Profit Sector: Harvard, Cornell, and Stanford among Those Lured by $10 Billion Potential," *Matrix: The Magazine for Leaders in Higher Education*, online edition, 1, no. 4 (November 1, 2000).

possibilities of the nascent e-learning market.[3] These initiatives were both inspired and shaped by the belief, held by many, that there was great pressure on universities to adapt to the digital age, and that those that did not act quickly would lag behind the competition.

More specifically, Fathom and AllLearn developed at a time when the traditional roles of the university and audiences for higher education were increasingly questioned. As management consultant Peter Drucker provocatively stated, "thirty years from now the big university campus will be a relic. Universities won't survive in their present form. The main reason is the shift to the continuing education of already highly educated adults as the center and growth sector of education."[4] Both Fathom, a for-profit enterprise of partner institutions from the United States and United Kingdom, and AllLearn, a not-for-profit consortial effort aimed at its member universities' alumni, were high-profile attempts to generate revenue through fee-based access to digital courseware. Fathom and AllLearn are no longer extant (they were officially shuttered in 2003 and 2006, respectively), but their progress was closely followed at the time, and their influence is evident in the development of later online courseware projects.

Fathom

Fathom was the brainchild of Michael M. Crow, then executive vice provost of Columbia University, and Ann Kirschner, a PhD in English and former head of NFL.com who would serve as Fathom's

---

[3] A 2000 Merrill Lynch white paper estimated "that the U.S. market for online higher educational alone will grow from $1.2 billion in 1999 to $7 billion in 2003" (quoted in Zemsky, Robert, *Making Reform Work: The Case for Transforming American Higher Education*, New Brunswick, NJ: Rutgers University Press, 2009, 145). A 2001 article by Diana Oblinger noted that dot-com education company "Ecollege . . . traded at $200 million of market capitalization on its first day of trading" (Oblinger, Diana, "Will E-business Shape the Future of Distance Learning?" *Open Learning: The Journal of Open and Distance Learning* 16, no. 1 (February 2001), 18.

[4] Quoted in Atkinson, Richard C., "The Globalization of the University," speech delivered at Nagasaki University of Foreign Studies, Japan, May 26, 2001, http://www.rca.ucsd.edu/speeches/japanspc.pdf.

chief executive. In the late 1990s, Columbia's leadership was strategically considering its use of technology. Crow characterized this period as an "upbeat, optimistic opportunity moment" that Columbia could seize, as the university was eager to be a player in what administrators saw as an emerging field. According to Crow, the idea for Fathom—an online repository of educational and course content from Columbia and elsewhere geared toward a general audience—arose because at the time, "we were trying to figure out a way to put Columbia out there on the web externally."[5]

Kirschner was hired in late 1998 and started at Columbia in January 1999, working with Crow to develop a strategic plan for the university's internet presence.[6] Fathom was one of several concurrent digital efforts spearheaded by Crow, whose portfolio of responsibilities was designed to "take [Columbia's] knowledge, incubate it, and project it" out to the public.[7] These efforts were soon organized into a group called Morningside Ventures, led by Kirschner, which investigated potential online companies or business ventures that Columbia might create. By the end of 1999, the bulk of those efforts were focused on Fathom,[8] a digital startup intended to offer the outside world an unprecedented window into the institution. As Columbia Provost Jonathan Cole told the *Chronicle of Higher Education*, "what Fathom is trying to do is to recreate in virtual space the kind of possibilities that one can usually get only from being at a great university or a great museum."[9]

The strategic planning process that resulted in Fathom's creation was motivated by impulses both to break new ground and to ward off potential competition in the online environment. President George Rupp described the pressure Columbia felt to establish an online presence as a reaction to "a lot of hype about the internet." "Someone was going to capture that space," Rupp noted,

[5]Interview with Michael Crow, 12/22/08.
[6]Interview with Ann Kirschner, 8/10/09.
[7]Blumenstyk, Goldie, "Knowledge Is 'a Form of Venture Capital' for a Top Columbia Administrator," *Chronicle of Higher Education*, online edition, February 9, 2001.
[8]Interview with Ann Kirschner, 8/10/09.
[9]Carr, Sarah, and Vincent Kiernan, "For-Profit Web Venture Seeks to Replicate the University Experience Online," *Chronicle of Higher Education*, online edition, April 14, 2000.

"and we wanted to do it first, even if it was more complicated and more difficult to be ahead of the curve."[10] For Crow, Fathom also presented an opportunity to gain an edge against competitors and "differentiate Columbia from other Ivy League schools," which would appear comparatively "slow and stodgy" in their unwillingness to take their content online.[11] Kirschner summed up the Fathom leadership's sense of the web's promise when she told the *New York Times* in 2000 that, when it came to teaching, "the Internet is the hottest new game in town" and discussed Fathom.com's "potential to be a category killer."[12]

In addition to the positive opportunities the internet presented, Columbia's leadership also saw Fathom as a defense against potential threats. Kirschner recounted an anecdote from Fathom's planning phases in which Stephen Friedman, the former chair of Columbia's board of trustees, once "had a nightmare that Microsoft would buy up all the faculty of Columbia and other leading universities and basically destroy the system of higher education. And so some of this was a defensive strategy" to provide faculty with a venue to explore online opportunities through Columbia-sanctioned channels before they were poached by outsiders.[13] There was also concern about protecting Columbia's institutional interests in the online space by guarding against individualized faculty efforts. In an open letter to the faculty announcing that the provost's office would coordinate all digital media initiatives generated at the university, Rupp wrote that in all of Columbia's new online ventures, "it is of the utmost importance that the Uni-

---

[10]Interview with George Rupp, 8/7/08.

[11]Interview with Michael Crow, 12/22/08.

[12]Quoted in Arenson, Karen W., "Responsible Party: Making Education an Online Brand," *New York Times,* online edition, April 23, 2000.

[13]Interview with Ann Kirschner, 7/28/08. The example was particularly compelling in this context, as Microsoft had conquered the encyclopedia format when it launched Encarta in 1993; it therefore seemed plausible at the time that the corporate world might encroach on university content as well. (Of course, Encarta has since gone the way of Fathom, ceasing production of new editions in the summer of 2009.) William F. Massy and Robert Zemsky expressed the prevailing belief at the time that "if traditional colleges and universities do not exploit the new technologies, other nontraditional providers of education will be quick to do so" (Massy, William F., and Robert Zemsky, "Using Information Technology to Enhance Academic Productivity," white paper prepared by Educom's National Learning Infrastructure Initiative [NLII], http://net.educause.edu/ir/library/html/nli0004.html, 2).

versity protect Columbia's name and its reputation for academic excellence. If we are not careful, if individual Schools or faculty members act as 'free agents' and neglect our collective need to maintain standards of quality, we may do damage to the University as a whole."[14]

Columbia was determined to stake out an early position for itself in the era's rapidly evolving marketplace, developing web-based courses to proactively enter the online environment and avoid being left behind. In this sense, Fathom seems to have grown from the premise that in a competitive, fast-paced market, the best defense is a good offense. As Columbia professor and Fathom course instructor Stephen Murray put it, "we all recognize that there are risks, as when you jump into a flooded river and don't know if you might drown. But there are risks involved with sitting on the sidelines and letting peers pre-empt the field."[15]

Though Columbia was less wealthy overall than some of its Ivy League counterparts, the financial rewards it reaped from technology transfer left it well positioned to take on such a significant and expensive endeavor.[16] A 2001 article in the *Chronicle of Higher Education* states that "Columbia ranked first among American universities in earnings from patent royalties for the past two years. Its royalty revenue for the 2000 fiscal year was more than $143 million. Columbia almost certainly will lead the pack again in 2001."[17] These monies formed the Strategic Investment Fund, which could

---

[14]Rupp, George, from "Current Communications: President's Office," February 29, 2000, http://web.archive.org/web/20000817225454/http:/www.columbia.edu/cu/president/current.html. Rupp went on to say that "while we do not compete directly with for-profit educational enterprises or for-profit publishing companies, we are not completely insulated from the forces at work in these markets and are therefore well advised to be vigilant in protecting Columbia interests while we are also both prudent and creative in projecting the Columbia identity into this domain."

[15]Quoted in Carr and Kiernan, "For-Profit Web Venture."

[16]Rupp said that when the idea for Fathom arose, he thought that it was something Columbia might be uniquely suited to do: "In some ways [the thinking behind Fathom] was part of the way we thought about Columbia: we were scrappers, we had an endowment that was like 20 percent of Harvard's, but we had a fair amount of flexible monies from our intellectual properties—largely from a small number of very, very lucrative patents. So we felt that this was something that the more staid institutions were just not going to do—they were too fat and happy, too comfortable" to risk launching an endeavor like Fathom (interview with George Rupp, 8/7/08).

[17]Blumenstyk, "Knowledge Is 'a Form of Venture Capital.'"

be spent at Crow's discretion and comprised what he called "the largest amount of internal risk capital of any university in the United States."[18] Fathom's funding, approximately $25 million over three years, was drawn from this internal fund.

Fathom was organized as a profit-seeking business with a dot-com domain name. From the beginning, it was intended to play a dual role: broadening access to Columbia's content while also providing a revenue stream back to the university. As Provost Cole said, "our motivation is to be entrepreneurial. We've been giving it away for generations. Now we want to get a fair return, always so we can reinvest it."[19] Just as patented technologies and scientific discoveries yielded dividends back to the parent institutions, Cole's statement indicates that Columbia was beginning to think of professors' course content as a product that, monetized appropriately, might have the same lucrative potential.[20] According to an April 2000 item in the university's student newspaper, the *Columbia Daily Spectator*, "Cole said that distance education's financial benefits could even exceed those reaped from patents."[21] And when patent royalties were bringing in more than $100 million annually, it is perhaps no surprise that Columbia felt that the potential rewards were worth the risk and upfront investment that Fathom would require.

Fathom was a substantial business venture—at one point it had about 30 staff members—and its leadership was comfortable discussing the endeavor using the language of commerce and retail.[22] In

---

[18]Interview with Michael Crow, 12/22/08.

[19]Quoted in Arenson, Karen W., "Columbia Sets Pace in Profiting off Research," *New York Times*, online edition, August 2, 2000.

[20]There could be additional benefits to conceptualizing online education in the same way that universities have understood the role of technology transfer. As Michael Goldstein has observed, "As faculty became more successful in creating valuable discoveries, the best and brightest were defecting to commercial enterprises. The technology-transfer companies provided a new mechanism for sharing value while keeping the faculty member within the institution. The same opportunity exists in telecommunicated learning" (Goldstein, Michael, "A Capital Innovation for Making a Profit," *Times Higher Education*, online edition, December 17, 1999).

[21]Gerrard, David, and Jacob Kurlander, "Columbia U. Enters Distance Education Territory," *Columbia Daily Spectator*, reprinted in *University Wire*, online edition, April 3, 2000.

[22]Carlson, Scott, "Going for Profit and Scholarship on the Web: A Woman Who Made the NFL Hot Online Turns Her Attention to Higher Education," *Chronicle of Higher Education*, online edition, May 5, 2000.

a 2000 article, Kirschner described Fathom as "a marketing vehicle to put all the intellectual property together in an attractive format, and develop a large audience for it."[23] Kirschner also stated that with Fathom, "we're creating a knowledge mall," and referred to it as a "wholesaler" for member institutions' course content.[24] This tone extended beyond Kirschner to Crow, who described Fathom content as "very high-end stuff" compared to other material then available online. Crow referred to the site's intended audience—educated lifelong learners with the means and inclination to pay for general enrichment courses—as a "niche market," and said that at Columbia, "we use knowledge as a form of venture capital."[25]

One of the earliest decisions the Columbia leadership made in formulating Fathom was to create an association of multiple partner institutions rather than go it alone. Kirschner credits this decision to a "chance encounter" in 1999 with a visiting team from the London School of Economics (LSE) that was similarly contemplating online dissemination strategies for their institution's teaching and intellectual property. According to Kirschner, the decision to partner grew quickly and easily from the two parties' first interactions, and both were eager to see if other partners could be brought on board.[26] Although very much of Columbia, in order to attract consortium partners and distinguish itself from the university's other not-for-profit activities, Fathom was organized as a separate entity.[27] By the time its website (depicted in Figure 2.1) launched in 2000, Fathom was a partnership of ten leading cultural

---

[23]Singer, "Distance-Learning Ventures."

[24]Quoted respectively from Beiles, Nancy, "A League of Her Own," *Grok,* October 2000, 41, and interview with Ann Kirschner, 7/28/08. Kirschner said that, in theory, Fathom's long-term financial arrangement would allow universities to "retain the majority of whatever money they made; our idea was to take a transaction fee, and that's what would support the production costs that went into it."

[25]Quoted respectively from interview with Michael Crow, 12/22/08, and Blumenstyk, "Knowledge Is 'a Form of Venture Capital.'"

[26]Interview with Ann Kirschner, 8/10/09.

[27]Fathom's earliest office was located in Low Library, Columbia's main administrative building and the symbolic heart of campus, but it eventually moved to another site. As defined by a Columbia University Senate committee on online learning and digital media initiatives, "Fathom was a privately held C corporation in which the university was a majority shareholder and provided most of the funding" (Hane, Paula J., "Columbia University to Close Fathom.com," *Information Today, Inc.,* January 13, 2003, http://newsbreaks.infotoday.com/nbreader.asp?ArticleID=16813).

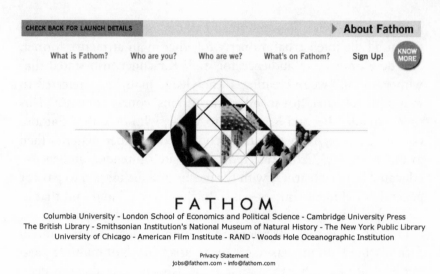

FIGURE 2.1 Fathom's pre-launch landing page (as it appeared on August 15, 2000).

Available at http://web.archive.org/web/20000815201751/http://www.fathom.com/.

institutions, pairing Columbia and the LSE with the American Film Institute, the British Library, Cambridge University Press, the National Museum of Natural History, the New York Public Library (NYPL), the RAND Corporation, the University of Chicago, and the Woods Hole Oceanographic Institution.[28] Initially, Fathom's leaders had wanted the consortium to consist only of Columbia and peer universities, but when attempts to sign on Harvard, Princeton, and Yale proved unsuccessful, other entities, such as libraries and museums, were brought on board.[29] While distinct from universities, cultural institutions like libraries and museums were thought to have sufficiently similar missions, as they were dedicated to lifelong learning and promoting access to knowledge and collections.[30]

Like the decision to launch Fathom in the first place, the choice to organize it as a consortium had both offensive and defensive

[28]The British Museum, the Science Museum of London, the University of Michigan, and the Victoria and Albert Museum were also very early Fathom partners.

[29]Interview with George Rupp, 8/7/08. According to Rupp, "we had a great deal of difficulty persuading our Ivy League confreres to join up."

[30]Interview with Ann Kirschner, 7/28/08.

rationales. In part, Columbia's partnerships were designed to increase the site's appeal by aggregating strong intellectual brands. Kirschner said that Fathom hoped to offer the widest possible range of products to its customers and that "Columbia preferred the model of strength in numbers and multiple brands," to provide "a teeming variety for the prospective customer."[31] But Fathom's consortial organization was also intended to turn potential competitors into collaborators. Its own promotional materials describe it as "a global e-learning company [that] works with leading educational and cultural institutions to project their teaching and research to an international audience."[32] Fathom's architects assumed that the field would soon be flooded with vendors trying to digitize and monetize intellectual content; they wanted to ensure that other institutions would be with them rather than against them.[33] One of the few requirements of partner institutions was that they sign an exclusivity agreement entitling Fathom to all of their future online content production.[34]

Given the variety of its contributing institutions, Fathom set out to publish online courses supplemented by an array of digital educational materials, including articles by professors, images, museum objects, and primary sources like documents and maps. The text-based courses were frequently enhanced by features like audio slideshows, animations, or interactive graphics, and some of the courses contained social networking elements like threaded discussions or moderated chats.[35] The site's content types and pre-

---

[31]Interview with Ann Kirschner, 8/5/08.

[32]"Background on Fathom," promotional one-sheet, Fathom.com, undated.

[33]According to Kirschner, "there were two ways to build the business: one was to get it deeply rooted in Columbia and then see where we were. The other was to expand it as fast as possible and to include as many institutions as possible, and we chose the latter in the context of 1999, in the belief that everything was going to happen so quickly that in two or three years every institution would have picked sides and gone somewhere" (interview with Ann Kirschner, 8/5/08).

[34]Interview with Michael Crow, 12/22/08.

[35]For example, a description of Professor Alan Brinkley's Fathom course entitled "America since 1945: The Politics of Anticommunism" stated that "the e-seminar makes use of multimedia elements including audio slideshows, period newsreels and television features that reflects [sic] the political atmosphere of the era, as well as additional text elements such as biographical entries, and primary documents" ("America since 1945: The Politics of Anti-Communism," http://web.archive.org/web/20021017143217/fathom.com/fks/catalog/course.jhtml?id=58705023).

FIGURE 2.2   Fathom course page, "Liberty and Slavery in the Early British Empire" with Professor Simon Schama, a joint presentation of Columbia University and the BBC (as it appeared on November 22, 2002).

Available at http://web.archive.org/web/20021213221251/www.fathom.com/fks/catalog/course.jhtml?id =2510. © 2002 Fathom Knowledge Network. All rights reserved.

sentation styles varied widely: content creation was decentralized, with each partner organization responsible for creating and providing its own content, which would be posted following approval by Fathom's Columbia-led academic council. Kirschner chose to work with "whoever would participate" at Columbia, where most of the early Fathom content was generated, but "if those faculty were big names, so much the better." The presence of some star faculty in Fathom courses (such as Alan Brinkley, Brian Greene, Kenneth Jackson, and Simon Schama, whose course page is depicted in Figure 2.2) indicates this desire to work with those whose reputations might attract customers.[36]

Fathom's initial offerings were primarily courses lasting about six hours, many of which cost $500 or more, but Kirschner said that Fathom.com also contained a great deal of free content.[37] Promotional material states that Fathom offered "over 600 courses, ranging from $50 to over $500," as well as "more than 80,000 free learning experiences including seminars, articles and reference entries across ten disciplines."[38]

Challenges Fathom Faced

Over the course of its life, Fathom met with a series of challenges that led to corresponding adjustments to its content. Although comprehensive figures regarding the site's usage statistics and total revenues are not available, all involved confirm that Fathom never attracted a sufficient number of paying customers and, consequently, revenues did not come close to matching the program's costs. This cannot be blamed on lack of attention to the site by the education press, which covered Fathom's launch and development quite closely; technology reporters also took note, naming the site "best learning portal" in *Yahoo! Internet Life*.[39] But Fathom had difficulty converting this attention into sales. Former Fathom CIO Bill Ying confirmed that the site received a great deal of traffic but said that the "conversion rate [of visitors to customers] was practically zero."[40] Indeed, articles discussing Fathom's closure reported that "in 2001, Columbia gave Fathom $14.9 million, while the venture earned $700,000 from fees from other institutions and

---

[36]Interviews with Ann Kirschner, 7/28/08, and Bill Ying, 7/11/08.
[37]Interview with Ann Kirschner, 7/28/08.
[38]"Background on Fathom."
[39]Carlson, Scott, "For-Profit Web Venture Shifts Gears, Hoping to Find a Way to Make a Profit," *Chronicle of Higher Education,* online edition, February 9, 2001.
[40]Interview with Bill Ying, 7/11/08.

sales revenue," and that while 65,000 people signed up for either a paid or free Fathom course, it "was not revealed how many were converted into paying customers."[41]

As a result of low initial revenues, Fathom undertook a series of (ultimately unsuccessful) adjustments to its model. The initial course offerings from Columbia were longer, more expensive to produce and to purchase, and included more high-tech multimedia offerings such as interactive graphics and streaming video. But by 2002, several years into the endeavor, Fathom courses became shorter, cheaper, and simpler as business continued to flag.[42] Kirschner said that after the site's initial launch, shorter e-seminar options were added in an effort to increase usage and generate revenues. These smaller units retailed for significantly less than the full e-courses and could be completed more quickly by the user. At the time, Kirschner defended the change: "we've broadened the kinds of courses in recognition of the fact that most people aren't familiar yet with online learning, so they need different price points. We need to introduce learners to the concept before they will commit money."[43] Fathom also began to offer short, self-paced courses free of charge—what Kirschner called a "free sample strategy"—to entice customers.[44]

Fathom suffered in its first year from a dearth of content. Many partners did not have digital materials ready to sell on the platform, and Fathom fell short of offering the "teeming variety" of content options that Kirschner had hoped the consortial structure would enable. The arrangement between Columbia and Fathom's other member institutions was designed to be mutually beneficial, with Columbia providing the vast majority of the funding and the other partners providing digital content in exchange for a share of

[41]Carlson, Scott, "After Losing Millions, Columbia U. Will Close Online-Learning Venture," *Chronicle of Higher Education,* online edition, January 17, 2003; Phillips, Stephen, "E-Outfits Go the Distance," *Times* Higher Education Supplement, *New York Times,* online edition, February 7, 2003.

[42]Interview with Bill Ying, 7/11/08.

[43]Quoted in Hafner, Katie, "Lessons Learned at Dot-Com U," *New York Times,* online edition, May 2, 2002.

[44]Interview with Ann Kirschner, 7/28/08. According to Kirschner, over 100,000 people registered for free courses.

the potential profits.[45] Describing the relationship between Fathom and the member institutions, Kirschner said that "the most important thing was the ability to use their name and their brand."[46] In other words, partners were chosen based on the prestige of their reputations, with little consideration given to the amount of digital content they were ready to contribute to the site. Despite the fact that Fathom amassed what Kirschner referred to as a "glittering group of institutions," all with reputable, well-known brands and access to valuable intellectual property, much of the content never materialized to the degree that had been hoped.[47] The resulting arrangement left Columbia in charge of providing much of the early content and nearly all of the money.[48]

The structure of Fathom's agreement with its partner institutions therefore posed a challenge to the ultimate success of the project. Columbia made the strategic decision not to force other Fathom partners to take on investment burdens, hoping that a low barrier to entry would attract consortium partners and might also allow Columbia to retain full control of the eventual profits as the sole initial investor.[49] But without a financial stake in the endeavor's success, the other partners had relatively weak incentives to deliver

[45]Interview with Ann Kirschner, 7/28/08. David L. Kirp put Columbia's contribution to Fathom's financing at "more than 90 percent" (Kirp, David L., *Shakespeare, Einstein, and the Bottom Line: The Marketing of Higher Education,* Cambridge, Mass.: Harvard University Press, 2003, 173).

[46]Interview with Ann Kirschner, 7/28/08.

[47]Ibid. For instance, the NYPL had originally planned to contribute half a million digital images to Fathom, but digitization took much longer than anyone had anticipated, and by the time the content was ready, Fathom had already shut down (interview with Bill Ying, 7/11/08). Columbia gave Fathom a five-year lease, but it was terminated only three years after its launch, so all involved may have been operating under the assumption that there was more time for the effort to prove itself than it actually had. Crow agreed with Ying that the partner organizations were slow in providing content (and that some did not produce much of anything) but noted that "it was all expected to take a very long time; we were very patient with developing this, because no one had ever done this before" (interview with Michael Crow, 12/22/08).

[48]"Columbia had the vast majority of the courses," according to Kirschner, when the Fathom platform was open only to consortium partners in the endeavor's early phase (interview with Ann Kirschner, 7/28/08).

[49]According to Rupp, "the strategy was to try to build a critical mass of content partners in order to make the site weighty enough that there would be a sense that it was *the* place to go. But that meant that there was a great value in getting people to join the consortium, and the odds of that were far diminished if we'd also said, 'OK, you have to pony up a few million dollars'" (interview with George Rupp, 8/7/08). Kirschner said that the LSE also

content in a timely manner. Kirschner said that in retrospect, financial contribution should have been a condition of participation in the
Fathom consortium, because "sometimes when things are free it's too
easy to get in and get out. I think it would have been better if they'd
had more skin in the game, so to speak. Because then when the going
got tough, to *then* ask them for any money was a fool's errand—it
should have been done at the very beginning but wasn't."[50]

The inadequate body of content on the site in its first years was
a major source of concern for the Fathom team, and the desire
to fully flesh out its offerings led to more serious changes to the
model. The original Fathom business plan called for content generated exclusively by the 14 consortium institutions. But as the consortium members were not producing content fast enough to hit
the designated benchmarks, the model was reworked in an attempt
to save the endeavor.[51]

In its second and third years of operation, Fathom began to allow courses created outside the consortium to be sold on the platform. To populate the site with content, Fathom turned to additional universities such as Penn State, Purdue University, and the
University of Florida, as well as to nonacademic organizations and
even corporate partners.[52] Fathom hosted a series of promotional
courses for MasterCard International targeted at young people
and worked with organizations like the AARP.[53] A February 2002
article reported that, "in a bid to market itself to corporate employees and job hunters," Fathom had also diversified its offerings
by establishing a "Professional Development Center," as seen in
Figure 2.3, with corporate training and professional development
courses created by for-profit education companies.[54] Kirschner said

had a small ownership stake in Fathom, but it was unique among the consortium members
in that respect (interview with Ann Kirschner, 8/10/09).

[50]Interview with Ann Kirschner, 7/28/08.

[51]Interview with Ann Kirschner, 8/10/09.

[52]Some of these online courses offered credit from those universities, and Fathom served
as a vendor, aggregating a range of courses and providing marketing (interview with Ann
Kirschner, 8/10/09).

[53]However, these courses were not available through the course directory on the Fathom
platform alongside the academic content (interview with Ann Kirschner, 7/28/08).

[54]The article also reported that "the arrangement brings several hundred new courses

FIGURE 2.3   Fathom Professional Development Center (as it appeared on November 22, 2002).

Available at http://web.archive.org/web/20021002222230/www.fathom.com/professionals/.

© 2002 Fathom Knowledge Network. All rights reserved.

that "when content came from AARP—things like how to choose health insurance providers or tracing trends in American healthcare —we were simply the course developer. . . . It wasn't an academic course, but it was a revenue-generator for Fathom."

Such changes to the site's scope were perhaps confusing from a branding perspective, as viewers drawn to Fathom by the Columbia, LSE, or British Library monikers might find courses and other

into Fathom's online catalog" (Arnone, Michael, "Fathom Adds Training to Distance-Education Offerings," *Chronicle of Higher Education*, online edition, February 22, 2002).

learning materials from very different sources. Frank Mayadas of the Sloan Foundation commented on this shift in Fathom's content: "this kind of training is aimed at a very different kind of customer . . . [and therefore] dilutes their brand. What do they want to be known for?"[55]

None of the efforts to adjust the content or pricing generated sufficient revenue, and as a result of these many changes, Fathom's original mission—which Rupp described as "seek[ing] to be a high-end Web learning environment that retains the form and style of intellectual discourse that typifies Columbia University"—grew obscured toward the end of the organization's life.[56] But from Kirschner's perspective, "entrepreneurship is a messy business, it just is. You think you understand what the business is going to look like, and then reality intrudes, and you either stand in place because you're paralyzed or you evolve. And we continued to evolve."[57]

Tensions also arose between Fathom, a revenue-seeking commercial venture, and the academic culture of the contributing institutions. Kirschner defended the decision to structure Fathom as a for-profit, claiming that "you would have trouble attracting a first-rate team in the year 1999 if you weren't a for-profit structure, because it was the go-go years of the internet."[58] But she also said that Fathom's for-profit status was the source of some tension within the broader academic community in which it resided, as she had experienced "the light going out in somebody's eyes when they found out that [Fathom] was for-profit."[59]

[55]Quoted in Arnone, "Fathom Adds Training." Rupp agreed, saying that when Fathom started allowing a broader group of institutions to contribute, "it was a point of departure for the organization, and I think that came at the point at which there was a failure of nerve or confidence in the original idea, and a kind of scrambling to see what kind of content we could enlist" (interview with George Rupp, 8/7/08).

[56]Rupp's open letter went on to say that Fathom was "intended as a kind of digital gathering place for those who cannot attend classes, lectures, and other events on campus but who want a sense of immersion in the intellectual atmosphere that characterizes a great research university" (Rupp, from "Current Communications").

[57]Interview with Ann Kirschner, 7/28/08.

[58]Ibid. At the time, paying huge salaries and offering stock options or other perks to programmers was the norm, and an organization like Fathom had to compete for technology staff with Silicon Valley at the height of the boom.

[59]Interview with Ann Kirschner, 8/5/08.

Fathom was a major priority of Columbia's executive vice provost and benefited from interaction with the provost, the board of trustees, and the university president—as Kirschner said, "it was totally led from the top."[60] But despite the backing of university leadership, the project did not necessarily enjoy widespread support from the faculty. Crow admitted that Fathom's team "got some pushback from faculty for even undertaking the thing. Some faculty, not all faculty, thought we would ruin the university with it because it was commercial."[61] This sense that an e-commerce project was fundamentally at odds with the university's core activities became increasingly apparent as time passed and Fathom failed to generate significant revenues. Columbia Professor Richard Bulliet said in 2001 that the administration's focus on digital ventures "has a marginalizing effect on the faculty," as much of a professor's teaching does not necessarily translate to an online product.[62]

A University Senate subcommittee on online learning and digital media initiatives then launched an inquiry into Fathom. Bulliet served as the committee's chair, saying that Fathom's business plan was still "in a state of flux" and that "the precise way in which this would become in the long run self-sustaining without infusion of University resources was never precisely laid out."[63] The 2002 report issued by the subcommittee advised that the university "fund initiatives that either make a profit, provide infrastructure for those that do, or reinforce the core missions of the university," and concluded that "it became apparent that Fathom did not meet these criteria."[64] In addition to expressing frustrations with the ini-

---

[60] Interview with Ann Kirschner, 7/28/08. Three members of Columbia's board of trustees also sat on the Fathom board (interview with Ann Kirschner, 8/10/09).

[61] Interview with Michael Crow, 12/22/08. A February 2001 article in the *Chronicle* mentioned that Fathom had some detractors among the Columbia faculty and quoted Columbia Law School Professor Eben Moglen as saying "Let's be real. Nobody who thinks seriously about the shape of Internet media thinks Fathom is going anywhere" (quoted in Carlson, "For-Profit Web Venture Shifts Gears").

[62] Blumenstyk, "Knowledge Is 'a Form of Venture Capital.'"

[63] Quoted in Casselman, Ben, "Columbia Committee Reports on Fathom.com's Difficulties," *Columbia Daily Spectator,* reprinted in *University Wire,* online edition, January 29, 2001.

[64] Beam, Chris, "Fathom.com Shuts Down as Columbia Withdraws," *Columbia Daily Spectator,* online edition, January 27, 2003. The committee issued a recommendation to the University Senate that proposed limiting Fathom's funding to "the minimum level to keep

tiative's inability to hit its revenue targets, a contingent of the Columbia faculty felt that the funds directed toward Fathom—which one Columbia professor referred to as "the only uncontrolled revenue stream of the university"—could have been better spent.[65] The subcommittee report said that Fathom had "failed to identify and capture a market segment sufficient to warrant the resources dedicated to [it]. . . . It is difficult to thus justify the expense of producing new online content, especially when it is completely separate from the instruction offered in Columbia's traditional degree programs," suggesting that Fathom had strayed too far from both the mission and the everyday academic activities of the university.[66]

Accounting for some of the skepticism that Fathom encountered, Kirschner claimed that "we did not have the core constituency that we really should have had [at Columbia], and we had enemies because people didn't understand what we were doing."[67] She spent a great deal of her time growing and tending to the trans-Atlantic consortium, and she felt that committing to that direction may have prevented Fathom from becoming sufficiently

basic operations going" and said that, in the long term, "Fathom should rethink its business model" (quoted in Hane, "Columbia University to Close Fathom.com"). Kirschner believed that "if we would have been selling courses in the thousands [per year] rather than the hundreds, that would have been evidence of a better acceptance curve" and some of Fathom's critics at Columbia might have been more patient with it (interview with Ann Kirschner, 8/10/09).

[65]Quoted in Blumenstyk, "Knowledge Is 'a Form of Venture Capital.'" Kirschner said that "probably the greatest grousing came from faculty who felt that they could see other purposes for the university's investment" (interview with Ann Kirschner, 8/5/08). Rupp agreed, recalling that within the Columbia community, Fathom elicited "more resistance among traditional academic people than many ideas, because it was a quite radical departure. And I think to the extent that it required funding, there was more resistance, because there were opportunity costs and that money could have been spent in other ways" (interview with George Rupp, 8/7/08).

[66]Arnone, Michael, "Columbia Senate Questions Spending on Fathom," *Chronicle of Higher Education*, online edition, May 10, 2002.

[67]Interview with Ann Kirschner, 7/28/08. Martin Trow has also noted that within institutions, tensions can often arise between intrepid individuals who enthusiastically embrace new technologies and business models and the otherwise stable and fundamentally conservative culture of the university: "in the great research universities, there is tension between the deeply conservative norms and structures of academic communities, senates, and decision-making processes on the one hand, and the readiness of individual members of those communities to initiate and experiment boldly in research and teaching and in responding to market opportunities on the other" (Trow, Martin, "The Development of Information Technology in American Higher Education," *Daedalus* 126, no. 4 [Fall 1997], 312).

rooted within the Columbia community. According to Kirschner, "we would have had to do a lot more than we did to establish Fathom as a shared mission that would benefit faculty, as well as the institution, as well as the students" at Columbia.[68] (This, for example, was the approach that MIT took to OpenCourseWare, as discussed in the following chapter.) Without a broad base of internal support or signs that it was on the path to profitability, Fathom found itself vulnerable following turnover in the offices of the president, provost, and executive vice provost. Columbia announced Fathom's impending termination on January 6, 2003, early in the tenure of President Lee Bollinger, who replaced Rupp following his resignation in the summer of 2002.[69] The article in the *Spectator* announcing Fathom's closure reported that much of Crow's former portfolio was being handled in the new Bollinger administration by Robert Kasdin, who in short order closed down both the Fathom initiative and Columbia's Biosphere 2 project—both highly visible beneficiaries of the strategic investment fund under Crow.[70]

Kirschner admits that in retrospect there were inherent contradictions in Fathom's approach, which had roots in both the for-profit and not-for-profit camps. "Fathom always had a bit of confusion in its mission because we had the really lofty mission of educating the world, but on the other hand Columbia was . . . judging us on our ability to be self-sustaining rather quickly—and you can't have it both ways," she said. "We could have been self-sustaining more quickly if we would have sold just anything on the site, but if we had sold just anything on the site we wouldn't have been proper stewards of Columbia's brand and its intellectual property."[71] MIT and other schools that subsequently explored online course dissemination avoided this tension by simply offering

[68]Interview with Ann Kirschner, 8/5/08.

[69]Carlson, "After Losing Millions."

[70]Beam, "Fathom.com Shuts Down." Prior to assuming his new role at Columbia, Bollinger was president of the University of Michigan, where in 2000 he had endorsed that institution's membership in the Fathom consortium (University of Michigan News Service, "U-M Joins Fathom," November 15, 2000, http://www.ns.umich.edu/index.html?Releases/2000/Nov00/r111500a).

[71]Interview with Ann Kirschner, 8/5/08.

the content for free, enabled by angel capital that did not carry the expectation that their projects would generate any revenue.

AllLearn

Founded in 2000 as a consortium of top institutions, including Oxford, Princeton, Stanford, and Yale, the Alliance for Lifelong Learning—renamed AllLearn in 2002—was designed as a collaborative approach to e-learning (see the site's homepage in Figure 2.4). As was the case with Fathom's founding, AllLearn's former director of academic programming Peter Bernstein said that member institutions chose to launch the initiative for "both offensive and defensive reasons."[72]

AllLearn's participating institutions were intrigued—as Columbia had been—by the apparent promise of the internet during the dot-com boom, and each of the partner institutions had explored and experimented with distance education efforts in some way.[73] The initiative offered participants a chance to enter the burgeoning realm of online learning, as well as to experiment with the use of technology in teaching. Kristin Kim, AllLearn's general counsel and later its second CEO, said that AllLearn's member universities were motivated by "the desire to really understand this space and to provide their faculty members with the opportunity to explore" the use of digital technologies, both in the classroom for internal audiences and in outward-facing projects.[74] This was also the recollection of Diana Kleiner, Yale's faculty liaison to AllLearn and a professor of art history and deputy provost for the arts; she said that when Yale began its involvement with AllLearn, "we didn't really know how it was going to go, but we thought that an institution like Yale need[ed] to be a leader" in this space.[75]

[72]Interview with Peter Bernstein, 4/28/09.

[73]Stanford had a commission on technology and teaching and learning in the 1990s that examined the role of the university in the digital age; the Association of Yale Alumni invested in a "Great Teachers Series" offering VHS tapes of lectures; and Oxford had historically supported a thriving continuing education program.

[74]Interview with Kristin Kim, 5/7/09.

[75]Interview with Diana Kleiner, 12/18/08.

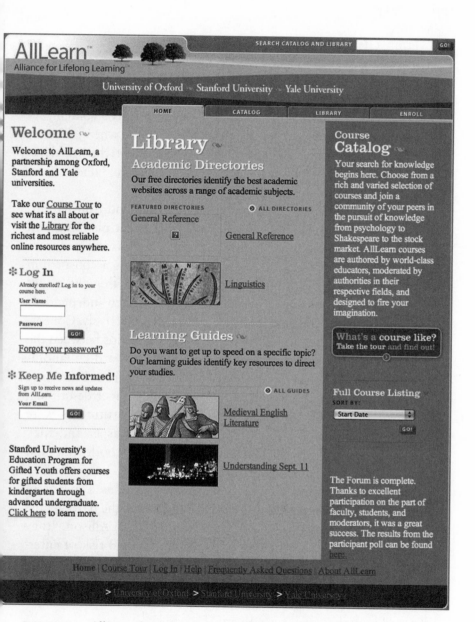

FIGURE 2.4   AllLearn landing page (as it appeared on November 20, 2002).

From a defensive perspective, many involved with AllLearn recall a shared concern among participants that online courses were the way of the future, and that if they did not develop a digital venture they risked being superseded by competitors—both peer universities and for-profit ventures that might siphon off faculty's content. As Princeton's then-provost Jeremiah Ostriker put it, when AllLearn was founded, "they were heady times. People thought: the world has changed, everything's going to be different, there [are] billions to be made with our franchise, don't get left behind."[76]

The idea for Fathom generated at Columbia, and Ann Kirschner and the Columbia team carried out significant planning and development work on the venture before partner institutions were brought on board. But AllLearn was structured as a consortium from its inception: although members had each thought about the digital space on their own and had undertaken independent precursor efforts, AllLearn itself was founded collectively. Consortium members were chosen via personal relationships between the presidents of the universities.[77] As a first step toward collaboration, Kleiner said that a group of representatives from Princeton, Stanford, and Yale discussed, and wrote a white paper describing, a potential joint effort. Once the four member institutions were in place, Stanford and Yale Presidents Gerhard Casper and Rick Levin tapped Herbert M. Allison, a graduate of both Yale and Stanford with a strong finance background, as AllLearn's CEO.

AllLearn's members viewed a consortial model as a means of spreading out the financial burden. As intrigued as the participants were by the potential of e-commerce, according to Allison, "they were concerned about the cost and the reputational risk of entering online learning. So they decided to band together to launch a venture that might have a different name and a broader funding base to reduce those risks, and yet still learn about these new media and how they might use them."[78]

---

[76]Interview with Jeremiah Ostriker, 7/24/08.
[77]Interview with Diana Kleiner, 12/18/08. Tristram Wyatt, Director of Distance and Online Learning at Oxford, confirmed that close personal ties between key leaders at Oxford and Princeton facilitated Oxford's entrance into the consortium (interview by Roger Schonfeld with Wyatt, 6/25/08).
[78]Interview with Herbert Allison, 3/11/09.

AllLearn considered its member institutions' alumni to be its primary audience. The site's promotional materials stated that "One graduates. To a degree. There's just no end to a great education," framing the initiative as a means of keeping alumni involved and engaged beyond their four years of college.[79] Graduates of these institutions were considered a prudent initial audience for AllLearn because they were likely to have both the will and the means to pursue enrichment courses from their alma maters.[80] In addition to mitigating risks and spreading the workload, AllLearn's consortial structure also allowed it to access a larger pool of alumni than any single institution could have separately—Allison estimated the combined alumni population of the four universities at 470,000.[81] And as was the case with Fathom, member institutions also realized that joining together could yield promising branding opportunities. According to Jeffrey Brenzel, then-director of the Association of Yale Alumni, "Yale, Princeton, Stanford, [and] Oxford [are] some of the most recognizable names in education in the world . . . so the idea was that it would enhance the credibility of the entire business."[82]

Both Fathom and AllLearn charged user fees for courses, but the similarities in the two business models basically end there. While Fathom was organized as a for-profit corporation, AllLearn.org was a not-for-profit 501(c)(3) association governed by its member universities. And unlike Fathom, which was intended to provide a revenue surplus back to member institutions above and beyond the initiative's operating costs, AllLearn attempted only to recoup its member institutions' investments, which included an initial con-

[79]In the press release announcing the initiative, Allison said that "the Alliance among four of the world's greatest universities has an inspiring mission. It will provide the schools' alumni around the world with ongoing access to the best in higher education, enriching their lives and helping them make the fullest contribution to their communities" (quoted in "Oxford, Princeton, Stanford, Yale to Invest $12 Million in Distance Learning Venture," News from Princeton University Office of Communications, September 28, 2000).

[80]Interview with Jeffrey Brenzel, 4/23/09. Kleiner added that because the initiative was experimental in nature, the participating institutions thought alumni would provide helpful feedback in the initial stage.

[81]Stanford Provost John Etchemendy recalled that in forming the AllLearn consortium, "we wanted it to be similar universities with a similar alumni cross section so we'd be dealing with alumni you could make assumptions about—targeting a fairly homogenous sector of the population" (interview with John Etchemendy, 8/19/08).

[82]Interview with Jeff Brenzel, 4/23/09.

tribution of $3 million in start-up capital from each of the four partners.

Work on AllLearn was divided between the central office in New York, headed by CEO Herbert Allison until 2002 and then by Kristin Kim, and the partner campuses, where liaisons worked with faculty and campus technology groups on course production and development. At its height there were 22 people working for the central office of AllLearn—a significant business effort on a par with Fathom.[83] Yet the language favored by the AllLearn team indicates that they tended to focus on its mission of providing valuable educational opportunities to alumni and to deemphasize its status as a business. According to Bernstein, the partners viewed AllLearn "as a way to fund- and friend-raise, and as a way to involve the alumni in the continuing life of the school."[84]

Because it intended to generate revenues through the sale of online courses, AllLearn was responsive to market indicators in selecting and developing its curriculum. In Kleiner's words, "we needed to make something that people would pay a few hundred dollars to take."[85] But in general, AllLearn stuck to the universities' core competencies in the liberal arts and did not veer into skill acquisition or professional training courses, as Fathom eventually did.[86] Content was chosen for inclusion in AllLearn based in part on a course's wide-ranging appeal, resulting in a set of offerings that favored current affairs and other marketable subjects like history survey courses (some of which can be seen in Figure 2.5, listing AllLearn's offerings in American Studies). Kleiner mentioned that among the site's most popular offerings was a one-day panel on the Iraq War with faculty from each institution, as well as a course related to *The Da Vinci Code*.[87]

---

[83]Interview with Herbert Allison, 3/11/09.

[84]Interview with Peter Bernstein, 4/28/09. Etchemendy echoed this sentiment, saying of the original goal of AllLearn that "it was an outreach effort for our alumni. More and more education isn't something you can think of as being done after four years" (interview with John Etchemendy, 8/19/08).

[85]Interview with Diana Kleiner, 12/18/08.

[86]Princeton's liaison Georgia Nugent said that with AllLearn, "we're focusing on our core—a liberal arts education—not education in the professional areas or certification programs" (quoted in "Alliance with Yale, Stanford, Oxford Paves the Way for Life-Long Learning," *Princeton Weekly Bulletin*, online edition, 90, no. 5 [October 9, 2000]).

[87]Interview with Diana Kleiner, 12/18/08.

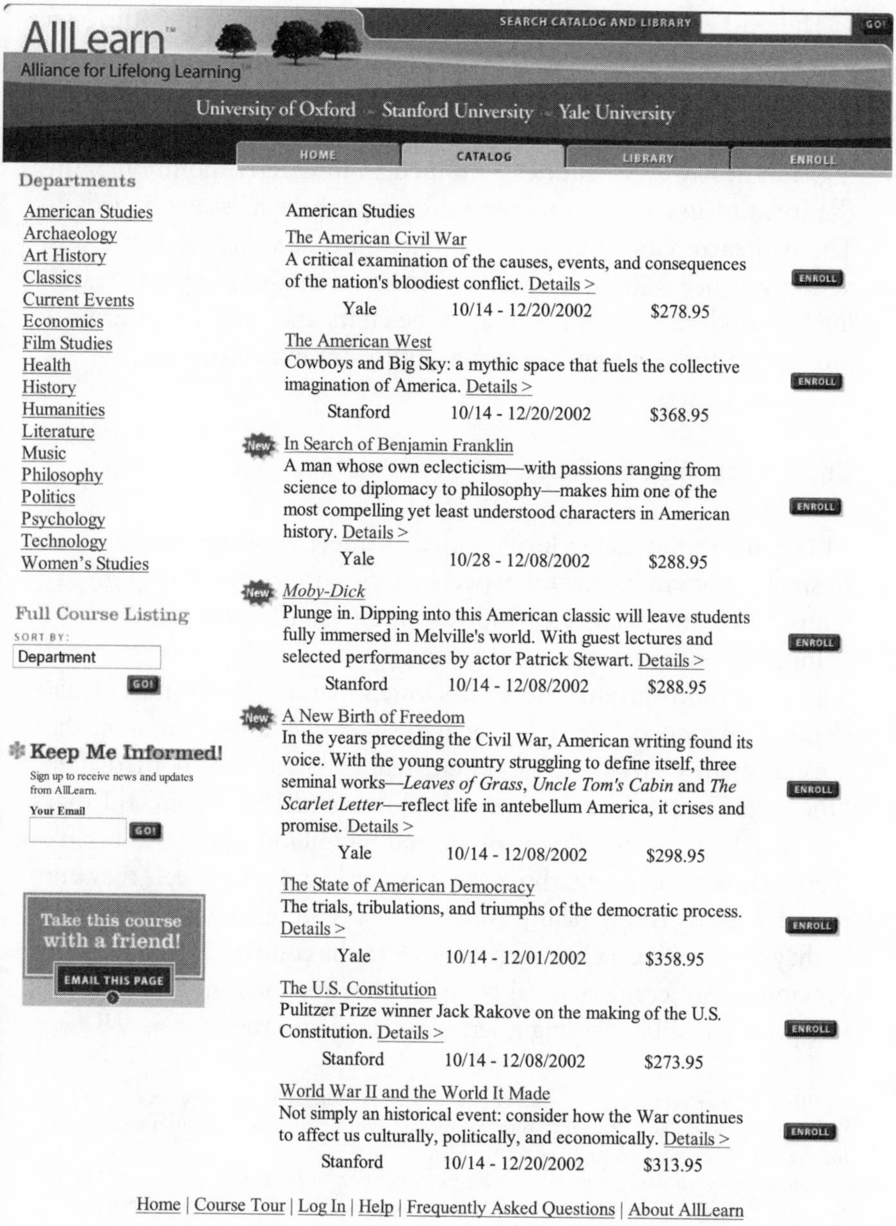

FIGURE 2.5   AllLearn list of course offerings in American Studies (as it appeared on November 20, 2002).

Available at http://web.archive.org/web/20021003223047/allianceforlifelonglearning.org/catalog.jsp?d=8.
© 2002 Alliance for Lifelong Learning, Inc. All rights reserved.

The AllLearn team approached course design in the spirit of experimentation: there was not a clear template for the courses, and each could contain different elements.[88] Courses were kept short to appeal to the working adults whom AllLearn was targeting, and nearly every course contained an interactive component in the form of live chats, threaded discussions, or message boards.[89] The AllLearn team shared the conviction that some kind of interaction was necessary to attract customers, though paying and training the moderators who managed the chats and message boards—mostly graduate students—was a significant expense.

Challenges AllLearn Faced

AllLearn's initial usage levels failed to meet expectations, and as business stagnated, several aspects of the model evolved in an attempt to create efficiencies and respond to market forces.

Initially, AllLearn courses were uniquely and elaborately designed with sumptuous production values, often making use of multimedia elements like video.[90] After Allison left AllLearn in 2002 to assume the presidency of TIAA-CREF and Bernstein departed shortly thereafter, "the organization was significantly downsized."[91] Allison said that AllLearn had operating costs of around $4 million a year, "so I think there was some concern about the cost level, and when I left they cut the costs pretty dramatically. And they really stopped any innovation —they were taking a cheaper approach to the courses."[92] Kristin Kim, previously AllLearn's general counsel, then assumed the chief executive position, implementing a series of changes to the model.

[88]Ibid. Kleiner said that "because we saw this as experimental, we were very willing to try a number of different things," so there were no firm or consistent minimum standards for the content or the look and feel of AllLearn.

[89]Interview with Paul Lawrence, 12/17/08. According to Kleiner, "we thought that for this to be exciting for people, there needs to be some kind of interaction" (interview with Diana Kleiner, 12/18/08).

[90]Interview with Paul Lawrence, 12/17/08. Lawrence, whose Center for Media and Instructional Innovation was responsible for producing the courses, described the more elaborate AllLearn videos as "mini-documentaries."

[91]Interview with Peter Bernstein, 4/28/09.

[92]Interview with Herbert Allison, 3/11/09.

With Kim at the helm, AllLearn began to shorten and simplify the design of its courses in response to early customer purchasing behaviors and feedback. Kim was also charged with reaching out to new, broader audiences for AllLearn, as the alumni pool alone did not provide the initiative with sufficient revenue to break even.[93] According to Kleiner, AllLearn's content and pricing models kept evolving because "we really didn't know what was going to work."[94] Courses were shortened to make them both more accessible to users and less expensive to produce, and AllLearn created week-long versions of its full courses "as a kind of teaser to encourage people to take the eight-week course if they liked it."[95] As a separate legal entity, AllLearn was perhaps positioned to be more nimble than projects governed within larger and more conservative structures like the traditional university. Yet in the end, these changes proved unsuccessful: in its five years of operation, All-Learn never came close to breaking even, and course enrollments always lagged.[96] According to Bernstein, "if we got over ten in some courses, we thought we were doing well. Some courses went up to 200, but usually if we got over 50 that was a best-seller."[97]

[93]In an article announcing Kim's ascendency to chief executive of AllLearn, Levin said "we've asked her to focus on building new audiences for the alliance and she's pursuing a wide variety of strategies for doing this" (quoted in Blau, Jessamyn, "Veteran Takes Over at AllLearn," *Yale Daily News,* online edition, February 6, 2003). Allison observed that the alumni's interest level was simply too low to support the endeavor. He said that when AllLearn sent direct mailings to the schools' alumni, "we thought we'd be able to get a one-half of 1 percent response rate, and we got about 0.3 percent, which wasn't quite enough" (interview, 3/11/09).

[94]Interview with Diana Kleiner, 12/18/08.

[95]Allison said that the courses were very labor-intensive for users, who were expected to do all the reading, post on message boards, and participate in chats—all of which he estimated required about seven hours of work per week. "This was much more of a time commitment than people probably thought it would be when they first signed up" (interview with Herbert Allison, 3/11/09). As for costs, "Courses [were] reported to have cost between $10,000–$150,000 to produce." As time progressed, AllLearn's costs veered toward the cheaper end of that spectrum. The mini-courses could presumably be offered to customers at a lower price point in order to drive up business. "Tuition fees were initially set at a standard rate of $195 for alumni and $250 for the general public, plus variable 'material fees' ranging from $11.95 to $49.95. . . . By June 2004–2005, tuition costs had risen significantly and varied by course," with several courses costing over $800 (Jokivirta, Lisa, "What Went Wrong with AllLearn?" *University Business,* online edition, June 2006).

[96]Between July 1, 2001, and June 30, 2002, AllLearn's total expenses were $6,424,438, while it earned $232,499 in revenue (Alliance for Lifelong Learning 990 form, filed 2003, http://www.guidestar.org/FinDocuments/2003/134/138/2003-134138834-1-9.pdf).

[97]Interview with Peter Bernstein, 4/28/09.

Given its failure to generate significant revenue, the initiative was officially shuttered in March 2006.

Early on, AllLearn began to show signs of strain between the consortium members, manifested most dramatically in Princeton's early withdrawal from the Alliance in November 2001. Princeton had originally agreed to participate because Ostriker, its provost, saw AllLearn as an intriguing experiment, but the university quickly came to feel that the costs were too high and the business model unfeasible. Describing Princeton's earliest involvement in AllLearn, Ostriker said, "I was excited about it. I thought and think that there is great potential for this. But I found the actual form that it was taking extremely frustrating, because we entered into a business organization, which had goals that were very different [from the university's]. . . . This was dot-com madness as far as I was concerned."[98] Ultimately, Princeton determined that it was not extracting sufficient value from the AllLearn arrangement and would be better off exploring educational technology on its own, focusing exclusively on its own students' needs.

In general, AllLearn's central organization did not cultivate uniformly strong relationships with all of its member institutions— the partnership with Princeton soured quickly, and while Oxford and Stanford may have been enthusiastic, their financial support of the endeavor did not remain consistent over time.[99] In addition to its outsized financial contribution to the partnership, some also said that Yale did more than its fair share of the work on AllLearn; a March 2005 item in the *Yale Daily News* reported that "AllLearn now offers about 60 courses—up from about 20 five years ago, and about 35 of them have been developed by Yale faculty."[100] So while the AllLearn consortium was designed to promote shared

[98]Interview with Jeremiah Ostriker, 7/24/08.

[99]Allison said that when it came time to reinvest in the endeavor beyond the original $12 million provided at the beginning, Oxford found itself simply unable to do so, and Stanford did not reinvest to the same degree as Yale. "This came down to Yale and Stanford funding it, and I put in money on behalf of Stanford, so it was really Yale and Herb" (interview with Herbert Allison, 3/11/09).

[100]Pacia, Raymond, "AllLearn Expands Reach," *Yale Daily News*, online edition, March 25, 2005.

responsibility for the endeavor—in terms of both finances and content—that ideal was not fully realized in practice.

Along with evidence of conflict among the partner institutions, AllLearn's corporate office and the member campuses were not always on the same page. For instance, during Allison's tenure as CEO, he suggested that AllLearn take on new partners to further distribute the content creation and investment responsibilities. He initiated conversations with other universities, including Brown, Cornell, and Duke, "but these schools did not want to get second billing to the four founders, and the four founders were not going to make them full members."[101]

AllLearn's central organization's vision for course development also diverged somewhat from those of the campuses. Bernstein explained that the on-campus technology shops that produced much of the AllLearn content were naturally interested "in looking at pedagogy for online teaching" and wanted to experiment with innovative—and often expensive—uses of multimedia in course development. But AllLearn's central office preferred to keep it simple and develop courses cheaply, because these inexpensive courses had demonstrated the greatest market success. Bernstein said of the Iraq course: "it cost us nothing to develop that, $5,000 or $10,000, yet that was the one that could attract the most students." He also said that "a creative writing course that was extremely low tech, where you spend nothing on bells and whistles or recorded lectures or anything" was one of AllLearn's most popular offerings.[102] Tristram Wyatt of Oxford agreed, saying that surveys demonstrated that the simple courses based on a book with online discussions worked better than flashy courses.[103]

---

[101]Interview with Herbert Allison, 3/11/09. Kim said that eventually an agreement was reached under which other universities could serve as AllLearn affiliates to offer courses to their alumni, but the "affiliate" status did not involve financial investment by those universities (interview with Kristin Kim, 5/7/09).

[102]Interview with Peter Bernstein, 4/28/09. The Iraq course was offered for free as a means of driving interest in the site. That—combined with the very timely nature of the topic (the course was offered in 2003, near the start of the Iraq War)—surely had much to do with its popularity.

[103]Interview by Roger Schonfeld with Tristram Wyatt, 6/25/08. Bernstein said that it eventually became clear that the presence of innovative multimedia features "wasn't a key

After Kim replaced Allison in 2002, the bulk of the course production shifted away from the individual campuses to the AllLearn office in New York. Kim defends this as a pragmatic business decision to bring down development costs, but some of the campus developers felt alienated by the move and thought course quality might suffer because of it.[104] Bernstein also reported some tensions based on the fact that the AllLearn team was composed of people from commercial backgrounds rather than academics, and he noted that there was occasional friction if professors wanted to create content that would not be marketable to AllLearn's audience. As Bernstein put it, when AllLearn looked for courses to develop, it "wanted the 'History of Christianity' or 'Jesus, the Man,' but something like textual analysis of the Dead Sea Scrolls just wasn't going to cut it."[105]

Allison felt that "these schools got along great on the presidents' level . . . but you get down to the working level and it's a bit of a different story." He believed that one of AllLearn's problems was that because it started from the top down, there was not necessarily sufficient buy-in at all the working levels. For instance, AllLearn focused most of its marketing efforts on direct mailings via alumni associations, but it encountered some resistance from the universities, which were concerned about inundating alumni with communications.[106] Additionally, some at these universities took issue with the expenses incurred by AllLearn. Allison confirmed that about six of AllLearn's employees were paid competitive cor-

---

metric of success," as some of the simplest courses were among the best-sellers (interview with Peter Bernstein, 4/28/09). Kleiner took a somewhat different view, saying that some of AllLearn's media-rich programming was highly praised and just as well subscribed as other courses that were less expensive to produce (interview with Diana Kleiner, 12/18/08).

[104]Kim said that AllLearn was looking for efficiencies, and that if it made sense for a campus technology shop to develop a course "and it was on competitive terms, we would use them. But if it wasn't on competitive terms and they couldn't match our estimate, we would use an outside developer," either someone working for the AllLearn central office or an additional vendor (interview with Kristin Kim, 5/7/09). For the developers' view, see interviews with Paul Lawrence and David Hirsch, 12/17/08.

[105]Interview with Peter Bernstein, 4/28/09.

[106]Allison said that the mass mailings through the schools' development or alumni relations groups were "very difficult to arrange," because the schools felt that if they contacted alumni often about AllLearn, "that's one less opportunity to touch the alumni up for money or something else" (interview with Herbert Allison, 3/11/09).

porate salaries to entice top talent to a non-profit start-up, and the initiative had its offices in the prestigious Graybar building in midtown Manhattan. Allison had come to AllLearn as the former CEO of Merrill Lynch, and some felt that his stance was too commercial for a university-based endeavor. Discussing the partners' decision to terminate AllLearn, Allison said that he thought they became nervous that—as was the case with Fathom—the initiative could become unpopular with their faculties, who might disapprove of the expenditure. "This was going to be a cause célèbre in the faculty senates, and I don't think the schools—understandably— had much of an appetite for that."[107]

Legacies of Fathom and AllLearn

Many aspects of Fathom's and AllLearn's closures were specific to each initiative's particular circumstances and those of its member universities. But the most common reason that leaders of both endeavors cite for the closures was a misunderstanding of customer behavior: namely, that there was not a sufficient market for fee-based online enrichment courses.

Ann Kirschner said that, going into Fathom, "I don't think that we understood enough about the audience for online courses, because the real audience is for credit-bearing courses, and we didn't have any of those to sell from our institutions." In the absence of credit, Fathom had to target lifelong learners, "and in an era pre-broadband, pre-videocasting and iPods and all the rest, that was a very limited audience."[108] As then-Provost Jonathan Cole told the *Columbia Daily Spectator,* "the question of what the threshold was in people's willingness to pay was never clear. It was very hard after the [dot-com] bubble burst, and after all the bubble consisted of a lot of enthusiasm that was probably not well-founded."[109]

AllLearn encountered the same issue. Allison had always understood the difficulties of trying to make money—even just enough to

[107]Ibid.
[108]Interview with Ann Kirschner, 7/28/08.
[109]Quoted in Beam, "Fathom.com Shuts Down as Columbia Withdraws."

break even—from non-credit-bearing courses. Brenzel said that "if you offered courses for credit, you would enter a completely different zone of consumer mentality, but unless and until the enterprise was willing to offer courses for credit, the personal enrichment thermostat is set pretty low in terms of what people are willing to spend."[110] When he was first approached about the AllLearn CEO position, Allison expressed concerns with the project's non-credit model, and he continued to discuss offering credits with the member institutions after the launch of the initiative. As Allison pointed out, "you can charge ten times more" for credit-bearing courses than for enrichment offerings.[111] With the universities' permission, he explored the possibility of certification through their continuing education schools and even of independent accreditation for All-Learn. But the member institutions had reservations, including the concern that offering credits to outsiders might be seen as unfair to their current enrolled students.[112] As Kim put it, when it came to granting credit for online courses, the member institutions "just weren't ready."[113]

From Kleiner's perspective, "the people [AllLearn] reached loved it, but we never quite got the business model right."[114] Others felt that the market for the sort of content offered by Fathom and All-Learn was very limited: Gary Bisbee, online education market analyst at Lehman Brothers, speculated in 2003 that Fathom lacked a sufficient market because "working adults trying to advance their careers don't care about Shakespeare"—at least not enough to pay for courses at a level that could support the endeavor.[115] It is perhaps no coincidence that many of the online courseware programs from elite universities that followed would be offered to the public at no charge, based on a perception that, when it comes to non-credit-bearing enrichment courses offered online, free is closer to the price the market will bear.

---

[110]Interview with Jeffrey Brenzel, 4/23/09.
[111]Interview with Herbert Allison, 3/11/09.
[112]Interview with Jeffrey Brenzel, 4/23/09.
[113]Interview with Kristin Kim, 5/7/09.
[114]Interview with Diana Kleiner, 12/18/08.
[115]Quoted in Phillips, "E-Outfits Go the Distance."

Another oft-cited explanation for the disappointing performances and ultimate closure of Fathom, AllLearn, and other contemporary initiatives involves changes in the broader economic climate. Discussing Fathom in his book on the marketing of higher education, Kirp writes that "the idea of the world's best universities making their knowledge widely available is seemingly irresistible. But in the marketplace, timing is everything, and Fathom's timing was off. A few months after the unveiling, venture capital essentially dried up for e-learning business; and the revenues anticipated from on-line courses hadn't materialized."[116]

Between the launches of Fathom and AllLearn in 1999 and their closures several years later, the dot-com bubble burst and the economy experienced a downturn after September 11, 2001, making it difficult for the flagging efforts to locate new investors. Several involved in both Fathom and AllLearn also shared the sense that when these initiatives began, the technology and networking landscape was not yet sufficiently well developed to meet their needs. Fathom's backers argue that the idea was ahead of its time, before internet learning as a concept and the technology to support it had really caught up with their ambitions; Kirschner maintains that the digital capabilities for online courseware are now "light years ahead" of where they were during Fathom's time.[117] It is also important to note that Fathom and AllLearn fared no worse than their contemporaries: NYUOnline, Virtual Temple, and most of the other for-profit courseware spin-offs that came out of selective universities at that time have all gone the way of Fathom.[118]

. . . .

Fathom and AllLearn laid the groundwork for other elite universities to enter the online courseware space. Both of these early initiatives were covered closely in the press, and in many ways their

[116]Kirp, *Shakespeare, Einstein, and the Bottom Line*, 174.
[117]Interview with Ann Kirschner, 7/28/08.
[118]Kirp writes that "The roll call of universities that joined forces with e-learning companies between 1998 and 2000 reads like a 'Who's Who' of higher education . . . among universities, Columbia's plight was hardly unique. Very few of the for-profits survived the dot-com crash; and by 2002, none of them had seen a profit" (Kirp, *Shakespeare, Einstein, and the Bottom Line*, 169, 182).

experiences shaped future endeavors—if only as a cautionary example. Peer institutions watched Fathom and AllLearn closely, and the programs have been cited as direct influences on a variety of later efforts, such as MIT OpenCourseWare (OCW). Yale has since launched a free and open courseware effort (profiled in Chapter 5), and Stanford has subsequently formed a partnership with iTunes U to distribute free content and has focused on its credit-bearing online engineering masters program.

Yale University Vice President and Secretary Linda Lorimer succinctly described the major lesson to come out of Fathom and All-Learn: "people are not going to pay a lot for informal education."[119] This has become the conventional wisdom among the emerging group of traditional universities interested in exploring online courseware distribution, many of which have decided not to attempt to charge for digital courseware in the absence of credit. Kleiner said that she greatly admires MIT OCW, a free and open effort that was announced a year into AllLearn's operation: "What they did was put out this idea that maybe institutions should think about . . . the greater good. And at the time, we stuck with what we were doing, but after a time it became clear that maybe their approach was the right one."[120] Looking back on Fathom, Kirschner believed it was simply ahead of its time and suggested that many of the concepts and principles behind it may still prove valid under different circumstances. "We are so much at the beginning of what online education is," she said. "But with these things you're either too early or too late, and I've found that it's better to be too early."[121]

[119]Interview with Linda Lorimer, 3/6/09.
[120]Interview with Diana Kleiner, 12/18/08.
[121]Quoted in Carlson, "Going for Profit and Scholarship on the Web."

3

FREE AND COMPREHENSIVE: MIT'S OPENCOURSEWARE

The Massachusetts Institute of Technology's OpenCourse-Ware (OCW) project, launched in 2001, set the standard for open-access online course materials as the first initiative of its kind. In what continues to be the highest-profile project in this field, MIT pledged to offer freely available web-based versions of syllabi, lecture notes, reading lists, assignments, and other materials for virtually all of its courses. OCW thus constituted a major institutional commitment to transparency, providing, in the words of former Provost Robert Brown, "a window into MIT on a very fundamental level"—its classrooms.[1]

Though the committee that initiated OCW did not set out to create a free offering, it opted to do so when consultant studies revealed that a fee-based effort, akin to Fathom and AllLearn, was highly unlikely to generate sufficient revenues. Subsequently, the project's open availability has become a cornerstone of its success. MIT President Charles Vest, OCW's key champion at the university, capitalized on the idea's novelty to parlay personal relationships with foundation leaders into an extraordinary amount of start-up funding. MIT OCW has also received ample attention from the Institute's peers and in the popular press. Though the open courseware field has expanded greatly in the years since OCW's launch (in part due to MIT's success in encouraging other institutions to follow its lead), it remains the best-known—and best-funded—initiative of its kind.

---

[1]Interview with Robert Brown, 10/27/08.

Origins and Development of OpenCourseWare

In the late 1990s, conversations regarding the changing face of the university in the digital age—similar to those that prompted the creation of Fathom and AllLearn—were taking place at MIT. When Robert Brown became provost in 1998, he and Charles Vest, the university's popular and long-serving president, agreed that MIT should think deeply about a possible online project, as the two shared the concern that "we had not found our place" when it came to "what technology-enabled education was going to mean to the Institute." Brown convened a campus Council on Educational Technology (CET), which he co-chaired along with Professors Hal Abelson, who had long been involved with both open-source software and educational technology projects, and Steven Lerman, director of MIT's Center for Educational Computing Initiatives since 1991. Brown said that at the time, MIT was keenly aware of e-learning efforts like Fathom, AllLearn, eCornell, and others, and that "there was a sense that other institutions were going to eclipse us" if MIT did not develop a similarly ambitious online project.[2]

When the committee began to meet, it was widely assumed that its eventual recommendation would be a revenue-generating model like others in the market at the time. Over several years, the CET strategy group engaged the consulting firms of Booz Allen Hamilton (BAH) and McKinsey & Company to conduct market research and develop potential models for an MIT online project. Several for-profit ideas were proposed and then discussed at a strategy group meeting in February 2000, with paid online course offerings targeted toward the school's alumni—very similar to the AllLearn model—rising to the top.[3] Yet after surveying alumni and investigating the competitive landscape, the BAH group delivered a final report to the committee in the summer of 2000 concluding that "such a project would place MIT in a non-traditional business

---

[2]Ibid.

[3]Vest confirmed that when the committee began to discuss online ventures, "the clear bias of people going in was that we ought to do something that [was] going to return revenue to the institution" (interview with Charles Vest, 9/30/08).

where it had little or no existing capabilities," and that an alumni audience would be insufficient to support a profitable venture.[4]

But interest in disseminating some form of MIT materials online had firmly taken root, and the committee was wary of returning to the provost empty-handed. According to Lerman, we "concluded that it was futile as far as making money, which prompted us to think about other things we could do."[5] The essential idea behind OCW—to publish MIT course materials online, but to give them away for free rather than attempting to restrict access and generate revenues—emerged at the very end of the CET's final report, which was submitted to the provost for review. Implicit in the report's recommendation that MIT pursue courseware within a "zero revenue model" was the stipulation that such courses would be purely recreational and non-credit-bearing, a decision that committee member Shigeru Miyagawa said stemmed from the group's desire to "not do anything to dilute the MIT brand."[6] The OCW idea was immediately embraced by Brown and then by Vest, who said that upon first hearing the idea he became "an instant convert."[7] In an early email to strategy group chairman Dick Yue, Vest wrote that he was "increasingly enthused about your basic recommendation. . . .

[4]Abelson, Hal, "The Creation of OpenCourseWare at MIT," *Journal of Science Education and Technology* 17, no. 2 (April 2008), 167. Vest said that BAH summarized its voluminous findings in a single PowerPoint slide, which essentially said that for a traditional university to engage in distance education would be "very complicated; it's going to be highly competitive, and it's very unlikely to make money" (interview with Charles Vest, 9/30/08).

[5]Interview with Steven Lerman, 10/31/08. According to Kirp, there was a direct connection between OCW and Fathom: "OpenCourseWare (OCW) emerged as a direct response to the temptations of the market. Late in 1999, as Columbia was readying the launch of Fathom, Ann Kirschner sought out prestigious academic partners. MIT was a top choice because of its stellar reputation in science and engineering, but when she approached the institute, she was rebuffed. MIT officials were skeptical about the market potential of digital education" (Kirp, David L., *Shakespeare, Einstein, and the Bottom Line: The Marketing of Higher Education*, Cambridge, Mass.: Harvard University Press, 2003, 179). MIT's rejection of Fathom was thus meaningful foreshadowing.

[6]Interview with Shigeru Miyagawa, 10/29/08. OCW's first director, Anne Margulies, noted that MIT does not even grant honorary degrees at graduation, so to her it seemed natural that the university would be disinclined to offer any form of credit to outsiders (interview with Anne Margulies, 10/28/08). Lerman said that when the idea was first presented to faculty, "the language of publishing was widely used" to describe OCW, and "when you publish a textbook and someone reads it, they don't expect to get credit" (interview with Steven Lerman, 8/3/09).

[7]Interview with Charles Vest, 9/30/08.

done properly, it could be a serious act of national/international leadership. It certainly will change the equation."[8]

In the context of the contemporary online educational landscape, MIT viewed OCW as a break from the emerging commercial model and a bold step in a new direction. This open approach—which emerged only after the profit-seeking model was deemed infeasible—allowed MIT to enhance its online presence by offering unrestricted access to its courseware.[9] Although interest in making educational materials freely available to the world was not the original driver for MIT's exploration of this space, the open-access ethos found many supporters at the university. Lerman recalled that "in effect, it was almost a political statement at the time it was announced. There was a lot of movement to commercialize and capitalize upon these resources at the time, and OCW was a counterweight to that."[10] The initiative's first grant proposal distilled this aspect of OCW's self-presentation as an altruistic foil to the profit-driven activity that had infiltrated the education sector, stating that it "aims not to bolster financial capital, but to advance human capital in places within and beyond the Institute's current reach."[11]

With the idea on the table and the enthusiastic commitment of the CET to move forward, the next step was obtaining funding for the project. When the concept was first presented to him, Vest proposed that if MIT were to commit to OCW, the effort should be a comprehensive publication involving the entire faculty and curriculum.[12] Early estimates (which later proved outsized) suggested that an online effort to publish digital versions of each of

[8]Charles Vest email to Dick Yue and other members of the committee, October 28, 2000.

[9]As Curtis J. Bonk summarizes in *The World Is Open*, "the business plans of other universities attempting to enter the for-profit side of e-learning did not make sense. The economics simply did not add up. And MIT did not care to make an investment in an area where it could not be a leader" (Bonk, Curtis J., *The World Is Open: How Web Technology Is Revolutionizing Education*, San Francisco: Jossey-Bass, 2009, 165).

[10]Interview with Steven Lerman, 10/31/08.

[11]"MIT OpenCourseWare: A Proposal Submitted to the William and Flora Hewlett Foundation," April 27, 2001, principal investigators Harold Abelson, Robert A. Brown, and Steven R. Lerman, 1.

[12]Interview with Steve Carson, 7/30/09. Lerman said that Brown was also very enthusiastic about making OCW a comprehensive project (interview with Steven Lerman, 8/3/09).

the university's courses would cost $100 million, so securing suitable funding was a necessary early step.[13]

Vest personally instigated early funding conversations, traveling to New York in the fall of 2000 for breakfast with William G. Bowen, then-president of the Andrew W. Mellon Foundation and a long-time acquaintance. During their first meeting, Bowen expressed interest in the idea and also encouraged Vest to reach out to Paul Brest, president of the Hewlett Foundation, as another potential funder. Bowen had recently delivered the annual Romanes lecture at Oxford on "The University in a Digitized, Commercialized Age," asserting that universities are unique institutions with singular missions and are at great risk if they behave too much like businesses—tempting as such an approach might become in the new digital environment.[14] MIT OCW may have therefore been precisely the sort of program that would have intrigued Bowen at the time.[15]

Following auspicious discussions with funders, members of the subcommittee took the idea to a wider circle of their colleagues within MIT, circulating information on OCW in the final months of 2000 in preparation for meetings with the department heads and a vote by the MIT faculty—which came down in favor of supporting OCW—in February 2001.[16] Although the early talks with the Hewlett and Mellon Foundations were promising, MIT's grant funding had not yet been awarded when the initiative was announced on April 4, 2001, in a front-page story in the *New York Times*.[17] In that article, the project was described as a comprehensive publication of all MIT courses and a long-term commitment

[13]That figure appears in Goldberg, Carey, "Auditing Classes at M.I.T., on the Web and Free," *New York Times*, online edition, April 4, 2001.

[14]Bowen, William G., "At a Slight Angle to the Universe: The University in a Digitized, Commercialized Age," http://www.mellon.org/news_publications/publications/romanes.pdf/view.

[15]Fathom CEO Ann Kirschner said that she also approached the Mellon Foundation about funding around this time, but Bowen "was concerned about the for-profit structure," and no funding from Mellon materialized (interview with Ann Kirschner, 7/28/08).

[16]Abelson, "The Creation of OpenCourseWare at MIT," 169.

[17]The Hewlett Foundation awarded an initial $5.5 million to MIT on April 30, 2001, and by June the Mellon Foundation had contributed in kind, giving OCW a total of $11 million in start-up capital.

by the university.[18] Committing to OCW so fully and publicly was a bold move on MIT's part, but that same audacity, coupled with the altruistic potential of the OCW concept, may have been what intrigued the funders to take risks of their own in supporting it. Brest characterized investment in OCW as a "big bet" for Hewlett, but one that might pay huge dividends in what he called a "very promising area."[19] Ira Fuchs, the program officer who oversaw OCW's grant at the Mellon Foundation, confirmed this.[20] According to Fuchs, decision makers at Mellon "really bought into the ambitious and unique nature of doing all 1,800 courses. . . . Although we did hear from others who thought that MIT was only proposing to do what they would have done for themselves—for me, the unprecedented, comprehensive nature of the project was worthy of Mellon funding."[21]

OpenCourseWare's Content and Organization

Versions of nearly every course taught at MIT have now been published on the OCW site (pictured in Figure 3.1), totaling 2,000 courses and counting. Each course may be represented by a variety of materials, including syllabi, reading lists, lecture notes, and video or audio lecture recordings. By providing these materials, MIT allows the home user to access some of the same content used

---

[18]Goldberg, "Auditing Classes at M.I.T." The article states that OCW is "a 10-year initiative," and the original grant proposal states that "MIT is committed to the creation of OCW as a sustained Web site representing the content of subjects taught at MIT" ("MIT OpenCourseWare: A Proposal," 14).

[19]Interview with Paul Brest, 8/20/08.

[20]At the time of writing, Fuchs, along with Charles M. Vest, William G. Bowen, and Paul Brest, served on the board of directors of ITHAKA, the not-for-profit parent organization of Ithaka S+R, whose staff initiated and executed the research that resulted in this book.

[21]Interview with Ira Fuchs, 12/2/08. Those in charge of the Open Educational Resources program at the Hewlett Foundation reported receiving similar feedback: "We have heard faculty from other institutions say that they have looked at the MIT-OCW site and wondered 'What's the big deal?' They argue that they themselves put course materials online for anyone to view. The 'big deal' is that never before has one institution or a number of them placed core instructional materials from a substantial number of courses online, in one place, in a coherent and searchable format, to be used worldwide" (Smith, Marshall S., and Catherine M. Casserly, "The Promise of Open Educational Resources," *Change* 38, no. 5 [September–October 2006], 12).

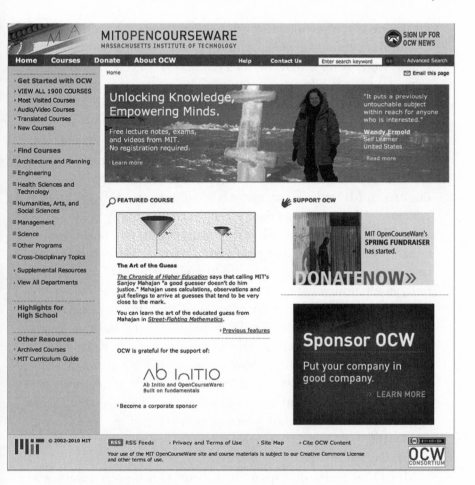

FIGURE 3.1 MIT OpenCourseWare landing page (as it appeared on May 11, 2010).

Available at http://ocw.mit.edu/OcwWeb/web/home/home/index.htm. © 2002–2010 MIT. License: Creative Commons BY-NC-SA.

by MIT students in their coursework. But proponents of OCW have always been very careful to stress, in their own statements and in the site's explanatory text, that OCW does not constitute MIT's entrance into the distance education space: there is no credit associated with OCW courses, and OCW is not a path to an MIT degree. Steve Carson, OCW's external relations director, said that "prior to the whole OpenCourseWare idea, people were trying to fill the need for certification—that's what distance learning is all about. But I think the recognition of the committee that proposed OpenCourseWare is that there's a really severe need for just access to content [and] information in the absence of certification."[22]

The OCW team therefore maintains that the project's mission is to provide some of the pieces of an MIT experience without attempting to replicate that experience at a distance.[23] This distinction is clearly written into OCW's first grant proposal, which states that "OCW is not a course, but it is courseware; it is not a door to an MIT education, but it is a window on MIT educational content."[24] The attention paid to explaining not only what OpenCourseWare is, but also what it is not, was an important way in which the OCW team assuaged early concerns about the project: namely, that giving away the core knowledge of MIT to just anybody might undercut the university's primary operating model—or worse, might nullify the prestige value of the school's degrees. The *Times* article announcing OCW posits that MIT students might resent having to pay tuition when their courses are being offered online for free, but it quotes Vest as saying that "Our central value is people and the human experience of faculty working with students in classrooms and laboratories, and students learning from each other, and the kind of intensive environment we create in our residential university. . . . I don't think we are giving away the direct value, by any means, that we give to students."[25]

MIT OCW's offerings span the Institute's entire curriculum, and this comprehensiveness is perhaps the initiative's most striking feature. The OCW team cites several motivations for the decision to publish MIT's full course catalogue, as opposed to selecting particular courses. The site is organized by academic department, with all MIT departments represented. OCW's first director, Anne Mar-

---

[22]Interview with Steve Carson, 10/27/08.

[23]Carson described OCW with a metaphor: "We're not trying to recreate the classroom environment: you don't get the experience of interacting with the faculty member or of interacting with the students—it's the footprints of the beast, but not really the animal itself" (interview with Steve Carson, 10/27/08).

[24]"MIT OpenCourseWare: A Proposal," 1.

[25]Goldberg, "Auditing Classes at M.I.T."

gulies, said that by not restricting the program to only the "star courses," some of the university's "hidden jewels"—lesser-known but nonetheless excellent professors or courses—have had the same chance to find an audience as the more famous MIT courses.[26] Vest said that the MIT faculty like to think of the institution as "all at one level," without strengths and weaknesses among departments and faculty members.[27] Steven Lerman, then-chair of the MIT faculty, agreed that OCW's decision to procure materials from all of the courses helped to maintain good relations between the initiative and the faculty—a key consideration, as faculty participation was voluntary. "Politically, it made sense," he explained, "because you don't have to choose your favorite children . . . if you get the entire faculty to buy in."[28]

While the vast majority of courses taught at MIT are represented on OCW, the amount of content present for each course is not uniform; the depth varies widely from course to course, from the robust—complete archive of video lectures, extensive notes, homework and test questions—to the relatively sparse, as depicted in Figure 3.2—a syllabus, a reading list, and little else. Brown said that in formulating the OCW concept, the consensus was that "the power came from striving to do all, with the total understanding that different content lent itself at different levels to doing this effectively, and some of it would be pretty thin."[29]

Such unevenness may be a necessary consequence of the initiative's comprehensive nature. Miyagawa said that MIT recognized the trade-off: "when you have as many courses as we do, it's unavoidable that there will be such inconsistency. As long as there are enough courses that are deep enough to be useful, if there are some that are sort of stark, that's part of the deal."[30] In 2003, several years into the project, OCW instituted some minimum standards

[26]Interview with Anne Margulies, 10/28/08. Margulies also believes that publishing the entirety of the university's curriculum allows the site's users to see how individual courses fit together to create programs of study.
[27]Interview with Charles Vest, 9/30/08.
[28]Interview with Steven Lerman, 10/31/08.
[29]Interview with Robert Brown, 10/27/08.
[30]Interview with Shigeru Miyagawa, 10/29/08.

MITOPENCOURSEWARE
MASSACHUSETTS INSTITUTE OF TECHNOLOGY

Home   Courses   Donate   About OCW   Help   Contact Us   Enter search keyword   [GO]   Advanced Search

VIEW ALL COURSES

Home > Courses > Anthropology > Anthropological Theory > Course Home

Course Home
Syllabus
Calendar
Readings
Study Materials

Download Course Materials

Translations*
繁體字

Send us your feedback
Cite this course
Email this page
Newsletter sign-up
Donate
[SHARE]

21A.110 Anthropological Theory

As taught in: Spring 2003

The death of Captain James Cook at Kealakekua Bay, Hawaii. (Archival photograph by Sean Linehan, courtesy of the National Oceanic and Atmospheric Administration.)

Course Highlights

This course includes a general guide to reading social sciences texts effectively, located in the study materials section.

Course Description

This course introduces students to some of the major social theories and debates that inspire and inform anthropological analysis. Over the course of the semester, we will investigate a range of theoretical propositions concerning such topics as agency, structure, subjectivity, history, social change, power, culture, and the politics of representation. Ultimately, all theories can be read as statements about human beings and the worlds they create and inhabit. We will approach each theoretical perspective or proposition on three levels: (1) in terms of its analytical or explanatory power for understanding human behavior and the social world; (2) in the context of the social and historical circumstances in which they were produced; and (3) as contributions to ongoing dialogues and debate.

Level:
Undergraduate

Instructors:
Prof. Susan S. Silbey

Course Highlights
Course Description

DONATE NOW

WHY I DONATE

" OCW is an extensive and valuable resource for both students and teachers."

Franco Frazzoli
Educator
Italy

[Read more ►]

Get the Latest

Get updates on new OCW courses and features.

>> SIGN UP for our E-Mail Newsletter

*Some translations represent previous versions of courses.

FIGURE 3.2   MIT OpenCourseWare course page, "Anthropological Theory" with Professor Susan S. Silbey (as taught in spring 2003). The basic elements of a typical, text-based OCW course are visible in the navigation tabs on the left: the course includes a syllabus, calendar, reading list, and brief guide to reading social science texts.

Available at http://ocw.mit.edu/OcwWeb/Anthropology/21A-110Anthropological-TheorySpring2003/CourseHome/index.htm. © 2002–2010 MIT. License: Creative Commons BY-NC-SA.

for all OCW courses in an effort to avoid publishing what Margulies called "Swiss cheese," or "courses full of big holes that wouldn't be valuable to anybody."[31] Every OCW course should now have at least three elements—planning materials, subject-matter content, and learning activities—though the definition of what fits these categories may vary.[32] In recent years, MIT has become increas-

---

[31]Interview with Anne Margulies, 10/28/08.

[32]Interview with Steve Carson, 10/27/08. Planning materials could include the course syllabus or calendar; subject-matter content could be lecture notes, a reading list, or readings; an example of learning activities would be homework problems.

FIGURE 3.3   Still from MIT OpenCourseWare lecture video, Physics 8.02, lecture 1 with Professor Walter Lewin (as taught in spring 2003).

Available at http://ocw.mit.edu/OcwWeb/Physics/8-02Electricity-and-MagnetismSpring2002/
VideoAndCaptions/detail/embed01.htm. Permission provided courtesy of MIT. © 2002–2010 MIT.
License: Creative Commons BY-NC-SA.

ingly focused on incorporating more video content into the OCW site (see, for example, Figure 3.3), though only about 60 courses, or 3 percent of the total corpus, contained video elements at the time of writing.[33]

To create such a large repository of content, the fledgling OCW organization needed both an orderly operation and buy-in from the faculty. In OCW's earliest days, while its grant funding was pending, the project was run by an interim management board headed by Lerman. That board determined that a large team with

---

[33]OCW production manager Kate James said that video lectures for six full courses are published each year (interview with Kate James, 10/28/08). According to Steve Carson, as of December 2009, 33 courses have full video lectures, with every course meeting recorded, and about 30 more contain some video elements (interview with Steve Carson, 12/9/09).

a professional manager would be necessary for OCW to make the ambitious launch goals set by its founders: to mount 500 MIT courses in the project's first two years. Based on the interim board's recommendation, the OCW organization was given structural autonomy within MIT as a distinct office reporting to the provost.[34]

The search for a suitable executive director commenced when the grant funding became available; it resulted in the hiring of Anne Margulies, a former CIO of Harvard. Margulies joined the MIT staff as the first full-time OCW employee in May 2002 and was charged with delivering a 50-course pilot by September of that year.[35] Margulies recalls that in those first months the operation was run "like a start-up," with a combination of consultants and independent contractors helping to assemble the courses while Margulies contemplated the permanent staff positions that OCW would need. OCW courses were produced in phases, with the first 500 completed in October 2003 at the time of the site's official launch and 1,550 by 2006; the goal of publishing 1,800 courses, constituting virtually all of MIT's curriculum, was achieved in 2007.[36] The staff has fluctuated accordingly, reaching about 50 people at the height of the "ramp-up" phase when OCW expanded from 50 courses to 500 within a year.[37] The project currently has 22 full-time employees and 3 consultants, including an executive director (Margulies was succeeded by Cecelia d'Oliveira, formerly OCW's technology director, in 2007), an external relations director, a publication director, an intellectual property supervisor, a production manager, and a handful of department liaisons.

---

[34]Margulies and Brown said that in the beginning, some had thought that OCW might logically be housed in the educational technology department, but that a strategic decision was made to have it report to the provost (interviews with Anne Margulies, 10/28/08, and Robert Brown, 10/27/08). Cecilia d'Oliveira, OCW's second director, feels this is the best and most logical choice: to her OCW has always been a content-focused publishing project rather than a technology project (interview with Cecelia d'Oliveira, 10/29/08).

[35]Abelson, "The Creation of OpenCourseWare at MIT," 171.

[36]MIT OpenCourseWare, "About OCW: Our History," http://ocw.mit.edu/OcwWeb/web/about/history/index.htm. The number of courses continued to grow to include those newly added to the MIT catalogue, as well as updated versions of existing courses.

[37]Interview with Steve Carson, 12/9/09. This figure does not include an outsource team of seven or eight individuals in India doing data entry and supporting OCW's course management system.

From the outset, OCW was intended to be a comprehensive endeavor, yet faculty participation was to remain voluntary. When the project was announced in April 2001 as a commitment by MIT to "post sites for all its courses," total faculty cooperation was by no means guaranteed.[38] But the core group of faculty responsible for the idea had already begun an extensive internal communications campaign on OCW's behalf. During the winter of 2000, with funding for the initiative pending, some subcommittee members distributed informational memos and discussed the project with representatives from each of MIT's academic departments.[39] As it turned out, faculty willingness to participate was less of an obstacle to OCW's success than had originally been anticipated.[40] These early meetings were successful, and the MIT faculty voted to support moving forward with the initiative in February 2001.

The project began publishing the courses of the most willing professors and progressed from there.[41] Many participants in the 50-course proof-of-concept in OCW's first year were members of the planning committee or their close colleagues. Some 500 courses were mounted in the second phase, the OCW pilot, and Margulies explained that at that point an effort was made to represent the breadth of the MIT curriculum by publishing courses from every department, including large lecture courses and small seminars.[42] Early faculty participants received stipends of $3,000 per course for contributing, though stipends were reduced to $2,000 by 2005 and ceased after 2006.[43] Margulies said that stipends were seen as "a way to encourage early adopters . . . to build early momentum" around contributing materials, and that the intention was always

[38]Goldberg, "Auditing Classes at M.I.T."

[39]Abelson, "The Creation of OpenCourseWare at MIT," 169.

[40]According to Vest, it was assumed that lack of willingness to share materials openly would be the greatest source of faculty resistance, but in fact no significant numbers of faculty expressed concern with that aspect of the project (interview with Charles Vest, 9/30/08).

[41]Margulies said that to reach that initial goal of 50 courses, "we took whoever would be willing to publish, and we had to talk them into it" (interview with Anne Margulies, 10/28/08).

[42]Margulies said that when OCW had published around 1,200 courses, it reached a tipping point at which professors began to reach out to them about participating (interview with Anne Margulies, 10/28/08).

[43]Lerman, Steven R., "Recommendation of the OCW Faculty Advisory Committee on Sustaining OCW into the Future," September 12, 2005, 2.

to phase them out over time as the production process became more efficient and faculty participation more common.[44]

The OCW team's guiding principle for securing faculty participation has been to make the production process as easy on them as possible, ensuring that the required time commitment was minimal and that faculty would have support from a professional staff. Once professors make the raw materials that they are already using in their courses available to the OCW team, the staff handles the remaining steps of the process: digitizing the materials, creating additional materials when necessary, addressing intellectual property concerns (for a more detailed discussion of this and other projects' handling of such issues, see Chapter 8), and posting the content to the site.

Faculty participation was also strongly encouraged by senior academic leadership, up to and including the university president. Vest said that the university's administration was "heavily involved" in OCW and felt "the obligation to build much of the support for it" within the Institute.[45] Clearly an institutional priority, OCW reports in at the provost's level, a decision which Margulies felt was a key element of its organizational efficacy.[46] As president and provost at the time of OCW's founding, Vest and Brown exercised direct, personal leadership when it came to OCW, actively championing it both within and outside the university.[47] When it came to securing funding for the project, Vest took it upon himself to initiate con-

---

[44]Interview with Anne Margulies, 8/17/09. Of the stipend, Margulies said, "I think it was pretty important in the early stages, [because] when the project started we had to aggressively recruit and win over . . . one faculty member at a time." The funding was intended to "help the faculty cover the investments they were making in graduate students that were helping them work on their materials" to ready them for inclusion in OCW.

[45]Interview with Charles Vest, 9/30/08.

[46]Lerman remembered that when Vest announced OCW as a permanent activity of MIT, "he sent a clear message institutionally that this was a presidential priority" (interview with Steven Lerman, 10/31/08). Margulies emphasized that "what I cared about was that it reported in at a senior level, because it would get high-level support that way" (interview with Anne Margulies, 10/28/08).

[47]Vest also made frequent mention of OCW in published articles and speeches. Brown remarked that he was emotionally invested in OCW from the beginning, and Vest said that his role in the project "was driven by the fact that I instantly was in love with this concept, so that's a reason that I threw my weight behind it" (interviews with Robert Brown, 10/27/08, and Charles Vest, 9/30/08).

tact with foundations, and Brown was the principal investigator on the original grant proposal. Miyagawa called Vest's role in the OCW project a rare display of "academic leadership exerted in a direct and useful fashion," and Margulies considers the involvement of MIT's administration to be the linchpin of OCW's success: "I don't think this ever would have happened at any place but MIT, or under any leadership but Chuck's. . . . Faculty come up with great ideas every day, but the leadership Chuck showed to seize this idea was really extraordinary."[48]

Though Vest and Brown have both left MIT, OCW continues to receive attention from administrators at the highest level. According to Lerman, "one of the virtues of Chuck Vest's unequivocal commitment was that it was passed on to future presidents and provosts," a legacy bolstered by the fact that Vest dedicated not only his presidency but the institution as a whole to establishing OCW as "a permanent feature of the MIT academic program."[49] Despite the turnover in these key posts, OCW continues to play a major role in the external conversations that the current president, Susan Hockfield, has about MIT. Current provost Rafael Reif summed up the administration's commitment to the initiative this way: "OCW is so much a part of MIT—we're all extremely proud of OCW."[50]

Impact of OpenCourseWare

In a 2004 article he authored in the *Chronicle of Higher Education,* Vest defined the audience for OCW materials as incredibly heterogeneous: "a faculty member at a new engineering university in Ghana, a precocious high-school biology student in suburban Chicago, a political scientist in Poland, a literature professor in up-

[48]Interviews with Shigeru Miyagawa, 10/29/08, and Anne Margulies, 10/28/08.

[49]Interview with Steven Lerman, 10/31/08; Lerman, Steven R., Shigeru Miyagawa, and Anne Margulies, "OpenCourseWare: Building a Culture of Sharing," in *Opening Up Education: The Collective Advancement of Education through Open Technology, Open Content, and Open Knowledge,* ed. M. S. Vijay Kumar and Toru Iiyoshi, Cambridge, Mass.: MIT Press, 2008, 220.

[50]Interview with Rafael Reif, 10/30/08.

state New York, or an executive in a management seminar down the hall at MIT will be able to use the materials our professors rely on in teaching our full-time students."[51] But Margulies and Vest both said that the audience originally envisioned for OCW was primarily other educators, and that the OCW team was surprised to eventually learn that more "self-learners" were using the materials than teachers.[52]

There has always been an emphasis on the developing world as a key audience for OCW. The first grant proposal states that "we expect OCW to be of particular value in developing countries that are trying to expand their higher education systems rapidly. . . . The OCW materials will be able to jump-start curriculum improvements in these countries."[53] Lerman echoed this sentiment in the press conference announcing OCW, saying "we hope our materials will be translated. Developing countries need information, and they need to develop infrastructure and institutions."[54]

The main appeal of OCW rests on the premise that these course materials will be useful to individuals around the world. But the OCW staff admits that much of the site may not be suitable for the average learner. According to Margulies, "the material starts with the assumption that you have to be an MIT-caliber student to be able to use [it]; it's not at all for your average student."[55] When asked if the site's current offerings are geared toward any specific group, Carson responded that "in going for breadth, I think we probably skewed to the side of educators by covering the entire curriculum. The bare bones version of a course is only going to be useful to educators and educational administrators who are developing curricula. . . . But you need a relatively deep amount of

---

[51]Vest, Charles M., "Why MIT Decided to Give Away All Its Course Materials via the Internet," *Chronicle of Higher Education,* online edition, January 30, 2004.

[52]MIT OpenCourseWare, "2005 Program Evaluation Findings Report," June 5, 2006, http://ocw.mit.edu/ans7870/global/05_Prog_Eval_Report_Final.pdf, 11.

[53]"MIT OpenCourseWare: A Proposal," 14.

[54]"MIT to Make Nearly All Course Materials Available Free on the World Wide Web," press release, MIT News, April 4, 2001. OCW materials have subsequently been translated into more than ten languages, through formal translation partnerships or independent efforts.

[55]Interview with Anne Margulies, 10/28/08.

content in a course for independent learners to make use of it," and many of the OCW versions lack that necessary depth.[56]

From the beginning, OCW did not plan to offer users any kind of interaction with MIT professors or graduate students, avoiding the asynchronous threaded discussion or live chats that characterized Fathom and AllLearn courses.[57] On the one hand, this limited the scope of the project in a way that allowed the OCW team to stay focused on its publishing mission and minimize distractions—and in a university full of people with personal and professional interests in technology, OCW has not allowed itself to become bogged down in unnecessary technological complexities.[58] But on the other hand, the lack of interactive features on OCW has also necessarily limited its impact: as Vest himself said in his first press conference on OCW, "real education requires interaction, the interaction that is part of American teaching."[59]

From the beginning, MIT has felt an obligation to undertake self-evaluation efforts to track its user demographics along with levels and patterns of usage. But understanding usage scenarios for freely available online content has often proved quite challenging. Mar-

---

[56]Interview with Steve Carson, 10/27/08. "I would say about a third of our courses are primarily useful only to educators. Another third are useful to both educators and students, and then there's a final third of our courses that really support independent learning in a significant way."

[57]From the perspectives of some of the AllLearn team, MIT's format was a step backward, as they considered interaction a key source of value for AllLearn. In a *Yale Daily News* article covering the launch of OCW, Yale President Richard Levin discussed the difference between MIT's plans and those of the Alliance, saying "We would use the Internet to create online discussions, and our thinking is much more interactive. The MIT approach is just making it available to anyone who wants it" (quoted in Ladine, Bret, "MIT to Offer Access to Materials Online," *Yale Daily News*, online edition, April 5, 2001). Stanford Provost John Etchemendy agreed, saying that in MIT's case, "Putting course materials online is really just a step beyond what universities have always done," resulting in what he saw as less innovative offerings than AllLearn's (interview with John Etchemendy, 8/19/08).

[58]The majority of the course content is delivered in PDF files, and the "back-end" technology is also simple and straightforward, built using off-the-shelf commercial software products (although Margulies said that Microsoft donated substantial resources to customizing their back-end software). The fact that OCW did not use open-source technology drew some criticism, but Margulies defends it as an expedient business decision—evidence of the professionalized, deadline-driven working environment surrounding OCW's production process (interview with Anne Margulies, 10/28/08).

[59]"MIT to Make Nearly All Course Materials Available."

gulies said that "when we got grant funding, we knew we were going to have to have measurable results to report," but "figuring out
how to measure and evaluate results was *hugely* difficult."[60] OCW
first approached outsiders to investigate usage by issuing a request
for user studies proposals, but after a series of unsuccessful partnerships, concluded that they would be better off conducting the
research themselves.[61] To date, that research has centered mostly
on gathering demographic information through surveys and web
analytics, as well as employing survey methodologies to understand the uses to which the OCW content is put.

The original grant proposal states that concerning "the usage levels of OCW, we have not yet established clear, quantitative goals,"
and the organization never developed a specific number of users
they wanted to reach with the material.[62] An evaluation conducted
in 2009 revealed that users were geographically dispersed, with 54
percent of visits originating from outside the United States. The
report also broke down users by type, with 43 percent identifying
themselves as self-learners, 42 percent as students, and 9 percent
as educators.[63] As of July 2010, the OCW website claimed the site
has received "100 million visits by 71 million visitors from virtually every country" since its launch, averaging 1 million visits per
month.[64]

When it comes to the effect that OCW has had outside of the
MIT community, OCW's proponents are confident that their work
has been meaningful worldwide, though the specifics or the scale

[60]Interview with Anne Margulies, 10/28/08. D'Oliveira agreed, saying "you've got to
prove to your funders what they're getting, and the more money you're getting from them,
the more imperative that evaluation is" (interview with Cecilia d'Oliveira, 10/29/08).

[61]Interview with Anne Margulies, 10/28/08. According to Margulies, the various interested parties were concerned more with using OCW to conduct academic research than with
answering the questions about user behaviors that were important to MIT.

[62]"MIT OpenCourseWare: A Proposal," 15.

[63]MIT OpenCourseWare, "2009 Program Evaluation Findings Summary," http://ocw.mit
.edu/ans7870/global/09_Eval_Summary.pdf.

[64]MIT OpenCourseWare, "About OCW: Site Statistics," http://ocw.mit.edu/about/
site-statistics/. In a 2008 publication, Lerman, Miyagawa, and Margulies wrote that "in addition, there are over 100 mirror sites in Africa and Asia that deliver MIT content to users
who have limited Internet access. And users have downloaded complete course packages for
off-line use over several million times" (Lerman, Miyagawa, and Margulies, "OpenCourse-
Ware: Building a Culture of Sharing," 216).

of that impact is difficult to determine. While internal benefits to MIT may have been an acknowledged consequence of the OCW project from the beginning, the external impact was always viewed as paramount. Vest wrote in 2004 that "the real pay-off of what we hope will become the open-courseware movement will be its effect on educators and learners around the world."[65] The language of the original grant proposal's sections dealing with impact reveals both MIT's vast ambitions for OCW's effects on the wider world and a lack of clear metrics for systematically assessing that impact. The proposal's authors state that "we believe that in the long run, OCW, like other successful contributions to education, will lead to greater equality and improvements in economic performance, but these long-term, ultimate outcomes are impossible to isolate and measure."[66]

Though web analytics can give the OCW team a sense of the traffic levels their site is receiving, whether or not OCW has actually made a difference in teaching, learning, or the state of global education is a more complicated issue. Margulies said that OCW has always known that it was important to collect data on impact—not only on who was using the materials and how, but also on whether the site was actually creating meaningful change in individual lives or institutions—but that the team knew that it would take time to develop a methodology for that sort of inquiry. "Because our audience is the world, it's not like we could measure test scores or worldwide educational achievement, or even the achievement of our users. With OpenCourseWare, we couldn't have a control group, so our impact data is still somewhat anecdotal."[67]

When assessing its global impact to date, OCW has relied heavily on the voluminous—yet unscientific—feedback it has received.[68] The tens of thousands of overwhelmingly positive emails that users

[65]Vest, "Why MIT Decided."

[66]"MIT OpenCourseWare: A Proposal," 15.

[67]Interview with Anne Margulies, 10/28/08.

[68]As Vest stated in 2004, "since we announced OCW, we have received more than 13,000 e-mail messages from around the world endorsing our vision and the potential benefits of sharing knowledge freely" (Vest, "Why MIT Decided"). D'Oliveira said that OCW's "impact may not be scientifically provable, but we love getting the anecdotal feedback on a daily basis from people who tell their stories. There aren't many jobs I've had where you

have sent to OCW since its launch have convinced MIT that it has created something of true value. "I think it's had—in some cases—a genuinely transformative and profound impact on lots and lots of individuals who have used it either to dramatically improve their teaching or to advance their learning," Margulies said. "The accumulated over-the-top feedback that we get convinces me that it's been enormously positive."[69] User surveys have tried to generate some data on impact, and a detailed Program Evaluation Findings Report conducted in 2005 found that "80 percent of visitors rate OCW's impact as extremely positive or positive; 91 percent expect that level of future impact." The report also states that "visitor intent to return to the site is a strong indicator of perceived impact . . . 76 percent of first time visitors and 88 percent of returning visitors indicate that they will definitely return to the site."[70] But the method of surveying visitors to the website who have volunteered to complete questionnaires necessarily limits respondents to a self-selected portion of the user population and excludes nonusers altogether.[71] While OCW has received positive feedback on all of the indicators of impact it has established, it has nothing to benchmark this level of usage and these reactions against—no way to evaluate if positive feelings translate into an impact commensurate with MIT's hopes for the program.

Immediately following the program's launch, community expectations for OCW's impact were sky-high. In his 2001 President's Report, Vest said that "the reaction to its announcement has been astounding. Some have likened it to the Gutenberg printing press and to the Great Library at Alexandria. This is a bit hyperbolic

---

get that many continual insights into the results of your work" (interview with Cecelia d'Oliveira, 10/29/08).

[69]Interview with Anne Margulies, 10/28/08.

[70]MIT OpenCourseWare, "2005 Program Evaluation Findings Report," 4, 62.

[71]Education scholar Diane Harley's research has emphasized this problem, and she notes that "both online surveys and TLA (transaction log analysis) are prone to overlook the universe of non-users. An understanding of non-users and their motivations can be extremely valuable for planning and development" (Harley, Diane, and Jonathan Henke, "Toward an Effective Understanding of Website Users," *D-Lib Magazine* 13, no. 3–4 [March–April 2007], http://www.dlib.org/dlib/march07/harley/03harley.html).

for my taste, but even as clear-eyed an observer as IBM's CEO, Lou Gerstner, recently stated to Wall Street analysts: 'What do you think happened when MIT put its entire course catalog on the Net, for free? If that didn't send a shiver through the higher education system in the world, I don't know what will.'"[72] But several years into the project, interpretations vary as to whether these early ambitions for OCW have yet been realized. A 2007 report to the Hewlett Foundation reviewing its investments in Open Educational Resources calls OCW a "world-changing project."[73] But Ira Fuchs of the Mellon Foundation takes a more tempered view. Although he credits the OCW concept with great potential for future transformative impact, in assessing the project's system-wide impact to date he said that "if you take away OCW completely, I'm not sure that higher education would be noticeably different."[74] A decade after OCW's launch, it is too early to determine whether the idea will fundamentally alter the way that universities disseminate knowledge—and if so, how.

More concretely, MIT OCW has served as a model for course dissemination efforts at other institutions, spurring the creation of over 200 similar projects at universities around the world (though it is important to note that some similar open projects, such as Rice University's Connexions or webcast.berkeley, profiled in Chapter 6, had quietly begun prior to OCW). From very early in OCW's history, its proponents have sought not only to publish MIT's catalogue of course materials but also to encourage other institutions to do the same. At the press conference announcing OCW, Vest said that "this is about something bigger than MIT. . . . We would be delighted if—over time—we have a world wide web of knowledge that raises the quality of learning—and ultimately, the quality of life—around the globe."[75] As suggested, success for the initiative in

[72]Vest, Charles M., "Disturbing the Educational Universe: Universities in the Digital Age —Dinosaurs or Prometheans?" Report of the President for the Academic Year 2000–01, http://web.mit.edu/president/communications/rpt00-01.html.

[73]Atkins, Daniel E., John Seely Brown, and Allen L. Hammond, "A Review of the Open Educational Resources (OER) Movement: Achievements, Challenges, and New Opportunities," report to the William and Flora Hewlett Foundation, February 2007, 8.

[74]Interview with Ira Fuchs, 12/2/08.

[75]"MIT to Make Nearly All Course Materials Available."

the eyes of its founders hinged on both creating the OCW product and serving as a model for others to emulate.[76]

The OpenCourseWare Consortium (OCWC), launched in 2005 with a planning grant from the Hewlett Foundation, represents OCW's efforts to turn an idea into a movement. OCW began fielding requests from other universities—with early interlocutors including the Johns Hopkins University, Tufts University, and Utah State University—to tell its story and describe its processes. In OCW's early years, this outreach function was managed at a personal level by the project's leadership, but Carson explained that by 2005 the conversations involved so many outside participants that they were becoming unwieldy.[77] According to Margulies, "as we started to help people do what we were doing, a natural next step was to formalize it and organize ourselves."[78] Following an initial planning meeting in February 2005, the Consortium had its first official meeting that September and established three objectives for itself: to "extend the reach and impact of OpenCourseWare by encouraging the adoption and adaptation of open educational materials around the world," "foster the development of additional OpenCourseWare projects," and "ensure the long-term sustainability of OpenCourseWare projects by identifying ways to improve effectiveness and reduce costs."[79]

Until recently, the Consortium was basically run as a subsidiary of MIT. The OCWC's first director, John Dehlin, was hired in 2006 as an MIT employee reporting to Carson, and grant funding from Hewlett was awarded to MIT on the Consortium's be-

[76] Abelson said that while sparking worldwide interest in the creation of OCW was included in the first grant proposal as one of OCW's original intended outcomes, "the Hewlett Foundation gave specific funding for more aggressive action in the community," so in later phases OCW went further in that direction using grant money allocated for that purpose (interview with Hal Abelson, 10/31/08).

[77] Carson said that once the level of interest hit a tipping point, "we decided to bring everybody together to talk about the idea of forming a consortium, and that way we're creating channels for Tufts to talk to Johns Hopkins to talk to Utah State, because they're facing different challenges than we were, because we had a lot more money to throw at our problems than they had to throw at theirs" (interview with Steve Carson, 10/27/08).

[78] Interview with Anne Margulies, 10/28/08.

[79] Carson, Steve, "The Unwalled Garden: Growth of the OpenCourseWare Consortium, 2001–2008," *Open Learning: The Journal of Open and Distance Learning*, online edition, 24, no. 1 (February 2009).

half, giving MIT final authority over how it was to be spent.[80] In July 2008, the Consortium was incorporated as a 501(c)(3) organization independent of MIT (a structure that allows it to manage its own finances), and its leadership has shifted to a governing board composed of representatives from various member institutions, with Carson serving as its chair.

The Consortium currently includes several hundred institutions of higher education, with its most robust growth coming from non-English-speaking regions, particularly Asia. But elite U.S. institutions have not been particularly receptive to the OCW concept. Margulies said that when she and Provost Brown first discussed OCW's potential to inspire similar projects, they had assumed that public institutions in the United States would be early adopters. "Instead, we found that people got more excited about OpenCourse-Ware the farther you got from Cambridge—it was people from the other side of the world who really embraced the concept."[81] Carson agreed, suggesting that MIT's involvement with the Consortium has been "both a blessing and a curse": he believes that the MIT name has been a draw for some, while others have resisted joining for fear of appearing to be following MIT.[82] Time will tell in which direction the Consortium ultimately develops, but to date OCW's original vision of fellow American universities joining in droves has not been fulfilled.

The OCW project has been carried out in a coordinated and centrally planned manner, and now that OCW has become an established entity, the initiative may be evolving into a more prominent strategic element for MIT as an institution. Assessing OCW's internal value to the Institute, Carson said, "I think it started out as a strategic approach toward positioning MIT in the online world, but it's proved to be a tool that's useful in a great many other ways."[83]

---

[80]Interview with Steve Carson, 10/27/08.

[81]Interview with Anne Margulies, 10/28/08.

[82]Interview with Steve Carson, 10/27/08. While some elite U.S. institutions involved in online open courseware projects, such as the Johns Hopkins University and the University of Notre Dame, have joined the Consortium, others, like Carnegie Mellon and Yale, have not. Vest, Carson, and Margulies attribute those universities' decisions to a sense of competitiveness that makes them reluctant to appear to be in MIT's shadow.

[83]Interview with Steve Carson, 10/27/08.

Indeed, some of the "other ways" in which OCW could benefit the MIT community were present in its founders' minds early on, and they have taken on greater importance in recent years. Margulies said that the OCW team may have initially "underestimated" the benefits that the project would have for MIT, although "it's not as if they didn't have an inkling . . . that it would have a subtle and secondary beneficial impact on improving the educational materials at MIT, and therefore MIT students would benefit."[84] Brown and Abelson confirmed that the potential internal impacts of OCW were an important early component of the project and were especially valuable in convincing faculty to participate. Brown said that "when we went to sell it internally, it wasn't about doing something philanthropic or noble for the world, as much as transforming educational content internally."[85] Abelson agreed that planners felt they had to demonstrate to faculty that their own students would benefit from their participation in OCW. When first discussing the OCW concept with faculty, "the thing we had to fight was the notion that we were doing this for altruistic reasons. . . . We had to explain how [OCW] would give MIT a view of itself," Abelson said.[86]

Many contend that OCW has positively affected teaching and learning at MIT. As Brown put it, the presence of a course's written materials on OCW "pushes the faculty in the direction of 'How do I best use the contact hours so that people learn?' which is clearly critical."[87] The 2005 survey showed that many professors felt that contributing to OCW improves their teaching: of the MIT faculty surveyed, 32 percent agreed that contributing to OCW "improves their teaching materials."[88] Margulies suggested that the reason for this could be that faculty pay more attention to the quality of their course content when they know those materials will be shared with a world audience.[89] OCW has also permitted faculty to look closely at colleagues' teaching materials and to identify gaps be-

---

[84]Interview with Anne Margulies, 10/28/08.
[85]Interview with Robert Brown, 10/27/08.
[86]Interview with Hal Abelson, 10/31/08.
[87]Quoted in Goldberg, "Auditing Classes at M.I.T."
[88]MIT OpenCourseWare, "2005 Program Evaluation Findings Report," 4.
[89]Interview with Anne Margulies, 10/28/08.

tween concepts covered in lower- and upper-level courses, evaluating the curriculum as a whole perhaps for the first time. Lerman said that a comprehensive publication like OCW has been somewhat of a uniting force for the MIT faculty: "OCW is one of the few things that all the faculty do together. I couldn't get 5 or 10 percent of them to come to a faculty meeting, yet 90 percent of them have licensed their materials to OCW."[90]

OCW also receives significant use on MIT's campus and has generated positive feedback from students.[91] The 2005 Program Evaluation Findings Report states that "in all semesters for which the OCW site was available, the heaviest use from the MIT domain coincides with registration week," suggesting that MIT students are using it as an "enhanced course catalogue" when selecting their classes. "Additional traffic spikes occur during mid-term and finals weeks, suggesting use of the site by students in preparation for examinations."[92] OCW also benefits the Institute by preserving teaching materials.[93]

In response to OCW, MIT has received a great deal of positive —even glowing—attention from the press, due in no small part to the novelty of the open courseware concept when the project launched.[94] Some of OCW's press coverage emphasized the Institute's first-mover advantage. For instance, a 2003 article in *Wired* magazine definitively states that prior to MIT's launch of OCW, "no institution of higher learning had ever proposed anything as revolutionary, or as daunting," and that with OCW, "MIT earned

[90]Interview with Steven Lerman, 10/31/08.

[91]In his 2007 article, Abelson wrote that "of 600,000 monthly visits to the MIT OCW web site in September 2006, 25,000 originated from within MIT itself, a substantial number, considering that there are only about 13,000 students and faculty at MIT, and only 23,000 MIT network users in total" (Abelson, "The Creation of OpenCourseWare at MIT," 173).

[92]MIT OpenCourseWare, "2005 Program Evaluation Findings Report," 51.

[93]"By digitally archiving our faculty's course materials, we are preserving a record of MIT's continuously evolving curriculum" (Vest, "Why MIT Decided"). When OCW courses are updated, the old versions are moved to MIT's institutional repository, where they are permanently archived. Links to those courses remain on the OCW website, so the older versions are still openly available (interview with Kate James, 10/28/08).

[94]As an indicator of impact, the 2005 Program Evaluation Findings Report states that "OCW is increasingly cited in professional and popular literature as an influential open educational sharing project," referencing "more than 300 articles in global media" (MIT OpenCourseWare, "2005 Program Evaluation Findings Report," 4).

the distinction as the only university forward-thinking enough to open-source itself."[95] The volume and quality of press attention that MIT's initiative has received may also owe something to the OCW team's media savvy. While OCW does not devote funds specifically to marketing activities, it has been shrewd in its dealings with the media and employs two full-time external relations professionals. MIT leaked the OCW story to the *Times* before the funding had been officially secured—a bold move, and one that guaranteed that the Mellon and Hewlett Foundations' eventual role in supporting the project would not detract from MIT's primacy in that front-page coverage.[96]

OCW has yielded reputational benefits for MIT in the eyes of the world at large and the school's own alumni. As one article noted, "in some academic circles, MIT was viewed as making a masterful PR move. If so, the scheme worked brilliantly, because most of the world applauded."[97] This international appeal of OCW—and, by extension, MIT—was affirmed by MIT's provost and president. According to Reif, OCW is "a way to stay connected with the globe," and Hockfield said that "when we talk about global reach, OCW is a big part of our global reach."[98] Vest also offered that OCW has been useful for strengthening ties between MIT and its alumni. He reported in 2004 that in his travels discussing the initiative, alumni have told him that, "because of OCW, they have never been prouder of the Institute."[99]

[95]Diamond, David, "MIT Everyware." *Wired,* online edition, September 2003.

[96]Abelson explains the timing of OCW's announcement this way: "Announcing Open-CourseWare had originally been planned to coincide with the foundations' funding approval. But as the spring of 2001 progressed, word of the proposed initiative—which, after all, was being widely discussed on campus—began to get around, and there had been inquiries from the local press. So the administration decided to engineer its own news release in a way that it could control the timing, and contacted the *Times*. The early announcement, as it turned out, proved beneficial, even though it was a bit of a risk, since the proposal to the foundations, submitted shortly after the announcement, was able to highlight some of the enthusiastic responses" (Abelson, "The Creation of OpenCourseWare at MIT," 171).

[97]Diamond, "MIT Everyware."

[98]Interviews with Rafael Reif and Susan Hockfield, 10/30/08. Vest said that once the initiative was up and running, "it became clear that this was going to be a very international project, which most of us liked, because this was also the time in which every university [was] beginning to worry about how to globalize, and we felt this was a very efficient and effective way of doing that" (interview with Charles Vest, 9/30/08).

[99]Vest, "Why MIT Decided." According to the alumni survey conducted as part of the

Some members of the MIT community are also confident that OCW has played at least some minimal role in incoming first-year students' choice to attend the university. At the first OCW press conference, Vest asked rhetorically: "Am I worried that the Open-CourseWare project will hurt MIT's enrollment? No. In fact, I am absolutely confident that providing this worldwide window onto an MIT education, showing what we teach, may be a very good thing for attracting prospective students."[100] The 2005 report corroborates that hypothesis, stating that surveys of current students, faculty, and a sample of alumni showed that "71% of students, 59% of faculty members and 42% of alumni use the site, [and] 35% of freshmen aware of OCW before deciding to attend MIT were influenced by it."[101] But in Provost Reif's opinion, a program like OCW has limited powers in areas like attracting students: "I don't think a student comes to MIT for OCW, so I don't think it has attracted students to come who wouldn't have come already. I do think it's increased our prestige around the world—but I don't know that it's had an impact on measurable things like attracting talent to come."[102]

OpenCourseWare and Sustainability

A large and complex endeavor with a production process reliant on many individuals, OCW has required an ample budget over the years, most of which has been provided by outside funding. The Hewlett and Mellon Foundations "initially committed $11 million for the pilot phase of OpenCourseWare and have since awarded an additional $15 million."[103] When the grants were initially made, they were outliers within both the Mellon and Hewlett Foundations'

2005 Program Evaluation Findings Report, "a strong majority of the MIT alumni (83%) believe the OCW site greatly enhances or enhances MIT's reputation" (MIT OpenCourse-Ware, "2005 Program Evaluation Findings Report," 59).

[100]"MIT to Make Nearly All Course Materials Available."

[101]MIT OpenCourseWare, "2005 Program Evaluation Findings Report," 3.

[102]Interview with Rafael Reif, 10/30/08.

[103]Lerman, Miyagawa, and Margulies, "OpenCourseWare: Building a Culture of Sharing," 221.

typical portfolios. Mellon gave two large grants and then curtailed its financial involvement with online courseware, but the Hewlett Foundation completely retooled its program areas following the OCW award, which program officer Catherine Casserly called the "anchor grant" of the Foundation's new Open Educational Resources division.[104] As of July 2009, the OCW program has cost $33,707,000, of which $6,523,000 has been provided by MIT, not including the university's substantial in-kind contributions to the OCW project (e.g., office space in MIT buildings, portions of administrators' time).[105] The OCW staff projects that the cost of operating the project in future years will be $4 million annually.[106]

In the early days of OCW, plans for the initiative's long-term sustainability were not of primary importance.[107] Bowen said that he and members of the Mellon Foundation's board had been unsure all along about OCW's sustainability, and that "Chuck [Vest] didn't know himself, he just sort of hoped that somehow all would work out." While the board did grant OCW's proposal, Bowen said that concerns about the project's long-term financial viability were always present, and "I don't know that there's been an answer [to the question of sustainability] to this day."[108] Lerman confirmed this, saying, "we have had more meetings than I can count to discuss sustainability—it is the single real unsolved problem of OCW."[109] In recent years, the impending expiration of the project's grant funding has heightened the sense of urgency associated with the problem.

[104]Interview with Catherine Casserly, 8/19/08. As previously stated, the Hewlett Foundation defines OER as "free tools and content" that "can include full courses, textbooks, streaming videos, exams, software, and any other materials or techniques supporting learning" (William and Flora Hewlett Foundation, "Education: Open Educational Resources," http://www.hewlett.org/oer). In other words, OER includes, but is not limited to, open courseware.

[105]Figures prepared by Jeff Lazarus, 7/2/09.

[106]Interview with Steve Carson, 10/27/08.

[107]Margulies said that the sustainability question was not a big part of the OCW team's thinking early on because they were so focused on simply getting the project off the ground: "we were always cognizant that it was looming out there, but we didn't really have a plan, and we couldn't devote much time and attention to it until we were midway through the ramp-up phase" (interview with Anne Margulies, 10/28/08).

[108]Interview with William Bowen, 7/23/08.

[109]Interview with Steven Lerman, 10/31/08.

Reliant as OCW was on foundation funding, it was always clear to members of the team that such awards would be temporary, and funding sources would eventually have to shift. An inquiry into OCW's financial future was conducted by the OCW Faculty Advisory Committee in 2005, resulting in a recommendation for a financial arrangement in which MIT's General Institute Budget would support a portion of OCW's operating costs, with additional funds raised by the OCW team. According to that recommendation, "the case for sustained financial support of OCW publishing rests on the internal educational benefits that the program provides to the Institute's overall educational mission."[110] As OCW looks to its parent institution to cover more of its operating costs moving forward, attention is turning increasingly toward enhancing the benefits that OCW offers the Institute. According to d'Oliveira, a project without direct local benefit might be too easily considered expendable during times of financial crisis, so "now there's a big new focus on 'how do we increase the benefits to MIT?'"[111] For now at least, the case seems to have been made to the administration that OCW is an important part of the educational experience at MIT. Provost Reif said that "clearly it's being used, not just by people in Africa, but by people right here at MIT. MIT students benefit from it, and that to me is very important—we need to worry about our kids first."[112]

All involved agree that perpetually updating OCW's offerings must be part of its sustainability plan, requiring that funds be devoted not only to adding new courses but also to refreshing existing materials. The first proposal mentions the need to continue to update courses in the Steady State phase (the period following the completion of the 1,800th course), aiming for "a complete renewal of each course's Web site, on average, every four years."[113] Hockfield believes it is absolutely necessary to continue updating OCW, as she does not want to become complacent and allow the

[110]Lerman, "Recommendation of the OCW Faculty Advisory Committee," 3.
[111]Interview with Cecilia d'Oliveira, 10/29/08.
[112]Interview with Rafael Reif, 10/30/08.
[113]"MIT OpenCourseWare: A Proposal," 24. According to Steve Carson, since 2007 OCW has been updating about 130 existing courses each year (replacing the old versions), as well as adding about 70 new courses per year (interview with Steve Carson, 12/9/09).

site's quality to deteriorate. "One of the wonders of the internet world is that everything evolves so fast, so for OCW to continue to be relevant and continue to be attractive, it needs to innovate and keep up," she said. "What is core to MIT's education is that it moves with the field—[OCW] is on its way to the junk heap of history if we don't update it every year" to ensure that it remains accurate enough that MIT can be proud of it.[114] The OCW team also hopes to be able to keep the technology current as new options become available, as well as to eventually create additional functionality for the site.

Over the years, OCW has engaged in a series of preliminary efforts to add new features to the site while still pursuing the primary goal of creating a nearly complete online publication of MIT courses. OCW partnered with an outside organization to add message boards to the courses, though the chats were later abandoned due to lack of interest. More successfully, OCW has added a "Highlights for High School" portal to direct students and teachers to the material on the site most suitable for secondary school coursework or preparation for Advanced Placement examinations. Other innovations have included a program to distribute OCW on hard drives to areas of the globe with connectivity problems, adding audio and video content to the site, and contracting with secondary distribution channels like iTunes U and YouTube.

Fiscal year 2009 was the first in which OCW had to operate without funding from the Hewlett Foundation. The project's current operating costs—to maintain the site, add new courses, and update and augment existing courses—are $4 million per year; half of this is provided by funds designated in MIT's budget, while the other half must be raised.[115] A major gift of $6 million from Ab Initio, a software company founded by an MIT alumna, has ensured that operating costs are covered for three additional years,

[114]Interview with Susan Hockfield, 10/30/08.

[115]Reif explained that the annual $2 million given by the Institute's central funds to OCW is a permanent item in the budget and need not be requested each year. He added a caveat: "We cannot imagine what happens if the MIT budget has to shrink, but I don't know what that means for OCW any more than I do for the electrical engineering department or anything else we fund. Once something's in the budget, it doesn't have to be justified every year; it's just part of what we do" (interview with Rafael Reif, 10/30/08).

but the Institute has not settled on a concrete plan for generating revenue beyond that.[116] The OCW team agrees that a number of avenues for funding OCW should be explored simultaneously. Perhaps chief among them is pursuing donations, a strategy that has already met with some success. In addition to the large Ab Initio gift, Carson said that in 2007 OCW generated almost $100,000 in online donations. In the fall of 2009 OCW launched a naming opportunities program so that individual donors could sponsor particular courses.[117] Other ideas for future sustainability efforts include soliciting and accepting corporate sponsorship for OCW, with an eye toward building an endowment.[118] Vest remarked that, going in, "we did not have a clear model, but we were pretty confident that if it was successful, we would find a way to keep it going."[119] Moving forward, it remains to be seen how successful OCW can be in generating the funds it requires, and how the current necessity of focusing on fundraising may affect its core publishing effort.

• • • • • • • • • • • • • • •

Perhaps OCW's most significant contribution has been symbolic, in that it offers a new way of thinking about university content online, both within and outside the academy. At MIT, OCW has become the cornerstone of an ideological commitment to openness rooted in the university's core mission. Vest wrote in 2004 that "our challenge is simple: Can the decision makers of the world's leading educational institutions use what we are doing on our campuses to improve the lives of people around the world? History has proved that education and discovery are best advanced when knowledge is shared openly."[120] This sentiment is supported by MIT's more

[116]Interview with Steve Carson, 10/27/08.

[117]MIT OpenCourseWare, "MIT OpenCourseWare Diversifies Revenue Approaches," press release, January 28, 2010, http://ocw.mit.edu/about/media-coverage/press-releases/revenue/.

[118]Reif revealed that a member of MIT's development staff has been identified to aid OCW in fundraising: "that's a link that I wish had occurred earlier" (interview with Rafael Reif, 10/30/08).

[119]Interview with Charles Vest, 9/30/08.

[120]Vest, "Why MIT Decided."

recent institution-wide open-access mandate to begin making all products of the faculty's research openly available.[121] Externally, OCW has proved an influential exemplar. As John Dehlin, former head of the OCW Consortium, has said, "It's still not intuitive to share the learning. I think MIT's largest contribution is . . . putting this very simple idea of sharing the learning on the map in the public consciousness."[122]

Looking back on OCW's accomplishments to date, it is clear that the project's achievements in the realm of "intellectual philanthropy" have coincided with promotion of the university's brand: the project's successes are MIT's successes. Reflecting on OCW's founding with the benefit of hindsight, Vest concluded that "depending on your vantage point you could say MIT was arrogant, or you could say it was very generous, or that it was very far-sighted—probably some combination."[123]

---

[121]Albanese, Andrew, "Another First, as MIT Faculty Adopts 'University-Wide' Open Access Policy," *Library Journal Academic Newswire,* online edition, March 24, 2009. In September 2009 MIT joined four other universities in forming the Compact for Open Access Publishing Equity, through which the institutions committed to underwrite the contributions their own scholars make to open-access journals.

[122]Quoted in Chute, Eleanor, "How to Take a Course at MIT Free—At Home," *Pittsburgh Post-Gazette,* online edition, November 18, 2007.

[123]Interview with Charles Vest, 9/30/08.

4

DIGITAL PEDAGOGY: CARNEGIE MELLON'S
OPEN LEARNING INITIATIVE

The Open Learning Initiative (OLI) represents Carnegie Mellon University's distinctive approach to open online education. The project's first grant proposal to the Hewlett Foundation opens by stating an ambitious premise: "Carnegie Mellon is working to help the World Wide Web make good on its promise of vastly accessible and highly effective online education."[1] Building on Carnegie Mellon's past experiments with the use of information technology to improve educational efficiency and effectiveness, the initiative's 14 introductory courses provide users with self-contained rich online environments that profess to guide users—with the aid of interactive examples, embedded assessments, virtual labs, and constant feedback—toward the same learning outcomes as enrolled students taking the equivalent courses in person.[2]

The OLI seeks to expand access to instruction as well as to content. Rather than simply publishing professors' static teaching materials, as many other online courseware initiatives do, the OLI asks faculty to work with a team of experts to completely redesign their courses for web-based delivery. This interdisciplinary approach draws on Carnegie Mellon's institutional strengths in instructional

---

[1] "Four Courses, Millions of Users: Creating a New Paradigm for Online Education: A Proposal from Carnegie Mellon University to The William and Flora Hewlett Foundation," February 22, 2002, 2.

[2] Though heavily reliant on funding from the Hewlett Foundation, some of the courses in the OLI were direct beneficiaries of earlier experiments with technology in teaching that predate Hewlett's involvement in this space, such as those conducted through the Pew Charitable Trust's Program on Course Redesign (PRC) and the Mellon Foundation's Cost-Effective Uses of Technology in Teaching (CEUTT) program.

design, cognitive science, software engineering, and human-computer interaction. Because the creation of an OLI course is costly and requires an extraordinary time commitment from the faculty member (or "content expert" in OLI parlance), the OLI includes only a small fraction of Carnegie Mellon's curriculum—just over a dozen courses —and is limited to courses taught by particularly enthusiastic faculty.

The OLI's creators designed the project to achieve a concrete outcome: genuine, demonstrable knowledge acquisition on the part of the user. To that end, the initiative has focused heavily on assessment, undertaking a series of controlled trials to compare outcomes for students learning with the OLI to those achieved in a traditional Carnegie Mellon classroom setting. The results have been positive, and the OLI offers a much-publicized success story touted by the entire Open Educational Resources (OER) community.

Origins and Development of the Open Learning Initiative

A discussion of the OLI's origins must begin with the Hewlett Foundation's growing interest in supporting online educational content, as manifested in its first major OER grant to MIT Open-CourseWare (OCW) in 2001. Though the Foundation may not have been aware of it at the time, that investment was the first of many it would make in the open-education space over the next several years, ushering in a new focus for Hewlett's philanthropic activities. Following the awarding of the OCW grant on April 30, 2001, the recently hired team of Marshall "Mike" Smith and Catherine Casserly—respectively director and program officer of Hewlett's education division—were intrigued by the prospect of expanding the Foundation's portfolio of OER projects, and they spent the rest of that year conducting a series of site visits and conversations with interested parties.

In September 2001 this listening tour of universities engaged in digital learning initiatives brought Smith and Casserly to Carnegie Mellon, where they held meetings with Joel Smith, the university's CIO and head of its Office of Technology for Education (OTE), as well as with various members of the faculty and Provost Mark

Kamlet.[3] The Hewlett representatives did not arrive on campus with a specific project in mind, but their visit coincided with the events of September 11, 2001, and they found themselves detained in Pittsburgh several days longer than expected. As Provost Kamlet remembers it, "during that extended stay I had a chance to get a better sense of their vision about the importance of various forms of educational enhancement" in the digital environment, and in that week of talks the concept of a Hewlett-funded, Carnegie Mellon led OER project was seeded.[4]

While MIT brought the OCW concept to Hewlett already formed, the development of what would become the OLI was a much more collaborative effort with the Foundation. Carnegie Mellon had a long history of incorporating technology into educational environments, as well as particular institutional interest in interdisciplinary design processes and effective online pedagogies. The university was already a seasoned producer of online courses, having previously developed Carnegie Learning, Inc., a for-profit spin-off from the university that has been very successful in developing and marketing cognitive tutors—asynchronous computerized teaching tools that "[assess] the prior . . . knowledge of students on a step-by-step basis and [present] curricula tailored to their individual skill levels"—to teach middle school math.[5]

Following the September meetings, the Hewlett representatives returned to California expecting a proposal from Carnegie Mellon for a project merging the university's institutional expertise with the Foundation's funding priorities—interactive online courses that would be freely available to the public. According to Joel Smith, "Hewlett is the one that most pushes the open and free access thread; it was and is their fundamental goal. And the thread we were really pushing and continue to push is effectiveness, so essentially those two threads got woven together—open and free [online] education that is demonstrably effective."[6] Joel Smith headed

[3]Interviews with Joel Smith, 9/10/08 and 8/6/09, and Marshall Smith, 8/19/08.
[4]Kamlet, Mark, keynote address, Open Education Symposium, Carnegie Mellon University, March 10, 2008.
[5]Carnegie Learning, "Our Research Based Approach to Mathematical Success," http://www.carnegielearning.com/approach.cfm.
[6]Interview with Joel Smith, 8/6/09.

the effort to draft a formal grant proposal for the OLI over the next several months. That proposal, entitled "Four Courses, Millions of Users: Creating a New Paradigm for Online Education," was submitted to Hewlett in February 2002, and the first $1.9 million to begin work on the project was awarded that April.

The OLI is unique in the open courseware space in that it provides free access not only to content but also to instruction. The first OLI grant proposal states that "Carnegie Mellon is troubled by 'e-learning' drifting in the direction of cheap but ineffective products."[7] The initiative therefore set out to prove that a set of exemplary online courses could lead novice, unaffiliated learners to the same level of mastery over the material enjoyed by Carnegie Mellon students enrolled in a traditional course. By pursuing evidence-based, computer-assisted learning in rich online environments, the OLI's creators hoped to develop a system that would be "the *complete enactment* of instruction."[8] According to Joel Smith, this set of goals distinguished the OLI from the vast majority of online educational resources, open or otherwise, as most digital content "make[s] shockingly little use of what is in fact the best information available to improve education: scientific results from research studies in the learning sciences."[9] By rooting its course design in cognitive science and tracking user behaviors to constantly improve the product, the OLI is an attempt to utilize the online medium to its fullest advantage for distance education.

The OLI would need a home, and Joel Smith felt that the OTE was the obvious choice. In addition to his position as CIO, Smith was the office's director, so housing the OLI there would allow him to watch over the new initiative with minimal distractions from his other responsibilities. Because of the scope of the project, Smith decided early on that "this had to be somebody's full-

---

[7]"Four Courses, Millions of Users," 2.

[8]Thille, Candace, "Building Open Learning as a Community-Based Research Activity," in *Opening Up Education: The Collective Advancement of Education through Open Technology, Open Content, and Open Knowledge*, ed. M. S. Vijay Kumar and Toru Iiyoshi. Cambridge, Mass.: MIT Press, 2008, 174, 167.

[9]Quoted in Lederman, Doug, "In Search of 'Big Ideas,'" *Inside Higher Ed,* February 6, 2006.

time job," so a request to fund a high-level manager to oversee the OLI's day-to-day operations was written into the original grant proposal. The search for an executive director commenced almost immediately after the grant was awarded, and Smith recalled that he was interested in candidates with strong professional backgrounds and management skills: "not a cognitive scientist, not a content expert."[10] That search concluded with the hiring of Candace Thille, a veteran management consultant in the private sector, and work on the project had begun in earnest by mid-September 2002.[11]

The Open Learning Initiative's Content and Organization

The OLI's approach to content sets it apart from other initiatives in this space. As detailed in the previous chapter, MIT OCW has been careful to present itself as a purveyor of course *materials,* not courses—a caveat to ensure that users will expect to find only educational content, and not instructional support, on its site. But an OLI course attempts to create a complete learning environment online, using technology to replicate the kind of assistance with problem solving that traditional instruction provides.

Features like animations, interactive diagrams, virtual laboratories, and simulations create an immersive environment for OLI courses, using the unique properties of the web to encourage active learning.[12] But the most salient feature of OLI course design is found in the "mini-tutors"—simplified versions of the cognitive tutors developed through Carnegie Learning—embedded within the course content, through which students answer practice questions and receive targeted feedback.[13] These assessment tools test users'

[10]Interview with Joel Smith, 8/6/09.

[11]"Interim Status Report on Carnegie Mellon Open Learning Initiative," March 2008, 6.

[12]For instance, the causal and statistical reasoning course "includes 100 case studies and a 'causality lab' in which students simulate the process of collecting data to support or disprove a hypothesis" ("Carnegie Mellon Technology Will Reshape Curriculum of New Jersey's Centenary College," press release, *AScribe Newswire,* September 15, 2003).

[13]According to Thille, "the OLI mini-tutors behave in a similar fashion to cognitive tutors and to human tutors: making comments when the student errs, answering questions

comprehension at frequent intervals and are seamlessly integrated into the course content. As Anya Kamenetz writes of the OLI's feedback-based design approach, "it's what might happen in a classroom under ideal circumstances, with a teacher of infinite patience, undivided attention, and inexhaustible resources of examples and hints."[14] Thille feels that the mini-tutors create a learning environment much more conducive to learning than MIT OCW's, which provides users with raw materials but expects that they will engage in the actual learning entirely on their own, without the benefit of interaction or feedback.[15] Describing the OLI's attitude toward online pedagogy, Thille remarked that "we need to get away from the notion that assessment should only happen after some learning experience has happened—we can embed assessment in every learning activity."[16]

In addition to practice problems included in the OLI courses (see Figure 4.1 for an example from the OLI statistics course), students are also given the chance to complete self-assessments of their understanding at the end of each subunit, rating their confidence in their own ability to achieve the stated learning outcome (i.e., to answer a question or do a problem) from one to five. The results are

---

about what to do next, and maintaining a low profile when the student is performing well" (Thille, "Building Open Learning," 168).

[14]Kamenetz, Anya, *DIY U: Edupunks, Edupreneurs, and the Coming Transformation of Higher Education,* New York: Chelsea Green, 2010, 91.

[15]Interview with Candace Thille, 8/18/08. Thille conceded that users who are already educated at the college level may be able to teach themselves from the MIT OCW materials: "MIT is very good at supporting those kinds of learners. I don't think they're necessarily as successful at supporting novice learners who may not have good metacognitive skills and may not realize when they understand something and when they don't." The OLI tries to provide that service.

[16]Ibid. Information technology's capacity to improve learning had been discussed in education circles long before the OLI. As Massy and Zemsky noted in the 1990s, "IT enables self-paced learning with sensitivity to different learning styles and continuous assessment of student progress. . . . Allow[ing] teachers to pinpoint the areas where students falter—and in the case of some multimedia programs, those areas trigger further practice automatically so that students receive more instruction 'just in time,' when they need it most" (Massy, William F., and Robert Zemsky, "Using Information Technology to Enhance Academic Productivity," white paper prepared by Educom's National Learning Infrastructure Initiative (NLII), http://net.educause.edu/ir/library/html/nli0004.html, 3). Through the OLI, Carnegie Mellon's unique contribution has been to tap into this potential in a free and open online format.

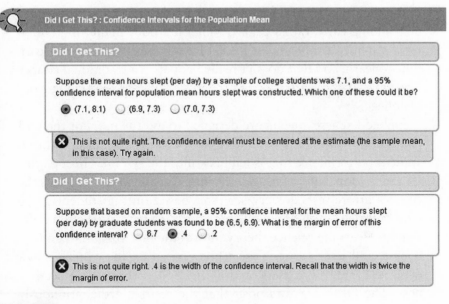

FIGURE 4.1   Open Learning Initiative "Did I get this?" prompt from "Statistics, confidence intervals for popular mean." While progressing through the statistics course materials, one frequently encounters exercises like this to test the content that has just been outlined. Wrong answers to the questions are met with customized explanations as to where a student may have erred and prompts to try again.

Available at https://oli.web.cmu.edu/jcourse/workbook/activity/page?context=091b7b6d80020ca 60148692c01e42549. License: Creative Commons BY-NC-SA.

then displayed next to the self-assessment, so students can determine if they are accurately gauging their own level of confidence—leading to what Thille refers to as "improved metacognitive skills," or heightened ability to accurately gauge one's own level of mastery.[17] Oded Meyer, a professor of statistics at Carnegie Mellon and co-creator of the OLI statistics course, is a strong proponent of this feature. "Being able to reflect on your own knowledge is really important, and it happens all the time in the OLI course," Meyer said,

[17]Interview with Candace Thille, 8/18/08.

noting that it is helpful for students to isolate the gaps in their understanding early, rather than relying on a poor midterm grade to highlight such problems. In the OLI environment, "students learn how to learn, and that doesn't really happen in a traditional course. Learning how to learn is one of the main skills students can get out of college."[18]

Embedded assessments are designed to aid the users of the OLI courses, but they have an additional purpose: to collect data on student performance that is fed back into the system. Through this feedback loop, current usage informs subsequent iterations, as the courses are refreshed every semester based on the student usage data culled from the previous semester.[19] Expert instructional design and learning science theory inform the first version of an OLI course, and later versions are refined based on the empirical evidence collected from users on usability and instructional effectiveness. The OLI's creators posit that the courses are continuously improving, as the designers are able to make adjustments to areas that cause students particular confusion.[20]

The design of the OLI is informed by the principles of cognitive science, an area of expertise that faculty and researchers at Carnegie Mellon have cultivated and applied to teaching for decades. University President Jared Cohon said that Carnegie Mellon's interest in human-computer interaction and effective instructional design dates back to the influential work of computer science professor Herb Simon, one of the early innovators of artificial intelligence in the 1950s, so "this link between computing and psychology at CMU is very long-standing and very deep."[21] Many of the university's current applications of cognitive science to instruction come out of the Eberly Center for Teaching Excellence, headed by Susan Ambrose. The center was founded in 1981 with the aim of connecting

[18]Interview with Oded Meyer, 9/10/08.
[19]Interview with Joel Smith, 9/10/08.
[20]Interview with Candace Thille, 8/18/08. Thille said that every course is revamped every semester, "some to a great extent and some a more minor extent. That depends on what we learn from the data, how long the course has been in use, and the time the team has to devote to it" (interview with Candace Thille, 10/28/09).
[21]Interview with Jared Cohon, 9/10/08.

education theory to practice—bridging the gap between scientists in labs and professors in classrooms to see findings from cognitive science enacted in real educational settings.[22] Prior to the OLI's launch, Ambrose and Joel Smith had worked closely together for years, and Ambrose served as a consultant to the OLI in its early stages.

The Eberly Center works with Carnegie Mellon faculty to improve their teaching effectiveness, and its research on success factors for student learning—codified in the center's "Principles of Learning"—is incorporated into the OLI courses. For example, the Eberly Center has found that "goal-directed practice and targeted feedback are critical to learning," and that "students must learn to monitor, evaluate, and adjust their approaches to learning to become self-directed learners."[23] The embedded assessments and self-evaluations encouraged in OLI courses reflect these convictions. In classroom teaching, the Eberly Center encourages instructors to pace student learning to avoid cramming and to provide students with a great deal of support at the beginning and then progressively back off—principles that are enacted in the instructional design of the OLI courses.[24]

The OLI's asynchronous learning environment tends to support courses aimed at skill acquisition—topics on which students' progress can be evaluated objectively and in which there is a single correct answer. The OLI currently offers 14 introductory courses in science, math, and foreign languages—disciplines that correlate with Carnegie Mellon's institutional strength in engineering. The first Hewlett grant was awarded to develop one course each in statistics, causal reasoning, economics, and logic. A chemistry course followed in 2003, and subsequent introductory courses have been developed in the fields of engineering statistics, biology,

[22]Interview with Susan Ambrose, 9/11/08.

[23]Carnegie Mellon University (Eberly Center for Teaching Excellence), "Learning Principles: Theory and Research-Based Principles of Learning," http://www.cmu.edu/teaching/principles/learning.html.

[24]Interview with Susan Ambrose, 9/11/08. Ambrose calls the latter principle "scaffolding": providing intensive support when students are struggling and then gradually allowing them more autonomy. Similarly, the OLI mini-tutors provide fewer hints as students progress successfully through a course.

physics, empirical research methods, computational discrete mathematics, visual communication design, and French (Figure 4.2).[25]

To date, an OLI course has not been attempted in the humanities, and members of the OLI team hold opposing views regarding the feasibility of doing so. Joel Smith said there are no data on the efficacy of the OLI's methods for courses not based on skill acquisition, and Susan Ambrose, who is also a professor of history, admitted that she is "skeptical that [the OLI] would be an equally good format across all disciplines."[26] But Thille asserts that the application of OLI methods to a humanities course simply has not been tested yet.[27] Ken Koedinger, a professor at Carnegie Mellon's Human-Computer Interaction Institute who has done research and consulting for the OLI, pointed out that introductory courses in disciplines like history do involve some amount of fact retrieval, which could be served by an OLI-type environment, but he added that the problem lies in the course design methods. "One of the keys to success [in designing asynchronous online learning environments] is cognitive task analysis—having a deep understanding of the knowledge that differentiates an expert or good student from a novice or beginning student," Koedinger said. "And in a lot of humanities domains, teachers would say 'I know it when I see it, but I can't describe it'—and if you can't describe it, it's hard to design activities around it."[28]

When the OLI was launched in 2002, a few Carnegie Mellon professors had already begun to develop digital resources for their own local use.[29] The first Hewlett grant proposal identified some

[25]Open Learning Initiative, "Open and Free Courses," http://oli.web.cmu.edu/openlearning/forstudents/freecourses.

[26]Ambrose added that she cannot picture how her own course on immigration history could ever be adapted into OLI format (interview with Susan Ambrose, 9/11/09).

[27]Interviews with Joel Smith, 9/10/08, Susan Ambrose, 9/11/08, and Candace Thille, 11/17/08.

[28]Interview with Ken Koedinger, 9/8/09. The higher-education researchers William Massy and Robert Zemsky have weighed in on this issue, writing that "The areas that can profit most from IT-based strategies are those subjects that have a high volume of students, a standardized curriculum, and over whose content faculty are less possessive. . . . Some fields are not suited to extensive computer mediation, especially those concerned with questions of meaning and value, of culture and philosophy" (Massy and Zemsky, "Using Information Technology to Enhance Academic Productivity," 3, 4).

[29]Joel Smith said that these projects used funding from the departments or small out-

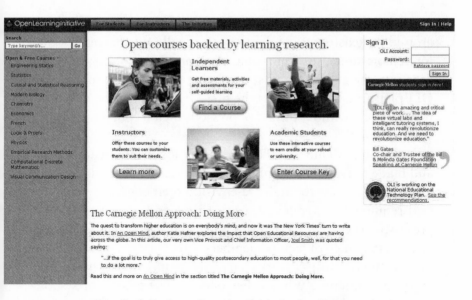

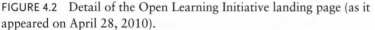

FIGURE 4.2   Detail of the Open Learning Initiative landing page (as it appeared on April 28, 2010).

Available at http://oli.web.cmu.edu/openlearning/. Permission provided courtesy of Carnegie Mellon. © 2010 Carnegie Mellon. License: Creative Commons BY-NC-SA.

of these technology projects, already under way in Carnegie Mellon classes, as good places to start developing OLI courses.[30] Three of the four courses named in that original grant—causal reasoning, economics, and logic—incorporated the preexisting online modules and virtual tools from those departments.[31] According to Joel Smith, those prior efforts had been piecemeal, and the technology-enhanced aspects of those courses were not designed for sufficiently robust delivery to open them up up to the world. As a result, much of the original $1.9 million OLI grant went

side grants from sources like the National Science Foundation (interview with Joel Smith, 8/6/09).

[30]Johnstone, Sally M., "Importing and Exporting Online Courses," *Change* 35, no. 4 (July 1, 2003).

[31]Both Pew's PCR (2002) and the Mellon Foundation's CEUTT program (2000) funded investigations into the uses of technology specifically in causal reasoning and statistics courses; some of the software developed under those programs has been integrated into the OLI in updated and expanded form.

toward improving what was already there: building up content around the existing technology to create full OLI courses designed for remote users, incorporating more principles of cognitive science into their design, and streamlining their delivery on a single OLI platform. Statistics was the first OLI course to be developed from scratch, without the aid of previous digital content that could be repurposed.[32]

According to Thille, "MIT's program took what already existed and made it available openly. At OLI, it's about engaging faculty in a design process to totally re-envision their courses," which she said requires "a *huge* investment of time and resources" for the professors involved.[33] Because the OLI course development process asks so much of faculty members, participation is entirely voluntary, and the project works only with faculty who come to them expressing interest. While other open courseware efforts showcase individual professors' talents as lecturers—or at least include syllabi and other materials that represent their individualized approach to their subject—OLI courses use what Thille calls a "team-based development approach," in which the faculty member's perspective is one among many that are incorporated into the course design.[34]

The development team for each OLI course consists of Thille providing project management, a Carnegie Mellon professor serving as the "faculty content expert," a software engineer, a designer with expertise in human-computer interaction, and learning scientists.[35] The intention to assemble this particular body of exper-

[32]Interview with Joel Smith, 8/6/09. Smith said that prior to the OLI grant, the existing course technologies were all "running on a server sitting under someone's desk. . . . From an information technology standpoint, all of these were fairly small-scale. They weren't designed for large-scale delivery across the internet, 24 by 7, potentially to tens of thousands of people." He explained that the OLI team approached the statistics department about creating a new OLI course from the ground up because "the department has a long history here of working with cognitive scientists to improve their traditional teaching," so it seemed like a natural fit. Oded Meyer confirmed that "statistics was the flagship course—it started from zero, and it tested and implemented all the elements that then went into other OLI courses" (interview with Oded Meyer, 9/10/08).

[33]Interview with Candace Thille, 8/18/08.

[34]Quoted in Vaidya, Akanksha, "Scientists Present Open Learning Interplay," *The Tartan*, online edition, March 31, 2008.

[35]Open Learning Initiative, "The Initiative: Team," http://oli.web.cmu.edu/openlearning/initiative/team.

tise was written into the first Hewlett grant, and Joel Smith said that the composition of the team flowed directly from the campus culture fostered by the Eberly Center's work: "It's very much the Carnegie Mellon approach to education."[36]

As a result of this intensive group design process, the bar for faculty involvement is set high in two respects: faculty must be willing to rethink and restructure their courses from the ground up, and they must also consent to collaborating with others to share authorship of the final product. As compensation for faculty involvement, funds are given to their department to cover one semester of release time, or the professor receives the equivalent in pay for teaching a summer course—though all involved confirm that creating an OLI course eats up far more time than a single semester, so much of the work goes uncompensated.[37] According to Thille, as a result of the significant time commitment required, the vast majority of OLI content experts are tenured, as it would be difficult for junior faculty to justify sinking so much time into a project like this rather than focusing on core activities.[38]

Such a labor-intensive design process results in a very high cost per course. Joel Smith called the OLI "extremely resource-intensive, especially given that our principle is that you never stop developing the course."[39] Between 2002 and 2008, the OLI received three grants from the Hewlett Foundation totaling $5.65 million, and additional funding has been provided by Carnegie Mellon (mostly in the form of in-kind support) and some much smaller grants tied to specific courses. Thille said that a new OLI course currently costs about $500,000 to develop—and that figure represents a decline over time, as some of the earlier courses cost over $1 million each.[40]

---

[36]Interview with Joel Smith, 8/6/09.

[37]Interviews with Oded Meyer, 9/10/08, and Candace Thille, 8/18/08.

[38]Interview with Candace Thille, 8/18/08. Meyer agreed, saying that he is on the teaching track at Carnegie Mellon, and that because the tenure and promotions process for that track does reward demonstrations of teaching impact outside the university, he will eventually reference his OLI work in that context. But he noted that "the tenure track is much more [about] counting papers and conferences and which journals you publish in," so his colleagues are less likely to find participation in something like the OLI to be beneficial when seeking promotion (interview with Oded Meyer, 9/8/09).

[39]Interview with Joel Smith, 9/10/08.

[40]Interview with Candace Thille, 8/18/08. A 2009 *Chronicle* item cited different figures, reporting that "initially, the cost per course was as much as $2 million, but that expense

The OLI has five full-time employees, including Thille and two software engineers, and the budget also covers fees to graduate student researchers and the time that professors and the staff of the Eberly Center devote to the project.[41] Given the human and monetary resources that must be brought to bear in developing a single course, it is not surprising that in its first eight years of operation, the OLI has created only about a dozen courses. The complexity of the OLI approach leads to an emphasis on quality over quantity. Thus, short of an overwhelming institutional subvention, it would be nearly impossible to imagine the OLI scaling up, as MIT OCW has done, to encompass its parent university's entire curriculum—assuming that all of the courses taught at Carnegie Mellon could even be taught by this method.

In contrast to initiatives like MIT OCW and Fathom, which can be seen as alternative publishing channels for university content, the OLI team is adamant that its project is not a publishing exercise. While Carnegie Mellon faculty take the lead in formulating the content of OLI courses, those courses are not replicas of the classroom versions—the level of functionality and interactivity contained in an OLI course requires considerably more transformation than simply uploading existing syllabi or lecture slides. As President Cohon noted, "what we set out to do and what we are doing is very different from MIT. I know what MIT's doing is not as simple as just dumping your syllabus on the web, but it's not much more than that: it's making available materials that already exist. We created a platform . . . that delivers a course, an educational experience—that's a very different thing."[42]

By providing an interactive course platform that adjusts to student performance and needs, the OLI serves a somewhat different purpose than many other online courseware projects: its function

---

has dropped to $1 million to $1.5 million" (Parry, Marc, and Karin Fischer, "How Obama's $12-Billion Plan Could Change 2-Year Colleges," *Chronicle of Higher Education,* online edition, July 17, 2009). Joel Smith said that he thinks the OLI has hit a wall in terms of its ability to lower the cost per course, and that it will probably not dip much below $500,000 (interview with Joel Smith, 9/10/08).

[41]Interviews with Joel Smith, 9/10/08, and Candace Thille, 8/18/08.

[42]Interview with Jared Cohon, 9/10/08.

is not to offer a window into Carnegie Mellon, because the course content has transformed in its migration to online format. According to Thille, the OLI "is not completely a representation of the way CMU teaches any one subject." But "the courses do represent a view of the world that CMU has—if you've completed an OLI course, you can be confident that you've covered the material in the same depth and breadth as it would be taught at Carnegie Mellon."[43]

Impact of the Open Learning Initiative

Substantive evaluation is a key feature of the OLI, and the program has devoted a great deal of resources and attention to testing its efficacy. As Joel Smith recalls, "Hewlett set the goal that these should be courses that [would allow] a novice learner anywhere in the world [to] get online and learn something without a faculty member"—and the program's success in achieving that goal would have to be tested.[44] Provost Kamlet has cautioned that a resource's good intentions and accessibility do not necessarily correlate with its efficacy: "just because [educational resources] are online or available for free does not mean they're very good."[45] Thille agreed that the OER field is plagued by a general lack of assessment, and that "there are lots of people throwing stuff against the wall, but how do you know that anyone's learning anything?"[46]

The OLI set out to prove that, in its case, real learning is occurring. The original grant proposal states that "we intend, in each of these courses, to leverage an entirely new opportunity presented by online courses for continuous gathering of evaluation data for both formative and summative assessment."[47] That grant also included funding for external evaluation, and Gaea Leinhardt from the University of Pittsburgh's School of Education was brought

[43]Interview with Candace Thille, 8/18/08.
[44]Interview with Joel Smith, 9/10/08.
[45]Kamlet, keynote address.
[46]Interview with Candace Thille, 8/18/08.
[47]"Four Courses, Millions of Users," 11.

in to evaluate the first four courses.[48] Subsequently the OLI developed an entire "evaluative portfolio," with dozens of research studies ranging from analyses of existing online courses to usability studies to "learning and effectiveness studies that use randomized controls" that compare learning outcomes of students in OLI courses to peers in formal classroom settings.[49]

The most significant evaluation efforts have been centered on OLI's statistics course, including learning effectiveness studies based on head-to-head comparisons of students in the OLI statistics course versus a traditional, in-person Carnegie Mellon statistics course in the fall of 2005 and spring of 2006. Outcomes were positive, with students in the OLI group performing on par with students in the control group.[50] The OLI team was eager to share these results with the Hewlett Foundation, which agreed that the findings were encouraging. When Mike Smith came to Carnegie Mellon in 2006 for a routine site visit, he discussed evaluation with Joel Smith and Thille and encouraged them to push these trials further by investigating whether the OLI courses might be not only just as good, but somehow better, than the traditional versions. He proposed that Carnegie Mellon conduct a study in which the OLI students had to cover the material much faster than the control group.[51]

Heeding Mike Smith's advice, in the spring of 2007 the OLI followed up its initial trials with a new study testing "an accelerated learning hypothesis" which stated "that learners using the OLI course in hybrid mode"—in which students have some face time with an instructor while simultaneously progressing through the

[48]Joel Smith credits Mike Smith at the Hewlett Foundation with the idea of bringing in an external evaluator: "I'm very sure that he and Cathy [Casserly] wanted someone independent of CMU to do the evaluation" in the project's early stages (interview with Joel Smith, 8/6/09).

[49]Open Learning Initiative, "The Initiative: Publications," http://oli.web.cmu.edu/openlearning/initiative/publications; Thille, Candace. "Building Open Learning," 176.

[50]During the course of that study, "in-class exam scores showed no significant difference between the traditional and online groups" (Lovett, Marsha, Oded Meyer, and Candace Thille, "The Open Learning Initiative: Measuring the Effectiveness of the OLI Statistics Course in Accelerating Student Learning," *Journal of Interactive Media in Education*, May 5, 2008, 7, http://jime.open.ac.uk/2008/14).

[51]Interviews with Joel Smith, 8/6/09, and Candace Thille, 8/11/09.

OLI modules—"will learn the same amount of material in a significantly shorter period of time with equal learning gains, as compared to students in traditional instruction."[52] The study found that the students in the accelerated study performed better on standard examinations than these in the traditional course.[53] The sample size of this first accelerated statistics study was quite small, consisting of just 25 students in the OLI group, but it was repeated at Carnegie Mellon in the spring of 2009 with twice as many students and achieved nearly identical results.[54]

The OLI team was pleasantly surprised at how well the accelerated OLI course measured up against the traditional version, and Thille said that the team came away from that study convinced that in hybrid mode, students can "learn more, better, faster, and less expensively."[55] Meyer, who taught both the control group and variable groups of students in the OLI accelerated study, said that teaching in hybrid mode—meeting with students twice a week, while they used the OLI on their own and completed the coursework in half the time—"was one of the best teaching experiences I ever had." Meyer recalled that the students who used the OLI came to class prepared to cover topics in greater depth than is usually possible, and as a result, "they gave me some of the best exam answers I have *ever* seen from students in an intro course, even when I taught it traditionally."[56]

Indeed, the OLI team originally envisioned unaffiliated, individual learners as the project's target audience. But the idea of a

[52]Lovett, Meyer, and Thille, "The Open Learning Initiative," 1. Mike Smith further explained the accelerated study as "an important randomized trial" in which "students in CMU's beginning statistics course were asked to choose whether they wanted to take the semester-long course with traditional lectures, weekly discussion sessions, and optional access to the statistics tutor software (the control group) or the same course with the tutoring software as the instructional medium, no lectures, two optional weekly discussion sessions, and only half as long to complete the entire course (Smith, Marshall, "Opening Education," *Science* 323 [January 2, 2009], 92).

[53]Students in the accelerated group also retained the information equally well when both groups were retested on the material the following semester (Lovett, Meyer, and Thille, "The Open Learning Initiative," 9).

[54]Interview with Candace Thille, 8/11/09.

[55]Interview with Candace Thille, 8/18/08.

[56]Interview with Oded Meyer, 9/10/08.

tiered usage structure was written into the original grant proposal. In accordance with the Hewlett Foundation's wishes, individual access would be offered freely and openly to any interested user, but Carnegie Mellon also proposed creating value-added features on top of the free content.[57] The proposal envisioned a version of the OLI containing "premium services," such as more fully developed assessments (quizzes and tests that can be graded instead of just incremental self-assessments) targeted to educators at other institutions who might use the OLI in their classrooms with their enrolled students.[58]

While this Academic Version has been an aspect of the OLI project from the beginning, it started as a secondary element to the OLI's primary purpose of serving individuals. But Thille said that the initiative currently "has two distinct populations that it tries to serve well" —individuals pursuing the OLI on their own and groups of students using it in conjunction with their instructors as part of enrolled courses.[59]

Confident in the power of the hybrid mode, after 2007 the OLI devoted more energy and resources to the Academic Version.[60] They built up the instructor materials, adding features like automatically generated feedback reports for instructors based on student performance on embedded OLI assessments; these allowed professors to target their teaching to address problem areas and tailor the classroom face time to students' specific needs. Thille considers this feedback loop to be the key value proposition of the Academic Version, writing that "the richness of the data we are collecting about student use and learning provides an unprecedented opportunity for keeping instructors in tune with the many

[57]Joel Smith recalled that these conversations centered on the question "If it's going to be open and free, what's a sustainability model that makes sense?" He compared the versioning option that the OLI proposed and pursued to Red Hat, which makes its version of the Linux operating system freely available under an open-source license but also sells value-added premium services and support to users of this software (interview with Joel Smith, 8/6/09).

[58]"Four Courses, Millions of Users," 10.

[59]Interview with Candace Thille, 8/11/09.

[60]Ibid.

aspects of students' learning."[61] The Academic Version now allows instructors who register their courses with the OLI to select and sequence content, even blending modules from different OLI courses, and it also empowers instructors to customize the course by gating aspects of the content to control the pace at which students move through the material.[62] Based on the embedded assessments, student feedback reports, or their own tests and quizzes developed to complement the OLI material, instructors "may assign applicable grades and or credit"—the OLI itself does not offer credits and cannot assign grades, but through the Academic Version students may receive credit for OLI work from their own institutions.[63]

Thille said that professors who participated in early OLI course development teams never envisioned it being used at Carnegie Mellon: "they thought their . . . students would get traditional education and they'd develop the open and free material for students who wouldn't be able to come to CMU."[64] But studies of the OLI's efficacy required some Carnegie Mellon faculty to utilize the courses, and student feedback has been positive, such that the courses or parts thereof are sometimes utilized during normal teaching. The design principles that make the OLI an effective method of teaching unaffiliated learners also make it a useful tool for Carnegie Mellon students; as Ambrose pointed out, "even at CMU we have really smart students struggling with intro classes, and this could help."[65] But on-campus use of the OLI is by no means university- or even department-wide, as it is still largely confined to the professors who created the courses in the first place.[66] Joel Smith said that Carnegie Mellon has done nothing to actively

[61]Thille, "Building Open Learning," 174.
[62]Interview with Candace Thille, 8/11/09. The modular construction of OLI courses was referenced in the original grant proposal ("Four Courses, Millions of Users," 10).
[63]Open Learning Initiative, "Frequently Asked Questions," http://oli.webl.cmu.edu/openlearning/initiative/faqs.
[64]Interview with Candace Thille, 8/18/08.
[65]Interview with Susan Ambrose, 9/11/08.
[66]Or, in some cases, those professors' immediate replacements, if they have subsequently moved on from teaching the introductory course (interview with Candace Thille, 10/28/09).

encourage other faculty to incorporate the OLI into their teaching, so adoption can happen only through "stumbling on it" or word of mouth.[67]

To date, the presence of the OLI does not seem to have significantly changed the Carnegie Mellon educational experience. The provost has served as an informal advisor to the project, but administrators have not gone out of their way to promote or advocate for the OLI in the way that President Charles Vest and Provost Robert Brown did for MIT OCW. Assessing the OLI's internal impact on Carnegie Mellon, Ambrose said that it is "still such a small number of courses that I think if you asked random teachers and students here, they really wouldn't know about it. It's gotten a lot more play nationally or internationally among certain interested communities than it has here—here the effect has been pretty minimal."[68]

The OLI team intended the data collected from students' progress through the material to serve as a "point of leverage for assessment and iterative improvement that is unprecedented in the history of higher education"—making the OLI an effective tool not only for students but also for researchers.[69] The OLI is a constant research cycle: cognitive scientific and instructional design research informs the production of the course, and the data collected through student use fuel research studies and inform the next iteration.[70] These OLI data are useful to some internal constituencies at Carnegie Mellon, such as the Eberly Center or the Pittsburgh Science of Learning Center, which is interested in applying the data to its academic research.[71] When asked if the OLI is a research project or a pedagogical tool, Joel Smith answered that it is "profoundly both" because of the virtuous feedback loop:

[67]Interview with Joel Smith, 9/10/08. In the summer of 2010, Carnegie Mellon piloted an OLI version of its seven-week "Computing @ Carnegie Mellon" mini-course on basic computing skills, which is required of all undergraduate students. Once the OLI course is in place, students will have the option of completing the requirement online.

[68]Interview with Susan Ambrose, 9/11/08.

[69]"Four Courses, Millions of Users," 11.

[70]Thille, "Building Open Learning," 169.

[71]"Interim Status Report on Carnegie Mellon Open Learning Initiative," 15.

by "turning teaching into a research activity," the OLI is both informed by and informs learning science research.[72]

Beyond the Carnegie Mellon campus, the OLI courses have been used by learners all over the world, both individually and in classroom settings. Between July 2006 and June 2010, there were 18,516 student registrations for the Academic Version—and 73,062 registrations for open and free courses—from 214 countries. In addition, the site received 356,293 anonymous visits in that period.[73] These numbers indicate that unaffiliated learners using the OLI far outnumber the students using it formally in their classes, but Thille is quick to remind that many may be using the OLI without registering, and instructors may be advising students to use it as individuals rather than registering the class and possibly incurring fees associated with the Academic Version.[74] According to a 2009 item in the *Chronicle of Higher Education,* there are about 300 classes around the world using OLI materials.[75]

Though the OLI did not set concrete goals for the level of usage the courses would receive, those involved have expressed some dissatisfaction with these numbers. When asked to list Hewlett's most successful grantees in the field of OER, Mike Smith cited the OLI as perhaps the most exciting, but remarked, "I don't think it's fully there yet . . . [because there is] not enough use."[76] Joel Smith agreed, saying that "the issue of adoption . . . just has not been addressed." According to him, the OLI has had real difficulties both on and off campus in "getting faculty other than the faculty who

[72]Interview with Joel Smith, 9/10/08.

[73]Figures obtained from OLI transaction logs (personal communication with Candace Thille, 6/28/10).

[74]Thille explained that not every course's Academic Version carries a fee. Only French, causal reasoning, formal logic, microeconomics, and statistics do, and the other courses are free even in the Academic Version. "The whole idea behind the fee is to be able to maintain and extend the course," so the courses that have some non-Hewlett funding associated with them do not need a maintenance fee (interview with Candace Thille, 8/11/09).

[75]Parry, Marc, "Obama's Great Course Giveaway," *Chronicle of Higher Education,* online edition, August 3, 2009. Thille emphasized that using the OLI at other campuses "is not an institutional decision, it's purely at this point in time an individual faculty decision" (interview with Candace Thille, 8/11/09).

[76]Interview with Marshall Smith, 8/19/08.

developed it to use it. There are some outside faculty using it, but there should be a lot more. Faculty in statistics and economics, for example, should look at this and say 'this is really an option for me.'"[77]

The OLI's low usage rates relative to other programs may be due in part to the initiative's complete lack of marketing: no efforts have been made to spread the word beyond Thille's and Smith's frequent talks at education conferences, and Thille reported that the marketing budget she requested in her second grant proposal to Hewlett was not funded. Some also speculate that usage has been hurt by the false perception that a teacher must surrender all control over his or her class if the OLI is used. Thille said that she is constantly finding herself taxed with explaining that the OLI is not trying to replace teachers—that, in fact, the initiative is a strong advocate of the hybrid mode as the optimal format for deploying the OLI.[78] Koedinger of the Human-Computer Interaction Institute said that for the OLI's level of usage to improve, users will need to "get past irrational issues that limit adoption," such as faculty's unwillingness to change or to accept and use something invented elsewhere.[79]

While the OLI's impact to date may be limited in terms of adoption, it provides a "proof of concept" that has made a strong impression within the OER community. The OLI's data-driven approach and proven efficacy are frequently cited as examples of OER's potential to increase access to quality education through technology. David Wiley, a professor at Brigham Young University and one of the strongest voices in the OER community, has said that "any time you want to show someone the power of open education, you don't take them to MIT, you take them to Carnegie Mellon," because in contrast to other open-educational content, "OLI is so obviously committed to really making sure that you learn from their material."[80] According to OER program officer

[77]Interview with Joel Smith, 9/10/08.
[78]Interview with Candace Thille, 8/11/09.
[79]Interview with Ken Koedinger, 9/11/08.
[80]Interview with David Wiley, 8/18/09.

Victor Vuchic, the Hewlett Foundation "gets[s] a lot of mileage out of" the OLI, often touting it as a success story for open education.[81] In short, the OLI seems to offer a model of a completely new direction for higher education: as Joel Smith said, "This is a potentially disruptive technology. So Carnegie Mellon could be placing itself—in terms of learning the technology—to really have an edge here."[82]

As this potential impact has gradually made itself clearer, the goals of the OLI have evolved, and Thille told the *Chronicle of Higher Education* in August 2009 that she aims "to fundamentally change the way postsecondary education is done in this country."[83] Though such a transformation has yet to be realized, there have been some recent indications that the OLI—or something like it—may be the way forward. The initiative has long been respected within the OER community, but until very recently, the popular press had taken little notice. Somewhat surprisingly, a program as innovative as the OLI has received only a tiny fraction of the press mentions accorded MIT OCW. The site's general lack of branding may be partially responsible: the Carnegie Mellon name and insignia are very discreetly placed on the site, and Thille said that this is intentional. "Even though the OLI's content is developed at CMU, I wanted it to be useful at other schools, so once you're inside the learning environment it doesn't scream Carnegie Mellon." Thille also said that when she came on board, she changed the initiative's formal name from the Carnegie Mellon Open Learning Initiative to simply the OLI—a decision that may have weakened its perceived connection to the university.[84]

But the OLI has recently garnered more public attention, as it was frequently mentioned in conjunction with President Barack Obama's proposed American Graduation Initiative to invest in community college education—particularly in the development of "a new online, open-source clearinghouse of courses so that com-

[81]Interview with Victor Vuchic, 8/20/08.
[82]Interview with Joel Smith, 9/10/08.
[83]Quoted in Parry, "Obama's Great Course Giveaway."
[84]Interview with Candace Thille, 8/18/08.

munity colleges across the country can offer more classes without building more classrooms."[85] Announced in July 2009, the Obama administration's proposal was viewed as a watershed moment by the entire OER community, as it marked the U.S. government's first serious display of interest in this space; though specific developers of the community college courses for the government repository were not named, there was strong speculation that "Carnegie Mellon, repeatedly cited by officials, might offer a model for the effort."[86]

Mike Smith—former head of the education division of the Hewlett Foundation and a veteran of the Carter and Clinton education departments—became a senior counselor to Education Secretary Arne Duncan in 2008.[87] Smith has been a long-time proponent of the OLI, and the timing of his recent employment with the federal government has coincided with the administration's new interest in the program.[88] He authored a major article on open education in the January 2009 issue of *Science,* in which he wrote that the OLI was the best example to date of "effective, high-quality, Web-based courses," and Carnegie Mellon received an inquiry regarding the OLI from the White House Office of Science and Technology Policy a few months later.[89] Candace Thille was invited to serve in a working group, co-chaired by Mike Smith, to formulate the 2010 National Educational Technology Plan. Released in draft form on March 5, 2010, the plan cites the OLI as an "[advance] in our understanding of how to design good OER."[90] Language

[85]Obama, Barack, "Remarks by the President on the American Graduation Initiative," July 14, 2009, Macomb Community College, Warren, Michigan; transcript released via Office of the White House Press Secretary, http://www.whitehouse.gov/the_press_office/Remarks-by-the-President-on-the-American-Graduation-Initiative-in-Warren-MI/.

[86]Parry, "Obama's Great Course Giveaway."

[87]Smith left his position at Hewlett as a result of term limitations.

[88]An item in *Inside Higher Ed* links the focus on open online courses to "the ideas of Martha J. Kanter, the under secretary of education. Kanter was previously chancellor of the Foothill De Anza Community College District," which is also a major Hewlett grantee (Jaschik, Scott, "U.S. Push for Free Online Courses," *Inside Higher Ed,* June 29, 2009)— another sign that Washington is now taking interest in the OLI.

[89]Smith, "Opening Education," 92; Parry and Fischer, "Obama's $12-Billion Plan."

[90]Office of Educational Technology, U.S. Department of Education, "Transforming American Education: Learning Powered by Technology," National Educational Technology Plan 2010, March 5, 2010, http://www.ed.gov/sites/default/files/NETP-2010-final-report.pdf, 73.

on the Obama administration's plans for community colleges was included in the hotly debated Health Care and Education Reconciliation Act of 2010. The administration's proposed $12 billion to aid community colleges—$500 million of which would have gone to developing freely available online courses over ten years—was reduced to $2 billion in the final legislation, and the specific provision for online courseware was removed.[91] Although economic realities prevented the proposed level of government investment in these strategies (at least at present), the import of gaining the president's attention and advocacy for a small and relatively low-profile initiative like the OLI should not be underestimated.[92]

The OLI set out to use technology to teach unaffiliated individuals, but its approach to course design may have unforeseen potential as a long-term source of cost-cutting for institutions of higher education. Provost Kamlet, an economist by training, has discussed cognitive tutors as an antidote to Baumol's "cost disease," which, when applied to higher education, postulates that college tuition will go up forever in the absence of a major innovation.[93] "Vast amounts of testing . . . indicates that cognitive tutors—done right—work better than traditional means of educating. But even if that were not so—even if they were only four-fifths as good—there could be a huge advantage in terms of cost savings."[94]

The remarkable innovation of this approach—and the possibility that it could, if correctly deployed, result in a meaningful shift in higher education—seems to finally be receiving the widespread attention it deserves. Richard K. Vedder, the director of the Center for College Affordability and Productivity, said that the stagnation that has defined the teaching field for so long may fi-

[91]Jaschik, "U.S. Push for Free Online Courses."

[92]Indeed, Hal Plotkin, a former community college administrator serving as an advisor to the Department of Education, told the *Chronicle of Higher Education* that "this legislation does enable us to move forward with our plans related to open online courses," though details on how much might be spent or what form the project would take given the slashed budget remained unclear (see Parry, Marc, "Agenda for Open Online Courses Can Go Forward, Federal Officials Say," Wired Campus blog (*Chronicle of Higher Education*), April 12, 2010, http://chronicle.com/blogPost/Agenda-for-Open-Online-Courses/22496/.

[93]Bowen, William G., "The Economics of the Major Private Universities," Carnegie Commission on the Future of Higher Education, Berkeley, Calif., 1968.

[94]Kamlet, keynote address.

nally be interrupted: "With the exception of—*possible* exception of—prostitution, I don't know any other profession that's had no productivity advance in 2,500 years." Online courses are "a way to kind of offer a new approach. It's applying technology to lower costs, rather than to add costs."[95] But realizing real savings from the OLI would require that faculty using the courses in hybrid mode take on more students per semester to maximize resources, or perhaps that they be replaced altogether by treating the OLI courses as standalone vehicles of instruction—a step that Carnegie Mellon has shown no inclination to take.

The Open Learning Initiative and Sustainability

As was the case with the OCW project, planning for long-term sustainability of the OLI was not a major concern in the early years; Joel Smith said in 2009 that "frankly it really wasn't until about a year ago that we thought we had enough product here—that's been tested and we really know works—that it's really time to turn to marketing and look at sustainability."[96] Both of these initiatives focused on developing their platforms and offerings in the early years and put off serious sustainability planning for later phases— a trait that seems consistent among many Hewlett OER grantees.

The Hewlett grant request template did require grantees to formulate some sort of sustainability plan, and Carnegie Mellon proposed that developing premium services—what has come to be known as the Academic Version of the OLI—could support the endeavor. The proposal envisioned the Academic Version generating

---

[95]Quoted in Parry, "Obama's Great Course Giveaway." In his 2004 book, Vedder expands on his point about stagnating productivity in higher education. He writes that "The productivity of university personnel is almost certainly falling, and it is clearly falling sharply relative to the rest of the economy. While it takes far less time for workers to make a ton of steel, type a letter, or harvest a bushel of corn than it did a generation ago, it takes *more* professors and college administrators to educate a given number of students" (Vedder, Richard K., *Going Broke by Degree: Why College Costs Too Much*, Washington, D.C.: American Enterprise Institute Press, 2004, xv).

[96]Interview with Joel Smith, 8/6/09.

revenue to sustain the project through a fee of $25 per student for those registered to take OLI courses as a group, and the OLI has basically adhered to that pricing.[97] But Joel Smith confirmed that, so far, those fees are not "at a level that provides us with income for sustainability."[98] Student fees from sales of the Academic Version of OLI courses generated only about $25,000 in the 2007–8 academic year—not nearly enough to cover the costs of a program with an annual operating budget of almost $1 million.[99] Thille said that the OLI routinely waives the fee if an instructor indicates that it might be a burden to the students, and that a sound billing structure for collecting these monies is not yet in place at Carnegie Mellon—implying that, as a plan for providing an income stream, the Academic Version is still rudimentary.

One possible path toward sustainability for any campus-run online courseware project involves significant institutional subvention from the parent university. As described in the previous chapter, MIT OCW received its first grant from the Hewlett Foundation a year before the OLI, and OCW's funding from Hewlett also expired a year earlier, at which point MIT's provost made an internal commitment to perpetually shoulder half of the project's operating costs. But President Cohon and Provost Kamlet do not feel that it is the university's responsibility to permanently fund the OLI out of pocket. According to Cohon, it is simply not an option for Carnegie Mellon to absorb the project's costs as a path to sustainability, because MIT's larger endowment provides it with more discretionary funds.[100] In addition to relative financial differences between the two institutions, some elements of the internal value

[97]For the proposed pricing see "Four Courses, Millions of Users," 13. The OLI website states that "some of our courses carry a small per-student usage fee that you would pay when you register. Depending on the course, this cost could range from $15–$60" (Open Learning Initiative, "Frequently Asked Questions").
[98]Interview with Joel Smith, 8/6/09.
[99]Interviews with Candace Thille, 8/18/08, and Joel Smith, 9/10/08.
[100]Interview with Jared Cohon, 9/10/08. According to the 2008 National Association of College and University Business Officers Endowment Study, Carnegie Mellon's endowment ranked 69th among American universities at just over $1 billion, while MIT's ranked 6th at just over $10 billion (2008 NACUBO Endowment Study results, http://www.nacubo.org/documents/research/NES2008PublicTable-AllInstitutionsByFY08MarketValue.pdf).

that OCW provides to MIT—branding, exposure, uniting the entire faculty through a common endeavor—are not shared by Carnegie Mellon's smaller and lower-profile OLI project.

Within Carnegie Mellon, there also seems to be some tension between the administration and the OLI directors regarding the project's sustainability if it remains perpetually open and free; Thille and Joel Smith are confident that it can become sustainable, but the president and provost have strong doubts.[101] Kamlet said that he is not sure if the OLI project can continue beyond the run of its Hewlett grants: "I hope it does, but I've pushed about as hard as I know how to push" for a sustainability model, and he does not think that those in charge of the OLI have heeded his advice. Perhaps this tension can be attributed to the project's very origins, as the open and free aspect was the Hewlett Foundation's contribution to the OLI concept[102]—not, as was the case with OCW, something that the president and provost immediately embraced and promoted to foundations.

The OLI's inability to develop and execute an effective revenue-generating mechanism is further complicated when one considers Carnegie Mellon's past success with monetizing other educational technology ventures. An entrepreneurial institution, Carnegie Mellon has made several forays into e-learning prior to the OLI. iCarnegie is a for-profit spin-off focused on executive training. And the Carnegie Learning company, launched as a research experiment in 1983 and commercialized in 1998, has also become profitable, with the product in use in 7 percent of U.S. public school districts.[103] As the company's chairman, Provost Kamlet is uniquely aware of the challenges involved in making an online learning venture self-sustaining, and he has serious doubts that a resource can grow and

---

[101]Joel Smith said the question of whether the OLI could always remain free and open is "a good-natured argument that's been there all along and continues to this day" (interview with Joel Smith, 9/10/08); Kamlet was less charitable in his description of the disagreements between his office and the OLI over the sustainability question.

[102]Interview with Mark Kamlet, 9/11/08. Kamlet said, "I didn't want to go the open route, but the terms of the funding dictate it. . . . I've had big arguments over the incorrectness of the Hewlett Foundation's religious beliefs in open source."

[103]Interview with Mark Kamlet, 9/11/08. According to the Carnegie Learning website, the product is used by 500,000 students in 2,600 schools (Carnegie Learning, "About Carnegie Learning," http://www.carnegielearning.com/company.cfm).

achieve its potential in the absence of revenues. Referring to the OLI, Kamlet said, "If it were so simple as take some money from a charitable organization, do the cognitive tutor, throw it up against the wall, and change the world, that would be great, but that's not my experience of how things typically work."[104]

Kamlet credits Carnegie Learning's success to the combination of sound science and an effective business model, in which school districts purchase the tutors for local use.[105] If it were more rigorously "productized," one could imagine the OLI someday achieving similar market penetration in higher education. In President Cohon's words, the OLI has always been more "focused on R&D rather than dissemination."[106] This emphasis on research may be a source of its value, but continuing to invest in constant research and inquiry for endless future iterations may not be the best path to sustainability. The OLI seems to have the makings of a strong product, but Kamlet is concerned that if the focus does not shift more toward marketing and dissemination, it may never reach the audience it should. Kamlet expressed interest in seeking venture capital to support the OLI, and maybe one day spinning it off as a separate entity akin to the iCarnegie and Carnegie Learning enterprises, but he feels that the terms of the Hewlett funding —dictating that versions of these courses must always remain free and open—may hinder his ability to attract investors.[107] Thille realizes that if venture capitalists were to be brought in to help productize the OLI and increase revenues, changes would be necessary, "but my concern is that the research cycle would be broken—what drives the next iteration of a course could be what's going to sell better, not what will help students learn better."[108]

---

[104]Kamlet, keynote address.

[105]Interview with Mark Kamlet, 9/11/08. An article in *Science* reiterates this point that the endeavor thrives due to the combination of its academic and business components, saying that the cognitive tutor's "creators say that ongoing improvements to the software would not have been possible without the steady revenue from sales or its enduring relationship to the university" (Bhattacharjee, Yudhijit, "A Personal Tutor for Algebra: Commercial Software Created in the Lab Anticipates Wrong Answers and Reinforces Needed Skills for First-Year Algebra Students," *Science* 323 [January 2, 2009], 64).

[106]Interview with Jared Cohon, 9/10/08.

[107]Interview with Mark Kamlet, 9/11/08.

[108]Interview with Candace Thille, 8/18/08.

The OLI's third and final Hewlett grant concluded on July 31, 2009, but within a month funding became available for a new project. In mid-2008 the OLI team began formulating the idea for the Community College Open Learning Initiative (CC-OLI), a new branch of the project that will explicitly address community college students and involve community college faculty in the design process. Thille said that she began discussions with program officers from the Gates, Hewlett, and Lumina Foundations in November 2008, and funding for CC-OLI from all three foundations became available in the summer of 2009. Development work on CC-OLI began in January 2010, and $4 million has been awarded for a three-year project.[109] Carnegie Mellon was the grant recipient for this project, and Thille will serve as its principal investigator, leading a team of faculty experts from various community colleges as well as Carnegie Mellon designers, software engineers, and learning scientists in developing four courses.

According to Thille, "the existing OLI courses have . . . a good starting foundation that we can build on and expand from, but there is adaptation that needs to be done for the new population." She said that the project will target community college courses that have low completion rates, with the goal of demonstrating a 25 percent increase in successful course completion over the run the project.[110] The planning of this venture predates the 2008 presidential election, so the OLI's foray into community college course development and the Obama administration's proposal to create online courses are coincidental. The proposed allocation for aid to community colleges, including provisions for open courseware, was decreased as the bill moved through the congressional legislative process in March 2010.[111] Should the concept remain a priority, however, the experience in working with community college

[109]Interview with Candace Thille, 8/11/09.
[110]Ibid.
[111]Lederman, Doug, "Student Loan Bill Scorecard," *Inside Higher Ed,* March 24, 2010. A blog post on the White House's Middle Class Task Force blog stated that the final bill will include "funding for community colleges to develop online courses" (Levine, Brian, "A Victory for Students and Their Families," Middle Class Task Force blog, http://www.whitehouse.gov/blog/2010/03/30/a-victory-students-and-their-families)—though at the time of writing, the amount of that allocation was unspecified.

faculty that the OLI will gain in the meantime may position it even more favorably if and when the government looks for grant recipients to develop courses for a national repository.[112]

This new funding for CC-OLI will allow the OLI team to continue their work in some form for at least three more years, but it has necessitated a change in direction. Thille said that Carnegie Mellon professors are beginning to come to her to request that their courses be part of the OLI, but she now has to tell them that they must secure their own additional funding, as there is no more discretionary money available for new Carnegie Mellon OLI courses. A few small outstanding grants continue to support the main OLI project: some NSF funding goes toward the assessment, improvement, and dissemination of several existing courses, and a grant from the Spencer Foundation to develop instructor feedback tools has yet to be fully spent. Some additional funding received in 2010 will also go toward working with Carnegie Mellon professors to create a "Concepts of Computer Science" course for the OLI.[113] But with those exceptions, the remaining funds are all earmarked for CC-OLI, and the future of the program at Carnegie Mellon remains uncertain.[114] In theory, Thille and Joel Smith as well as Kamlet would like to see the OLI project expand to include more Carnegie Mellon courses—Smith said that 25–50 would represent a "critical mass" of the university's core undergraduate courses—but at present there are no funds to support such an ambitious expansion.[115]

·················

All online courseware projects provide access to knowledge, but Thille thinks that the next step for the open-educational field "is in

---

[112]In April 2010 the Hewlett Foundation announced that it would play an advisory role to the Department of Education on issues relating to OER, indicating that its approach will likely exert further influence over the government's (William and Flora Hewlett Foundation, "News: The Hewlett Foundation's Role in Advancing Open Educational Resources," http://www.hewlett.org/news/hewlett-foundations-role-in-oer).

[113]Kresge Foundation, "Foundation Center: Grant Details," http://maps.foundationcen ter.org/grantmakers/grant_prosfile_page.php?nonp=1&nof=1&id=16902083&gmkey=K RES002. Thille said that the course will focus on introductory material aimed at undergraduates with nontechnical backgrounds (interview with Candace Thille, 8/11/09).

[114]Ibid.

[115]Interview with Joel Smith, 9/10/08.

using technology to make *instruction,* as well as materials, accessible to the widest possible audience of learners and, at the same time, *improve* teaching and learning."[116] This is the unique position that the OLI is trying to carve out for itself, and there is a mounting body of evidence to demonstrate that this approach is gaining traction and acceptance. In 2009 the U.S. Department of Education released a meta-analysis of all sufficiently rigorous studies on online education's effectiveness conducted since 1996 (including projects involving K-12 and professional training content, as well as higher education). It found that, "on average, students in online learning conditions performed better than those receiving face-to-face instruction," and that in blended settings—what the OLI calls hybrid mode—the outcome disparities were higher still in favor of the option that includes technology. While the OLI was not included in the meta-analysis (the sample sizes of its head-to-head trials were too small to meet its criteria), the study seems to confirm one of the OLI's central value propositions in finding that "online learning can be enhanced by giving learners control of their interactions with media and prompting learner reflection. Studies indicate that manipulations that trigger learner activity or learner reflection and self-monitoring of understanding are effective when students pursue online learning as individuals."[117]

Although prior studies had shown no consistent difference in learning outcomes between online instruction and in-person teaching, the 2009 government study declares online instruction to be even more successful, and it may result in a new appreciation for the efficacy of heavily interactive online courses. The findings led Arne Duncan to say that "this new report reinforces that effective teachers need to incorporate digital content into everyday classes."[118] This

[116]Thille, "Building Open Learning," 165.

[117]Means, Barbara, Yukie Toyama, Robert Murphy, Marianne Bakia, and Karla Jones, "Evaluation of Evidence-Based Practices in Online Learning: A Meta-Analysis and Review of Online Learning Studies," U.S. Department of Education, May 2009, http://ifap.ru/library/book440.pdf, ix, xvi.

[118]Quoted in Jaschik, Scott, "The Evidence on Online Education," *Inside Higher Ed,* June 29, 2009. John R. Bourne, executive director of the Sloan Consortium, which studies online education, believes that the most important thing about the study was that the Education Department was the source of the findings: "'I think this is incredibly significant,' he

remark could, if taken seriously by U.S. colleges and universities, be a strong endorsement for the use of something like the OLI's Academic Version. In sum, it seems clear that the OLI *model* has potential to take off, but the initiative's ability to realize that potential will depend on its capacity to achieve scale and build a strong user base.

---

said. 'Those of us in the business have thought these things for some time, but we have had enormous trouble convincing some folks' about the quality of online education. 'I think this will give more credibility to the things that have been said'" (quoted ibid.). The Department of Education's study has, however, been criticized by some for lacking sufficient rigor. Researchers at the National Bureau of Economic Research have expressed concern with the design of the meta-analysis, which included many underlying studies that did not include randomly assigned comparisons involving control groups (see Kolowich, Steve, "Seed of Doubt," *Inside Higher Ed,* June 22, 2010).

5

QUALITY OVER QUANTITY: OPEN YALE COURSES

Launched in 2007, Open Yale Courses (OYC) is Yale University's contribution to the open online courseware space. As of this writing, OYC offers 25 introductory-level courses, carefully selected to include some of Yale's most popular subjects and faculty members.

Professional-quality lecture videos are the cornerstone of OYC's offerings. Recorded live in the classroom with a videographer following the action, the videos attempt to faithfully capture the Yale student experience for the home user, enabling non-enrolled students to "audit" Yale courses virtually.[1] Reflecting the principle of quality over quantity, OYC provides a small number of courses that seek to embody the university's reputation for excellence. The OYC team stresses that all its courses are "full" and "complete," with a consistent presentation of the same curricular elements: video and audio versions of every lecture, searchable transcripts, syllabi, introductory summaries for each lesson, faculty biographies, and reading lists, as well as problem sets and other materials where appropriate.

OYC is a key component of Yale's broader digital strategy, which treats the university's web presence as a critical tool for expanding its global reach. Several internal initiatives are now in place to increase access to the university's collections, courses, and other resources, as a means of sharing Yale's intellectual assets with the world. The OYC team recognizes its potential to advance the uni-

---

[1] Yale Center for Media and Instructional Innovation, "Open Access to the Yale Classroom Experience," http://cmi2.yale.edu/projects.php?action=view_project&project=oyc&category=platform.

versity's brand among new audiences; due in part to the success of the project, Yale's leadership now views digital courses as a major area of interest.

Origins and Development of Open Yale Courses

The origins of the OYC initiative date back to the university's previous experience with AllLearn, discussed in detail in Chapter 2. AllLearn was a collaborative online venture undertaken in partnership with Oxford, Stanford, and briefly Princeton (before the latter's withdrawal during the initiative's early months). Yale "developed 24 full-length arts and sciences courses . . . , two writing courses, six Forums, and two mini courses" under the auspices of AllLearn.[2] That initiative struggled financially from its inception but was not officially terminated until March 2006—at which point its Yale contingent immediately began thinking of a way to somehow continue its efforts in this space. Yale President Richard C. Levin, who had served as the chair of AllLearn's board, and Diana Kleiner, a Yale art history professor and former faculty liaison to AllLearn, were the principal participants in the discussions leading to what would become the OYC effort. As Kleiner said, "President Levin and I said Yale needed to benefit from this experiment, but we left it very amorphous" and took some time to think through potential next steps.[3]

Involvement in AllLearn had taught Yale firsthand how costly such a venture could be, and from the beginning officials felt that a different approach to funding the project would be necessary if the university were to make a second attempt at online course dissemination. As Kleiner remembers, "all of us realized that [with AllLearn] we had tried to see if this could be a breakeven operation, and we learned that it wasn't so easy to do."[4] So this time around, Levin and Kleiner decided to seek grant funding for the

---

[2] "Proposal to the Hewlett Foundation Education Program," Yale University, Diana E. E. Kleiner, principal investigator, June 2006, 3.
[3] Interview with Diana Kleiner, 1/22/09.
[4] Ibid.

initiative. As the AllLearn project was winding down in 2005 and early 2006, those involved from Yale had been keeping abreast of broader developments in the online courseware space, particularly the support for OER initiatives from the Hewlett Foundation, where Levin had served on the board of directors since 1998. The open-access ethos championed by Hewlett and embodied by the projects it has funded is evident in the OYC concept: while in AllLearn Yale had been interested in charging an alumni customer base for access to online courses, Kleiner said that in crafting an approach to the new project, "we thought we'd try another experiment and say 'we just want to share this.'"[5] The Yale team submitted a proposal for an initial pilot phase of OYC, originally called "The Yale University Open Educational Resources Video Lecture Project," to the Hewlett Foundation in June 2006. That proposal credits both AllLearn and other Hewlett-sponsored free courseware initiatives like MIT OpenCourseWare (OCW) as its inspirations.

From the Hewlett Foundation's recent track record, it was apparent that funding was available for major universities willing to invest in open digital course dissemination projects—giving Yale reason to believe that the Foundation might be receptive to its proposal. Hewlett made its first grant in the field that would come to be known as Open Educational Resources (OER) in 2001, with a $5.5 million award to MIT OCW. At that time, much of the Foundation's education program budget was divided into subfields for higher education, elementary and secondary education, and Bay Area regional support. The higher-education area was somewhat diffuse at the time, encompassing eight different grant-making priorities as well as opportunity grants. The MIT OCW grant fell under the "using technology effectively" focus, which supported a wide range of technology-related projects, including digitization and digital archiving initiatives as well as online teaching tools and distance education efforts. In 2002 the education program underwent a major strategic planning process under its new director, Marshall "Mike" Smith, who led it from 2001 to 2008. In that same year, grants totaling $1.9 million and $1 million, respectively,

[5] Ibid.

were awarded to Carnegie Mellon's Open Learning Initiative (OLI) and Rice University's Connexions project.[6] By the end of 2003, the education program emerged from the planning process with the "open-content area" as a distinct component of the Foundation's grant-making agenda.[7]

In the following years, the number of grants in this area continued to grow. Creative Commons, a not-for-profit organization that provides free licenses to make intellectual property more accessible to end users, received $1 million from the Hewlett Foundation in 2003 to support development of the open licenses that Hewlett-funded open content carries, and Utah State University received the first of several grants to develop its own open courseware as well as the EduCommons software used by other grantees.[8] Grant recipients for open-content projects in 2004 included the Johns Hopkins University's Bloomberg School of Public Health and Foothill De Anza Community College. The year 2005 proved to be an important one in the evolution of Hewlett's interest in this space: the first meeting of the OCW Consortium was held at MIT in 2005, grants for suites of digital open courses were made to Notre Dame and Tufts, and the term "Open Educational Resources" was adopted to describe all the grants in this area that Hewlett was coming to define.[9] In the fall of 2005, Hewlett held a forum with the United Nations Educational, Scientific and Cultural Organization and the International Institute for Educational Planning to investigate

[6]Conceived in 1999, Connexions is a platform that enables users to view, author, or edit open content. Connexions utilizes an XML (Extensible Markup Language) format and modular organization to allow users to organize content as they see fit, creating unique "connections" across material to customize online courses that may also serve as digital open textbooks ("About Connexions: Philosophy," http://cnx.org/aboutus/index_html).

[7]*Hewlett Foundation Annual Report—2003*, http://www.hewlett.org/news/2003-annual-report, 14. In outlining the education department's areas of focus, new language emerged in this report regarding grants in technology. One of the department's five strategic components was now "using information technology to increase access to high-quality academic content" (ibid., 12).

[8]According to the Creative Commons website, "Creative Commons licenses are not an alternative to copyright. They work alongside copyright, so you can modify your copyright terms to best suit your needs" ("About: What Is CC?" Creative Commons, http://creative commons.org/about/what-is-cc).

[9]*Hewlett Foundation Annual Report—2005*, http://www.hewlett.org/news/2005-annual-report, 3.

usage and dissemination strategies for OCW materials worldwide. Of the education program's budget, $9.5 million (27 percent) was devoted to encouraging open courseware and other OER developments in 2005.[10] Any observer of this burgeoning field could see that the Hewlett Foundation was an enthusiastic supporter of open courseware projects developed at leading institutions. Yale Vice President and Secretary Linda Lorimer noted that the Foundation has "been ambitious in recognizing a vision for outstanding materials from universities being disseminated digitally" and that Hewlett's approach dovetailed well with OYC's own objectives.[11] Kleiner also acknowledged the importance of Hewlett's position in helping to inform Yale's own, saying that "because of the Hewlett interest in OER, we're all influenced by that messianic zeal."[12]

Yale viewed online courseware as a way to fulfill the knowledge-dissemination portion of its mission while increasing access to the university's resources. As Lorimer said, "if you look at the basic goals of a research university, almost everyone would say they [are] threefold. It's the creation of knowledge, the preservation of knowledge, and the . . . dissemination of knowledge." She added that this project would allow Yale to "take our intellectual treasury, which is manifested in classroom teaching, and have more people benefit from it than those who are tuition-paying students."[13] OYC would therefore offer Yale an opportunity to extend its reach beyond its own student population. Kleiner said that the period during which she and others were contemplating a new online venture, in early 2006, "was a time when . . . our acceptance rates were only going down."[14] If Yale could admit just a small percentage of interested applicants, the internet would allow it to expand digitally in a way that it could not expand physically.

[10]William and Flora Hewlett Foundation, "2005 Budget Memorandum: Education Program," 11.
[11]Interview with Linda Lorimer, 3/6/09.
[12]Interview with Diana Kleiner, 1/22/09.
[13]Interview with Linda Lorimer, 3/6/09.
[14]Interview with Diana Kleiner, 1/22/09.

The OYC team believes that the value of its courses derives from the close semblance of the online versions to the live versions reserved for Yale students, claiming that OYC offers the home user an accurate representation of the classroom experience. As Yale's Director of Marketing Stephanie Schwartz said, OYC delivers a "360-degree student experience" to non-enrolled learners who would never otherwise have access to it.[15] OYC's second proposal to the Hewlett Foundation states that "we also hope to highlight excellence and innovation in undergraduate teaching at Yale"—indicating that Yale believed it had something unique to contribute to the world.[16] Kleiner said they were motivated in part by a sense that "there's a lot of hunger out there for good knowledge online, and Yale could provide that."[17] This value proposition reflects a shift in Yale's conception of the intended audience for its online offerings: while AllLearn had been originally designed for an alumni audience, OYC was always considered a means of projecting Yale to far-flung audiences it could not previously reach.

The period during which the AllLearn and OYC concepts were incubated and launched was one of great prosperity for Yale University. In the years between President Levin's 1993 arrival and 2007, Yale's endowment outperformed that of every other American university and provided an increasing share of the operating budget, leading Yale to invest in a number of areas: maintenance of historic campus buildings that had been deferred for decades was finally carried out, a new campus was acquired to raise the university's standing in the sciences, and a new wave of investment was put toward improving conditions in the surrounding community of New Haven.[18] This financial security provided the sense of

[15]Interview with Stephanie Schwartz, 12/17/08.

[16]"Proposal to the Hewlett Foundation Education Program," Yale University, Diana E. E. Kleiner, principal investigator, April 5, 2007, 11.

[17]Interview with Diana Kleiner, 1/22/09.

[18]See Van der Werf, Martin, "Yale's Ambitious Renovation Tops Any Undertaken by a University," *Chronicle of Higher Education*, online edition, October 20, 2000; Fabrikant, Geraldine, "For Yale's Money Man, a Higher Calling," *New York Times*, online edition, February 18, 2007; Arenson, Karen W., "At Yale, a New Campus Just for Research," *New*

confidence and willingness to take risks required to acknowledge AllLearn's failure and quickly try again with an even higher-profile effort.

Given the challenges that AllLearn had faced in organizing and managing a cooperative effort among partner institutions, Yale decided this time to go it alone and rely only on trusted insiders to run the OYC initiative. Kleiner seemed a natural choice to lead the new project: not only had she served as Yale's faculty liaison to AllLearn, she was also former deputy provost for the arts, and this administrative and faculty experience positioned her well to span the two groups. She also had years of personal experience incorporating digital technology into her own courses, and she remains a strong supporter of the instructional role of media in the humanities, as well as other liberal arts disciplines.[19] To create the OYC courses, Kleiner worked with the production team that had been responsible for creating AllLearn courses at Yale: the Center for Media and Instructional Innovation (CMI2), led by Paul Lawrence. Other than Kleiner, who remains a full-time faculty member in Yale's history of art and classics departments in addition to her role as director of OYC, the project's full-time staff is "minuscule."[20] As principal investigator, Kleiner consults frequently with Yale Vice President and Secretary Linda Lorimer, who oversees Yale's portfolio of digital outreach activities and is one of President Levin's closest advisors.

The first phase of the OYC project was initiated in July 2006 upon receipt of the $755,000 that Yale requested from the Hewlett Foundation for a one-year pilot. Kleiner said that the grant was awarded "with a sense that if we came up with something good we could reapply" for more money to scale up the program in subse-

---

York Times, online edition, July 4, 2007; Gootman, Elissa, "An Intricate Bond: New Haven's Past and Future Are So Tied to Yale, But It Took 300 Years for the Two to Get Along," *New York Times,* online edition, February 18, 2001; and Paul, Noel C., "Beset by New Haven's Ills, Yale Revitalizes City," *Christian Science Monitor,* online edition, September 14, 2004.

[19]"Proposal to the Hewlett Foundation Education Program," June 2006, 7.

[20]Interview with Diana Kleiner, 2/25/09. One full-time technologist was hired to work under Kleiner during the pilot phase, and two additional employees have joined the OYC team since.

quent phases.[21] The nascent project was officially announced to the public in September 2006, and Kleiner and Lawrence and David Hirsch from the CMI2 created three courses in the project's first semester and four more in its second. Kleiner began her work without full-time assistance, but by the second semester of the pilot Jeffrey Levick, an instructional technologist, had joined the OYC team to coordinate the daily management of the production process. In April 2007 Yale submitted a second proposal to the Foundation and was awarded $2.25 million to create several dozen more courses over the span of three years. The OYC portal went live to the public in September 2007 and featured the seven courses created during the pilot phase.[22]

When the initiative was launched in 2007, some in the online courseware community viewed Yale as a latecomer to open education. But the OYC team feels that their timing allowed them to learn from peers' examples as well as to develop new strategies for their offerings that differentiate OYC from other efforts.[23] Hirsch said that by initiating this project in 2006, "we learned from what other schools had done and then added a little bit more, always trying to push ourselves to raise the bar."[24]

Open Yale Courses' Content and Organization

An Open Yale Course is a "multidimensional [package] of internet-based course materials," containing full video and audio recordings of each course, as well as written transcripts of those recordings. The site also contains course syllabi and reading lists, along with assignments or problem sets where appropriate. The initial proposal stated that while MIT had already made its "course architecture" available through OCW materials, Yale would seek to deliver "primary course *content*" in an openly available format.[25]

[21]Interview with Diana Kleiner, 1/22/09.
[22]"Proposal to the Hewlett Foundation Education Program," 9, 4.
[23]Interview with Paul Lawrence, 12/17/08.
[24]Interview with David Hirsch, 12/17/08.
[25]"Proposal to the Hewlett Foundation Education Program," 2, 5 (emphasis added).

For MIT OCW, the courses are mostly text-based, with written materials at the core of the offering, but Kleiner said that OYC considers those materials as mere supplements to the full video and audio recordings. MIT has been producing video for some of its courses for several years, but OCW external relations manager Steve Carson said that he admires Yale's contribution to the online courseware space: "They have done a really great job of putting up the material specifically for video."[26]

OYC cuts a broad swath across the liberal arts, with courses in fields ranging from philosophy to religious studies to physics (Figure 5.1). Although courses in the hard sciences are present, the corpus is weighted more heavily toward the social sciences and the humanities, reflecting Yale's relative institutional strengths and perhaps providing unique value in the online courseware space.[27] Some of the most popular courses on OYC include "Modern Poetry," "Introduction to the Old Testament," and a philosophy course called "Death." In the fall of 2009 Yale mounted an art history course—on Roman art and architecture, taught by Kleiner herself—which Lawrence called "a first in this space."[28] Art history courses (as well as those in music history, which Yale also explored in 2009 with a course entitled "Listening to Music") are rarely if ever posted by other producers of online courseware, perhaps due to difficulties associated with securing rights to the images on which the lectures rely.[29] For Kleiner, shown delivering an OYC lecture in Figure 5.2, the breadth of its course offerings is one of OYC's key merits, because "in an increasingly specialized world, it's important to underscore the liberal arts and the importance of critical thinking."[30]

[26]Quoted in O'Leary, Mary, "Popular Yale Courses on 'Net." *New Haven Register,* online edition, December 23, 2007. OYC's second grant proposal acknowledges that MIT is also providing some video for courses, but "MIT states that video is supplemental and not essential to the Institute's mission" ("Proposal to the Hewlett Foundation Education Program," April 5, 2007, 2).

[27]OYC's 2007 grant proposal asserts that "lecture videos made available to date [from other sources] have been drawn primarily from science and technology courses, leaving much of the breadth of liberal arts out of the picture" (ibid., 5).

[28]Interview with Paul Lawrence, 12/17/08.

[29]Courses in music are also heavily reliant on copyrighted intellectual property in the form of audio recordings, which can be problematic to post on the internet.

[30]Interview with Diana Kleiner, 1/22/09.

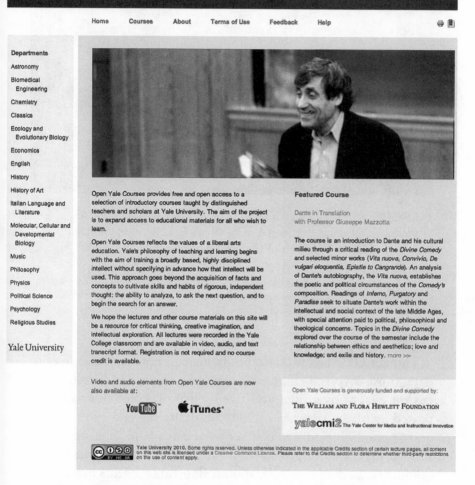

FIGURE 5.1 Open Yale Courses landing page, featuring ITAL 310, "Dante in Translation," with Giuseppe Mazzotta, Sterling Professor of Humanities for Italian (as it appeared on May 11, 2010).

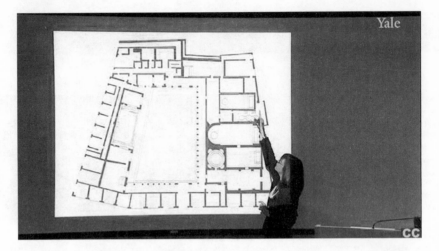

FIGURE 5.2   Still from Open Yale Courses lecture video, HSAR 252, "Roman Architecture," session 4, with Diana E. E. Kleiner, Dunham Professor of History of Art and Classics (as taught in spring 2009).

Available at http://openmedia.yale.edu/projects/media_viewer/video_viewer2.php?window_ size=medium&type=flv&title=HSAR%20252%20-%20Lecture%204%20-%20Prof.%20Diana%20E.%20 E.%20Kleiner&path=%2Fcourses%2Fspring09%2Fhsar252%2Fflash%2Fhsar252_04_012209. Permission provided courtesy of Yale University. © 2010 Yale University. License: Creative Commons BY-NC-SA.

Though OYC has produced only a small number of courses to date, those involved emphasize that the project has chosen to focus on quality over quantity. Twenty-five OYC courses had been posted as of the summer of 2010, and "by the end of the initial grant period, three dozen courses will be available."[31] Lorimer described OYC's approach as follows: "We're proud of the undergraduate experience we offer to baccalaureate students here, so we said we would like to have available for free something as close to the entire experience as you could have. And that of course is a distinctive proposition, different from at least the beginning of MIT courseware, where they had *fabulous* ambitions to have components of a huge number of courses, but not necessarily the entire complement of what constituted a course."[32] Both the OYC

[31]Yale Center for Media and Instructional Innovation, "Open Access to the Yale Classroom Experience."
[32]Interview with Linda Lorimer, 3/6/09.

and OCW teams stress the "completeness" of their respective projects, but with very different ideas of what "complete" means: OCW is comprehensive because it includes something from every class taught at the university, but OYC has instead focused its resources on achieving what Kleiner calls "a full revealing" of fewer courses.[33] As Yale spokesman Tom Conroy put it, "These are gavel-to-gavel presentations. We've put everything online that we could, and I think that's what makes this different."[34]

OYC courses are all introductory, originally intended for first- and second-year Yale students, and they include "some of the University's most popular undergraduate courses" taught by highly regarded scholars.[35] As the project director, Kleiner is primarily responsible for securing faculty participation, though she receives input from Yale's provost and dean of undergraduate education, as well as other administrators and faculty. Lorimer said that a real mark of the project's success is the fact that "some of our most distinguished faculty in the arts and sciences, those who are giants as scholars and who are commanding classroom teachers, have been participants in the Open Yale Courses."[36] In determining which faculty to approach, Kleiner leans toward those with strong reputations both on and off campus. "I keep my eyes open for people in the news," said Kleiner, who is interested in tapping Yale faculty who have demonstrated appeal beyond academia or their own specialized disciplines. But she cautioned that "a famous person who's a dullard in the classroom" would not be chosen, and said that wherever possible she wants to achieve "a mix of younger faculty and older faculty, men and women—you're looking for diversity if you can find it."[37]

---

[33]Interview with Diana Kleiner, 1/22/09.

[34]Quoted in Fischman, Josh, "Yale U. Puts Complete Courses Online," Wired Campus blog (*Chronicle of Higher Education*), December 11, 2007, http://chronicle.com/blogPost/Yale-U-Puts-Complete-Courses/3550.

[35]"Now Anyone Can 'Audit' Popular Yale Courses via Internet," *Yale Bulletin & Calendar*, online edition, 36, no. 13 (December 14, 2007).

[36]Interview with Linda Lorimer, 3/6/09. The first grant proposal promised that "Professor Kleiner will recruit faculty from among the most experienced and popular teachers at the undergraduate level" to create a suite of courses that "represent some of Yale's best teaching" ("Proposal to the Hewlett Foundation Education Program," April 5, 2007, 2, 12).

[37]Interview with Diana Kleiner, 1/22/09.

OYC emphasizes quality in the amount of materials produced for each class, as well as in the caliber of the faculty and the popularity of the course. But another key source of quality lies in the materials' production values. The OYC team attempts to create a finished product that conveys the Yale classroom experience to the home user as accurately as possible. To that end, OYC videos do not rely on automatic capture; instead, videographers are sent into the classroom to film the professor in the act of teaching, enhancing the naturalistic feel of the recordings. The resulting videos depict both the instructor and the visuals—slides, writing on the chalkboard—that he or she relies on to teach, allowing the viewer to see the relevant classroom material.[38]

Kleiner said that fundamentally, "we wanted everyone to be able to see and hear each lecture as if they were sitting in the classroom."[39] If press coverage of OYC is any indication, the team has achieved that goal. An article in *The Guardian* comments that "there are no concessions made for the camera, nor are corners cut," resulting in a viewer experience that is "as authentic as possible."[40] Describing Langdon Hammer's modern poetry course, technology writer Virginia Heffernan writes that "professors wear clip-on microphones but otherwise seem to conduct the classes just for the students. . . . Hammer can be seen distributing handouts and encouraging students to do their homework; he's not playing to the online bleacher seats or would-be book buyers. This is the real New Haven stuff."[41]

To help approximate the in-person experience via the web, OYC attempts to create TV-quality broadcasts. "The lectures have been captured using Sony's XDCAM HD (High-Definition) format, to ensure the highest quality of content production and delivery" to

---

[38]Lawrence explained that OYC courses are filmed with "a camera that is motivated; it actually follows the faculty member. It's a camera that reacts when a faculty member points or moves around the classroom" (interview with Paul Lawrence, 12/17/08).

[39]"Now Anyone Can 'Audit' Popular Yale Courses via Internet."

[40]Balakrishnan, Angela, "Reading Poetry at Yale . . . in My Sitting Room," *The Guardian,* online edition, April 29, 2008.

[41]Heffernan, Virginia, "The Camera-Friendly, Perfectly Pixelated, Easily Downloadable Celebrity Academic," *New York Times Magazine,* online edition, September 21, 2008.

provide a polished finished product for the user.[42] This, too, seems to be working, at least for Heffernan. In a piece for the *New York Times Magazine* in which she selects and describes her five favorite online courses, she writes "it's hard not to be biased in favor of the Open Yale courses . . . simply because they are presented in such a frank, nonfussy way. The silky audiovisuals start without graphic rigmarole and don't stall till they're over."[43]

In addition, the presentation of all OYC materials is kept consistent and intended to be user-friendly. Hirsch said that "we really want to make it easy for the user to find and use the content," leading to a high degree of standardization in the types and arrangement of materials from one Open Yale Course to the next.[44] According to Yale strategist David Schiffman, in contrast to other online resources that can appear a bit scattered, OYC "is a very high-quality, produced project with a consistent set of assets for every single course."[45] For instance, each element is fitted to a strict template, which Kleiner said was designed in part to achieve a clean look—a nontrivial consideration for a site that aims for intuitive navigation and visual appeal to achieve a seamless user experience.[46] Lawrence said that at the beginning of the design process, the team from the CMI2 drew on inspiration from the courses it had previously developed for AllLearn as well as materials from successful commercial outlets like the University of Phoenix.[47]

When the taping is completed, the production team engages in meticulous editing and polishing of the courses in postproduction before they are put online, a process which Lawrence considers unique. Full-text transcripts are created for each course to accompany the video and audio versions; Lawrence said that while Yale outsources the transcription process, "when they come back

---

[42]Yale Center for Media and Instructional Innovation, "Open Access to the Yale Classroom Experience."

[43]Heffernan, "The Camera-Friendly . . . Celebrity Academic." Of the five courses Heffernan highlights, two are from OYC.

[44]Interview with David Hirsch, 12/17/08.

[45]Interview with David Schiffman, 12/18/08.

[46]Interview with Diana Kleiner, 1/22/09.

[47]Interview with Paul Lawrence, 12/17/08.

they're still scrubbed to check for accuracy" to ensure that no mis-spellings or mistakes make their way into the text version of the lectures. Lawrence emphasized that the philosophy of focusing on quality over quantity has guided the entire OYC production pro-cess: "I think we're using the best of technology, and the best of human intervention, and it's connecting up well. Now does that scale to a thousand courses? No, it doesn't, but I don't think that's what this project is about."[48]

While a great deal of effort and labor goes into the creation and delivery of each Open Yale Course, Lawrence stressed the impor-tance of keeping the burden on Yale professors and students as light as possible. "We thought that the best thing we could do for Diana, who had to recruit these faculty, was to develop a process that didn't bump into [them]," he said. "That was something that we thought at times AllLearn might have done—not intentionally, but just by their production process they might have caused faculty to have to work harder than they should have. So we wanted at the very beginning to develop that production process that would streamline . . . the pro-cess for faculty." By bringing a live camera crew in to tape professors at the time and place they would normally teach, Lawrence hopes to minimize the impact OYC has on the faculty's workflow.[49]

The process of allowing faculty to view and approve their re-corded lecture content before it is published is also designed for their comfort: the CMI2 makes the raw footage available within days through a closed learning management system, so faculty can view it at their leisure without needing to come into the studio. Lawrence and his team also try to be conscious of not disrupting the Yale students who are in the classrooms during the tapings: "We did not want to interfere with that teaching that's going on in that classroom, because these are Yale undergrads that worked extraordinarily hard to get where they are, and we did not want to interfere with their learning by placing a camera in their faces—we try to be as unobtrusive as possible."[50]

---

[48]Ibid.

[49]Ibid. "We want faculty to feel that they're part of the project, but also to feel that it doesn't burden them on a daily basis."

[50]Ibid.

Kleiner said that overall the faculty recruiting effort has been well received: "In the pilot phase of the project, we achieved a high level of success in persuading members of the faculty to participate . . . of a total of ten faculty members approached to take part, seven accepted, and, of the three who did not, one member expressed interest in doing so in the future."[51] Yale faculty receive a small honorarium upon completion of an Open Yale Course in exchange for participating. Kleiner said that she "feel[s] strongly that there should be some incentive," though the compensation is "not significant enough for anyone to do it for the money."[52]

Impact of Open Yale Courses

OYC is considered key to several of Yale's strategic ambitions, including its desire to increase its global reach and expand its online presence. Global engagement has been a priority for Yale for the past decade, and a desire to increase its presence on the world stage has influenced nearly all of the university's activities. The Yale Corporation devoted its 1997 annual meeting to discussing the institution's global position, inaugurating a period of increased activity around international efforts. A *Wall Street Journal* piece on President Levin's tenure cites international issues as among the most significant in his portfolio. After assuming Yale's presidency in 1993, Levin first focused on improving the university's facilities, but "the second step was to go global, injecting international issues into every facet of the university, raising its profile abroad, forging joint ventures, expanding longstanding ties to China, pushing undergraduates to study overseas, recruiting foreign students and faculty. 'If we want to be a truly great university, we have to embrace the world,' he says."[53] A three-year strategic plan was implemented in 2005 to "internationalize" Yale through a series of

---

[51]"Proposal to the Hewlett Foundation Education Program," April 5, 2007, 8.
[52]Interview with Diana Kleiner, 1/22/09.
[53]Wessel, David, "Yale Safeguards Its Top Spot," *Wall Street Journal,* online edition, April 24, 2008.

strategic efforts at nearly all institutional levels. One of the main goals outlined in that document was to "position Yale as a global university of consequence" by "working to increase Yale's visibility around the world."[54] Although OYC is not explicitly named, many involved with the project cite it as a part of the university's efforts in this area.

The potential of a digital courseware project to help further Yale's internationalizing ambitions was clear from the beginning: Kleiner said that when she and Levin were considering the possibility of a new project following AllLearn, "we knew we wanted to stay in this arena, and it fit well with where Yale was at the time: our ambitions were global."[55] OYC's initial grant proposal states even more explicitly that "this undertaking aligns well with Yale's long-term aim to increase its engagement in the international community through student and faculty recruitment, educational outreach, research collaborations, and public service initiatives." The OYC team designed the offering with an international viewership in mind, selecting introductory undergraduate courses in order to "best serve the purpose of introducing lecture content to the open learning resource model, given the potential value of such courses to a broad range of users worldwide."[56] The CMI2 also attempted to use multiple technologies aimed at viewers with differing degrees of connectivity, language backgrounds, and abilities.[57]

OYC also functions to further the university's branding in the online environment. Interviewees defined the Yale brand as commensurate with excellence and considered it crucial that every facet of OYC enforce that aspect of the overall brand.[58] Stephanie Schwartz, who is Yale's director of both marketing and trademark

---

[54]Levin, Richard C., and Linda Koch Lorimer, "The Internationalization of Yale: 2005–2008," December 2005, http://world.yale.edu/about/pdf/Internationalization_Yale.pdf.

[55]Interview with Diana Kleiner, 1/22/09.

[56]"Proposal to the Hewlett Foundation Education Program," June 2006, 3, 5.

[57]"Lectures are available in audio-only format and in multiple video formats to accommodate low-bandwidth users. A full transcript of every lecture is provided as a resource for learners who do not have adequate connectivity to view the videos or for those who prefer to read the lecture content. Closed captioning is available on the videos to further enhance content accessibility" (Yale Center for Media and Instructional Innovation, "Open Access to the Yale Classroom Experience").

[58]Interviews with Lucas Swineford, 1/22/09, and Stephanie Schwartz, 12/17/08.

licensing and oversees OYC's promotional efforts, said that the decision to make quality paramount for OYC "was driven from a marketing perspective, because every time someone views something we made, they're consuming Yale, and the quality of their experience reflects how they think of us and the brand." While that excellence had previously been reserved only for the privileged few in New Haven, OYC allows Yale to project itself outward via one of its core activities—classroom teaching. Schwartz believes that "99.9 percent of the planet will experience Yale through the internet," and that online projects like OYC can therefore introduce Yale to new audiences that might not know about the university through other channels. "Depending on the market, Open Yale Courses reinforces people's perceptions of Yale or creates them, efficiently and cost-effectively," she said. "In places where we're already well established, this reinforces the ideas we hope they have of Yale. In places where people have never heard of Yale, viewing a course is their first interaction with Yale . . . and they'll have a positive experience, and I've just earned a customer." Given Yale's desire to reach far-flung audiences, Schwartz feels that "the digital impact—the impact we will have remotely on people—will play an increasing role in the development and enhancement of our reputation."[59]

Visual elements of Yale's branding—the university's name, logo, and signature colors—are prominently displayed on all content intended for digital dissemination. Every YouTube video associated with OYC has a Yale watermark to ensure that the materials convey their provenance and will receive proper attribution. Attention to consistent branding is conveyed in other design elements. The CMI2 did the graphic design for OYC, and Lawrence said that they wanted it to relate to Yale's main website, sending a strong visual message about the content's origins. "When people think of Yale, they think of blue, and this needed to have a close connection to our institutional branding. For an external audience, we wanted to stick with what makes Yale Yale, and blue is such an iconic color." Lawrence added that in designing the site, they were also

[59]Interview with Stephanie Schwartz, 12/17/08.

concerned with "keeping it clean," using streamlined fonts and a uniform look and feel for each course. Mistakes or sloppiness could not be tolerated because "we were carrying Yale's name with this, and we wanted to make sure it was something that connected well with the brand of the university."[60]

The press has been quite responsive to OYC. Articles in major media outlets have consistently described it as a major achievement. An item on *ABC News Online* stated that "While Yale is not the first to post classes online, it is providing special access by artfully videotaping lectures," and a February 2009 article in *The Guardian* claimed that "the most notable new step in democratizing higher education was recently taken by Yale University who initiated the Open Yale Courses in 2006—the first institution of its caliber to offer comprehensive online education for the general public."[61] *Inside Higher Ed* introduced its coverage of OYC by saying that "a handful of colleges intentionally make course materials available to anyone with an Internet connection, and now a major name may redefine expectations for online learning."[62] Despite trailing MIT OCW by five years, OYC has struck observers as a unique and valuable contribution to the online courseware space.

The experience of working on the OYC project has also pushed Yale to explore other digital dissemination efforts, which have become an institution-wide strategic priority. Kleiner recalled that within Yale, "it sparked thinking on the digital enterprise in general —I think this project served as a foundation and also a spur to the university on thinking about working on digital activities more broadly."[63] Lorimer agreed, saying that in the wake of the OYC project, "We've thought much more boldly about what Yale could be contributing to the world in terms of our intellectual assets." To develop ways that Yale might "disseminate more expansively its intellectual treasury," the university is working on a digital strategy

---

[60]Interview with Paul Lawrence, 12/17/08.

[61]Quoted in Urley, Sarah, "Ivy League Curtain Opened: Yale University Allows Free Access to Select Undergraduate Courses," *ABC News Online,* http://abcnews.go.com/Business/story?id=3997573&page=1; Minden, Sonia, "Higher Ed Goes Broadband," *The Guardian,* online edition, February 2, 2009.

[62]Guess, Andy, "Open Courses Open Wider," *Inside Higher Ed,* December 12, 2007.

[63]Interview with Diana Kleiner, 2/25/09.

to coordinate all of its previously disparate online efforts.[64] In addition to the OYC effort, Yale has recently created an Office of Digital Dissemination (ODD) tasked with aggregating and creating digital content aimed at an external audience, establishing a public face for Yale on the internet.[65] ODD Director Lucas Swineford said that in addition to marketing efforts on behalf of OYC, the ODD works to coordinate dissemination strategies for content from around Yale, providing some synergy to all the digital efforts that go on in various schools or departments.[66] As Lawrence observed, "this is an exciting time to be at Yale in terms of developing materials to be seen by an external audience."[67] These efforts are centrally driven and will soon be governed under an overall institutional strategic plan for digital activities.

As for Yale students, they of course have access to the lectures along with the general public, "and many watch the videos as a way of shopping classes."[68] Prospective students have spoken to Dean of Admissions Jeffrey Brenzel about OYC, which is linked on Yale's main admissions webpage: "We've had a fair number of high school students who have dipped into them and told us about it. . . . I can't quantify what the impact has been, but I think it's been positive." Brenzel characterized OYC as "a nice enhancement to the primary recruiting tools" that Yale uses to attract and inform prospective students.[69]

In assessing its external impact, OYC—like many online courseware programs—is heavily reliant on anecdotal feedback from indi-

[64]Interview with Linda Lorimer, 3/6/09.

[65]These efforts are centering on a platform for all of the university's freely available digital content called Open Yale. This platform will host a collection of preexisting materials culled from different sources and programs throughout the university. Lucas Swineford said that the goal of this portal "is to make all of these assets more discoverable" (quoted in Needham, Paul, "Digitization: Just a Click Away," Yale Daily News, online edition, October 30, 2008). The ODD is run out of the Office of the Secretary, which is responsible "for the public face of the university, and the way we look at digital dissemination is that it's about the public face of the university—we think of this really as a publishing vehicle" (interview with Lucas Swineford, 1/22/09).

[66]Ibid.

[67]Interview with Paul Lawrence, 12/17/08.

[68]Needham, Paul, "Cyber Yale: You and Me and Everyone We Know," Yale Daily News, online edition, February 20, 2009.

[69]Interview with Jeffrey Brenzel, 4/23/09.

vidual users. Lorimer admitted that when it comes to OYC's overall impact, "we don't yet have a scientific way to evaluate it. We have these testimonials, so certainly on both individuals and on some institutions, it's already had what seems to be . . . a serious educational impact."[70] Site usage statistics show that users reside all over the world, and this has indicated to the OYC team that Yale is contributing to global education. In Kleiner's words, "The testimonies are so positive that it's clear they're really changing people's lives."[71]

The OYC team had no specific usage goal when the site launched, aiming simply to reach as many users as possible. The first proposal stated that "at this time, we do not anticipate setting targets for participation for the project's pilot phase." According to Kleiner, they had seen the usage numbers for MIT OCW, which are available on its website: "We didn't think we'd be likely to get numbers that large because they were going with all of their courses, but that gave us a ballpark estimate of what might be possible." But she stressed that "this isn't a numbers game, since we're not making money off this; this is a gift we're giving to the world, so we want to see if we can bring that to as many people as possible." That said, the OYC team is happy with the level of usage the materials have received thus far. "We're being accessed by nearly every country in the world, over 190—the reach is really very, very broad," Kleiner said.[72]

The usage data come from analytics compiled by the OYC technologists, as well as pop-up surveys that have been placed on the site from time to time asking visitors to self-identify. OYC's project manager Jeffrey Levick reported in early 2009 that "since its launch in December 2007, approximately 850,000 unique visitors from over 190 countries around the world have accessed Open Yale Courses," and the university's press office has stated that "Open Yale Courses is one of the most frequently visited Yale websites."[73]

[70]Interview with Linda Lorimer, 3/6/09.

[71]Interview with Diana Kleiner, 2/25/09.

[72]Ibid. Regarding the initial proposal, see "Proposal to the Hewlett Foundation Education Program," June 2006, 12. Kleiner said that "We don't set a specific goal . . . our attitude is 'let's just keep moving forward and see how many we can reach'" (interview with Diana Kleiner, 2/25/09).

[73]Email correspondence with Jeffrey Levick, 1/15/09; "Yale University: Yale Doubles

A key effort to ensure the external impact of OYC courses has been through usage partnerships with institutions around the world. Although the courses are freely available and licensed under Creative Commons, Yale has also felt additional responsibility to encourage usage from specific sources. In a 2008 speech, Levin pointed out that "a novel feature of the Yale offerings is that we are not simply posting these courses and waiting to see who uses them. We have established partnerships with universities around the world, who are using all or part of our courses in their own undergraduate programs."[74] According to Lorimer, Yale's interest in targeting specific user institutions around the world has developed over time: "For the Open Yale Courses, at the beginning, we were not looking at audiences per se, we were looking at having it up there and letting anyone take advantage of it. . . . We're still doing that. We've realized now [that] if we're really going to have it be an extension of our underlying mission, we should be more intentional and more focused to supplement its ubiquitous availability by looking at partners who would actually use it for serious educational purposes."[75] Yale is interested in ensuring, through direct partnerships with ten universities around the world, that these other institutions will utilize the materials as a formal, structured part of their own curricula.

Yale's Office of International Affairs arranged many of these partnerships with foreign institutions with which it had established relationships, including the University of Bahrain, the University of Ghana, and Peking University. Lorimer also said that at Yale, "we have all kinds of international partnerships—student exchanges, faculty research projects, joint laboratories abroad—so this is another dimension of Yale's internationalization effort."[76] So far, arranging these partnerships has been the main effort to mar-

---

Number of Free Online Courses," press release, *M2 PressWIRE*, October 17, 2008. Unlike MIT OCW, OYC does not prominently feature its usage statistics on its website for public viewing.

[74]Levin, Richard C., "The Internationalization of the University," speech delivered May 6, 2008, Athens, Greece, http://opa.yale.edu/president/message.aspx?id=7.

[75]Interview with Linda Lorimer, 3/6/09.

[76]Ibid.

ket OYC.[77] According to Kleiner, "when you go to all the trouble of creating these, when you go to the Hewlett Foundation to get support from them, you want these materials to be used. The whole purpose is to make these as well known as possible to those who would find them most useful and who might not come across them on their own."[78]

It may seem contradictory to expend resources to increase usage of open and free materials, but when asked why Yale felt the need to take the extra step of creating these usage partnerships, Lorimer replied: "For impact. The issue is for impact. Yes, it would be great if [a user] in his free time . . . could find that many hours to study a physics course or a Greek history course for his general enlightenment. But if we're talking about liberal education courses, that requires a discipline that is very different from having a one-hour lecture netcast. They are intellectually demanding." Just as the OLI team feels certain that a "hybrid mode" combining online courseware with face-to-face instruction is the best environment for student learning, Yale feels that its offerings can have the greatest impact when they are incorporated into a student's own coursework. Lorimer said that Yale realized that "over time you might do much, much more if you look at these resources and find ways for other partners to take advantage of them. Again, freely and openly, but to be disciplined to ensure that they are actually being used."[79]

Although OYC aims to replicate the Yale student experience for a wider public, the university is not interested in offering credits for completing these courses, arguing that the online versions are not equivalent to a Yale student's educational experience. When the AllLearn venture was under-enrolled, ultimately fruitless discussions of offering university credits for online courses began, and Kleiner remarked that the conversation on the potential of credentialed online education has been ongoing for years. "But Yale is not

---

[77]Schwartz said, "We want to gain traction with these faculty who can make use of the stuff—that's been the crux of our effort in the first go-round" (interview with Stephanie Schwartz, 12/17/08).

[78]Interview with Diana Kleiner, 2/25/09.

[79]Interview with Linda Lorimer, 3/6/09.

seriously considering giving Yale credit for these courses. While we're willing to share what we do with the larger world, giving Yale credit for that and making it equivalent to what our students get is a slippery slope. . . . We may be giving away the classroom experience our undergraduates have, but what we're putting out is not a Yale education." Kleiner added that the OYC and enrolled experiences "are not equal, so giving credit for this doesn't make sense—if an institution like Yale is going to expect people to pay X number of dollars for a degree," the university could not make an equivalent experience available online and expect students to still be willing to pay a premium for the traditional version.[80]

However, Lorimer stressed that other institutions are welcome to incorporate the courses into their official curricula as a pathway to credit. She said that the credit Yale offers its own students is earned not just by attending lectures, but through examinations, term papers, and substantial engagement with faculty—none of which are possible through the current OYC model. But "partnerships mean that the other institutions can build Yale-standard education into their own provision," which Lorimer says is an important aspect of what Yale is trying to do. "I think the idea for where we are now is *yes,* you should get credit, but that doesn't have to be through Yale."[81] She noted that by partnering with the other institutions, Yale can feel confident that someone somewhere might be receiving credit for knowledge gained through OYC.

Open Yale Courses and Sustainability

OYC's costs are largely covered by the Hewlett Foundation grant, and there is some uncertainty as to the future of the project following the expiration of those funds in 2010. The first OYC proposal in June 2006 requested $755,000 for a year-long pilot phase to create seven courses. The second proposal, submitted April 5,

[80]Interview with Diana Kleiner, 1/22/09.
[81]Balakrishnan, "Reading Poetry at Yale"; interview with Linda Lorimer, 3/6/09.

2007, resulted in an award of $2.25 million over three years to capture several dozen additional courses, and two more staff members were allotted to the project. Lorimer said in 2009 that OYC's future is secure for the duration of the Hewlett grant, and "after that, we don't have plans exactly."[82]

Though the project's future finances are not entirely settled, there is reason to believe that Yale may be willing to assume the financial responsibility of supporting OYC internally.[83] The administration considers OYC a high priority, and the project enjoys the full support of the university president and consistent involvement from the secretary's office. Among the three most compelling reasons for the grant listed in the first proposal to Hewlett is "institutional commitment: University President Richard Levin, the other University Officers, and Yale College Dean Peter Salovey strongly support the proposed initiative and the underlying educational and social principles that it seeks to advance, which are consistent with the University's broad educational mission."[84] Kleiner characterized OYC as a "very high" priority for President Levin, who helped formulate the OYC concept along with her and was also the chair of the AllLearn board.[85]

Furthermore, several of the project's founding documents suggest that Yale representatives foresaw the need to become more financially committed to the project as time went on. The first grant proposal states that "if the project becomes sufficiently integral to Yale's overall teaching enterprise (for Yale undergraduates, graduate students, faculty, alumni), Yale may subsume some costs in its general operating budget."[86] The university further positioned itself as the project's potential long-term source of funding in the second grant proposal, explicitly stating that, "as the Project makes substantial progress towards completing its initial goals, the Uni-

---

[82]Interview with Linda Lorimer, 3/6/09.

[83]For instance, Lorimer said that Yale has recently funded a "brand new studio for the CMI2; we have a brand new office called the Office of Digital Assets and Infrastructure that has a healthy budget and a growing staff, so that we'll have all the infrastructure we need to support an expanded set of programmatic activities" (ibid.).

[84]"Proposal to the Hewlett Foundation Education Program," June 2006, 13.

[85]Interview with Diana Kleiner, 1/22/09.

[86]"Proposal to the Hewlett Foundation Education Program," June 2006, 9.

versity will consider subsuming a portion of the Project's ongoing costs into its operating budget," as MIT has already done by
supplying half of OCW's operating funds out of the provost-
controlled Institute budget.[87]

OYC's project staff has indicated that its long-term vision involves not just sustaining the existing content but also expanding
it in various ways. More broadly, the idea of digitally distributing the university's "assets" has become entrenched within Yale, and
the university's pursuit of similar projects to OYC is slated to increase in the coming years. According to Lorimer, Yale leaders are
strongly considering expanding online course offerings to include
content from all of its professional schools in addition to the undergraduate content developed for OYC. "I do believe that within
three to five years, we will find from other grant sources funds that
will allow us to supplement the arts and sciences courses currently
on Open Yale Courses with professional school courses—and that's
not only sustainability, that's going to be expansion." Lorimer can
imagine exciting possibilities for open courses in fields like public
health and medicine and said that in the future, "I would hope that
Open Yale Courses would have spawned a generation of new ways
to disseminate Yale's teaching, both in the professional schools as
well as the College."[88]

Interviewees were also careful to state that while some version
of the Hewlett-funded OYC courses must always be offered free
of charge, Yale is not against eventually creating revenue streams
to support other digital dissemination activities that the university
may pursue. Lorimer stated that "we don't have an objection to
contemplating that there will be some uses of these online teaching materials that will have a fee." She added that "Open Yale
Courses, four years from now, might be a whole lot more than
what Hewlett has funded here. It could become an umbrella brand
for . . . [content from] the law school. We don't have plans now, but
it's possible." And should the offering expand at Yale's expense, the
university is open to charging fees to recoup its costs. As Lorimer

[87]"Proposal to the Hewlett Foundation Education Program." Yale University, Diana E. E.
Kleiner, principal investigator. April 5, 2007, 18.
[88]Interview with Linda Lorimer, 3/6/09.

put it, "just like we have students that we charge tuition to, and students that we give full financial aid to, we think there are some courses—not the ones we developed in this round—where you can imagine it would be quite appropriate to have some charges." While Yale has not yet monetized any of its online curricular offerings, Lorimer said that "in this regard I think we might be different from some of the others, in that we're open to at least musing about . . . ways in which to monetize some of our dissemination initiatives to provide funding to do more of them."[89]

∙∙∙∙∙∙∙∙∙∙∙∙∙∙∙∙

Since awarding OYC's major three-year grant in 2007, the Hewlett Foundation has diversified its approach to OER by focusing on areas like open textbooks and online educational games as well as courseware, in addition to investing further in subject areas like public health and activities like assessment of outcomes. Although "early in the development of OER, Hewlett used name branding and elite universities to signal the quality of content,"[90] the Foundation has ceased funding individual institutions to produce their own suites of online courseware, and Yale may be one of the last such projects.

OYC's grant proposals indicate that the team has always understood the high likelihood that, after leveraging Hewlett funding to experiment with online courseware in a relatively risk-free manner, Yale would need to take over responsibility for financing the project at the termination of this grant. The acknowledged role that the university might play in ongoing funding may have contributed to the project's design from the outset: OYC serves external constituencies but is also deeply integrated into several of Yale's institutional objectives, particularly that of increasing Yale's exposure around the world. In President Levin's words, "we are pleased that so many people from around the globe have explored Open Yale Courses. . . . making part of the Yale classroom experience

[89]Ibid.

[90]William and Flora Hewlett Foundation, "2009 Budget Memorandum: Education Program," November 17, 2008, http://www.hewlett.org/programs/education-program.

accessible beyond the campus through the available technology is a significant emphasis of our growing digital presence."[91] It is therefore not surprising that Yale would begin to think of OYC as a pilot project for an expanded corpus of online course materials, utilizing the OYC concept as a vehicle for the university's broader future ambitions.

[91]Quoted in "Yale University: Yale Doubles Number of Free Online Courses."

6

A GRASSROOTS INITIATIVE:
WEBCAST.BERKELEY

When UC Berkeley professor Lawrence A. Rowe began webcasting his courses in the 1990s, his intention was not to create a university-wide digital dissemination effort. But what began as a proof-of-concept for an individual professor's research interests in internet video has since evolved into webcast.berkeley, a campus-based initiative offering audio or video recordings of nearly 550 courses by the spring of 2010.

Berkeley has undertaken the webcast initiative almost entirely without the aid of external funding from foundations or other partners. The initiative has a tight budget and small staff but strong ambitions to achieve scale, resulting in a production process focused on efficiency. webcast.berkeley's content offerings consist of simple audio and video recordings of Berkeley professors' classroom lectures, using minimal equipment and automatic capture techniques with limited editing. The project's initial goal was to use technology to benefit the university's enrolled students. Today webcast.berkeley's site is visited by users from all over the world, but it remains a student service first and a public service second.

Origins and Development of webcast.berkeley

The origins of webcast.berkeley can be traced back to 1995, when Rowe began webcasting a single course: his own. A technologist and the head of the Berkeley Multimedia Research Center (BMRC), Rowe had an academic interest in incorporating video into user interfaces and applications, and he began experimenting in that area in the late 1980s and early 1990s. At that time, several projects on the Berkeley campus dealt with the use of technology to capture courses, including a College of Engineering program to broadcast televised class sessions aimed at employees of Silicon Valley companies and a Berkeley Media Services operation that recorded university lectures on VHS tapes. Rowe observed that the taped lectures were "a cumbersome system," as students interested in using them for study had to physically check them out of the library, and viewing was necessarily limited to one student at a time. So he began to explore the potential of broadcasting lectures via streaming digital video.[1]

Internet video was in its infancy in the early 1990s, but many technology researchers were investigating possibilities for the transmission of video across networks. Rowe said that, to his knowledge, the first university to webcast course content was University College London in 1994. He was invited to speak there that year and was intrigued by the feedback he received from viewers around the world who had watched his talk online.[2] That experience, in addition to encouragement from a Berkeley graduate student, prompted Rowe to begin his own webcasting effort: the Berkeley Internet Broadcasting System (BIBS). He started with one of his own graduate seminars and developed a method for webcasting live courses, along with the software and user interface to view them.[3] His first seminar was disseminated live via the internet in January 1995. A 2008 *Educause Review* article claims this was the first time an entire course had been transmitted in this manner, and it generated interest: Rowe recalled that "on one or two occasions, we'd have as much as a hundred" people watching a live course.[4]

Rowe attributed his pursuit of webcasting to his own memories of furiously copying his professors' words in classes, not really paying attention to their meaning in his rush to keep up. He said the

[1]Interview with Lawrence Rowe, 6/8/09.
[2]Ibid.
[3]Rowe, Lawrence A., Diane Harley, Peter Pletcher, and Shannon Lawrence, "BIBS: A Lecture Webcasting System—Executive Summary," *BIBS Report Executive Summary*, June 2001, http://bmrc.berkeley.edu/research/publications/2001/160/bibs-exec.html.
[4]Edmonds, Victor, "Video Vision," *Educause Review*, online edition, 43, no. 5 (September –October 2008); interview with Lawrence Rowe, 6/8/09.

original goal was simply "making lecture material available on demand for study after the fact," as well as experimenting with creating the technology required to do so. Thus, webcast.berkeley was not initially conceived as a large-scale campus activity, but rather as an experimental component of a single professor's research agenda. But following the webcast of the first course, students close to the project encouraged him to think about including more classes, so he began to add courses in a piecemeal fashion. Rowe said that his response to early student interest in scaling up the project was "'OK, let's try it.' To be very honest, I viewed it as a test of the tools and I fully expected it to fail after four or five weeks. I never expected it to work."[5] Over the next several years, the number of courses webcast steadily increased—from seven in the fall of 1998 to ten in the spring of 1999 to fifteen in the spring of 2001—and in that time Rowe and his team experimented with several technological solutions and delivery platforms for the webcasts.[6]

Rowe posted his webcasts on the internet for all to see, but as the initiative's current steward Mara Hancock pointed out, "we didn't start this to be openly available." She said that the webcast project "stumbled into 'open' by accident—[Rowe] just never bothered to put it behind authentication."[7] In Rowe's recollection, there were two reasons for choosing to make the content publicly available: "One, I didn't have the resources to do a system that required logins and restrictions . . . it would have been horribly complex," because some 3,000–5,000 students were enrolled in the Berkeley classes webcast in BIBS's later years. The second reason was that "I had this fundamental belief that this is a public university funded by public money, and creating content and education is our mission, and so it seemed like publishing this worldwide on the internet was the right way to work towards that mission." Rowe said—and the then-provost confirmed—that he did not seek the Berkeley administration's permission to post the courses online

---

[5]Interview with Lawrence Rowe, 6/8/09. Rowe added that originally, "we didn't intend to do anything with classes per se; we were just trying to experiment and see what we could do."

[6]Timeline prepared by Lawrence Rowe, July 2009.

[7]Interview with Mara Hancock, 8/19/08.

for a world audience.[8] As the webcasting experiment evolved into a more coherent service program, open access to the content was retained.

Under Rowe's direction, the project operated out of the BMRC. But in the spring of 2001, after Rowe announced his plans to leave the university and the center was slated to close, it became clear that the webcasting program would need a new home if it were to continue. At the administration's request, the BMRC wrote a paper on BIBS to provide the Berkeley administration with information on the program's operations and impact on students, intended "to assess the costs and logistics of moving BIBS from BMRC to a permanently funded service organization on campus."[9] Following the completion and review of that report, Educational Technology Services (ETS)—the campus service arm also responsible for managing Berkeley's learning management system, campus radio, and audiovisual needs in classrooms—assumed control over the webcasting effort in the fall of 2001.

In its current form, webcast.berkeley's goals are twofold: First and foremost, it aims to serve Berkeley's students.[10] But beyond its chief purpose as a study aid, the webcast program has also provided a window for the world into the Berkeley educational experience. As former Executive Vice Chancellor and Provost Paul Gray—who oversaw the transition from BIBS under the BMRC to webcast.berkeley under ETS—has put it, "the internal student service was the thing that got us started, but it . . . snowballed." As time passed, it "began to dawn on us that it was a public service that we could do at very low incremental cost because of the web. So initially it was for student internal use, but over time we

---

[8]Interviews with Lawrence Rowe, 6/8/09, and Paul Gray, 6/9/09.

[9]Rowe, Lawrence A., Diane Harley, Peter Pletcher, and Shannon Lawrence, *BIBS: A Lecture Webcasting System*, Paper CSHE4'01, June 2001, http://bmrc.berkeley.edu/research/publications/2001/160/bibs-report.pdf, 2.

[10]According to ETS director Mara Hancock, "there are very few places where things are just done for students," but webcast.berkeley is an example of a tool to help students achieve success in their coursework (interview with Mara Hancock, 6/8/09). In the words of former project director Obadiah Greenberg, "this reinforces the digital bridge to our students, alumni, and the world, and allows us to explore new distribution channels" (quoted in Leung, Linda, "UC Berkeley Offers Course Materials on iTunes," *Network World*, online edition, April 25, 2006).

began to think of it as a public service at least as much as a student benefit."[11]

webcast.berkeley's Content and Organization

webcast.berkeley provides multimedia content in the form of recorded video lectures, audio-only versions of lectures, and screencasting, which combines professors' PowerPoint slides or other projected material with audio voiceover.[12] The site focuses on capturing lectures in audio-video formats and excludes written materials like syllabi, reading lists, or lecture notes. As Berkeley's Vice Provost for Teaching and Learning Christina Maslach said, webcasting lectures is a means of disseminating "the spoken word, but what we have not gone on to do is the MIT thing of doing all the course materials."[13]

The desire to publish the faculty's "spoken word" content within the confines of a limited budget has prompted webcast.berkeley to explore automating as many steps of the production process as possible. Rowe said that dating back to the earliest days of developing the BIBS project, "we thought a lot about what can we automate: what's the minimal set of hardware we can put into a classroom to capture the lecture?" with an eye toward scaling up the effort in the future.[14] Courses are now recorded via cameras and microphones that have been permanently installed in a limited number of Berkeley classrooms, and software has been written to automatically initiate recording at the appropriate time, convert the lectures to viewable formats, and even post the content to the program's secondary distribution channels like YouTube and iTunes.

The desire to, whenever possible, capture lecture content through these pre-installed devices—rather than sending live camera crews

---

[11]Interview with Paul Gray, 6/9/09.

[12]Screencasting, the newest element of the webcast.berkeley service, was introduced in the spring of 2009.

[13]Interview with Christina Maslach, 8/20/08.

[14]Interview with Lawrence Rowe, 6/8/09.

out to various locations, as Open Yale Courses (OYC) and increasingly MIT OpenCourseWare (OCW) have done for their video content—allows Berkeley to stretch its budget to cover the maximum number of courses.[15] As a result, the project's scope is substantial: though it is not comprehensive like OCW, webcast project manager Benjamin Hubbard said that as of the summer of 2009, 442 courses had been captured since 2001, with an average of about 55 courses per semester.[16] Hancock confirmed that the number of courses webcast each semester has risen steadily.[17]

With the exception of MIT OCW, no program profiled in this book covers its parent university's entire undergraduate curriculum, and therefore choices must be made concerning which professors and courses to include in its online courseware initiative. Each institution has approached this selection process differently in accordance with its local goals and strategic priorities. As we have seen, the Carnegie Mellon faculty selected by the Open Learning Initiative (OLI) must have the time and inclination to serve on a course development team, as well as teach disciplines that are a good fit for the OLI's mode of asynchronous digital pedagogy. At Yale, faculty asked to participate in OYC are renowned tenured professors who teach subjects of general interest to a wide public. Berkeley's "selection process" is quite different, and largely out of the webcast team's control: due to the reliance on automated technologies, only

[15] A technician is needed for video courses, to operate the controls that point the mounted cameras, but this is far simpler and less labor intensive than the recording process at Yale, which requires two live camera operators using portable equipment. webcast.berkeley does occasionally send camera people with Portapak equipment into classrooms, but they rarely use this method. According to Hubbard, occasionally "we do have a sort of hybrid approach; we will send camera people out to classrooms that aren't equipped. It's usually about three to five classes a semester, and we really try to limit it because it's very labor intensive, and what we're really focused on is providing a lot of value for a limited investment" (interview with Benjamin Hubbard, 6/8/09).

[16] Personal communication from Benjamin Hubbard, 6/16/09. By the spring of 2010, the number had increased to 548 courses (personal communication with Mara Hancock, 3/19/10).

[17] Although the number of video courses captured began to decline in late 2008, presumably due to departments' budgetary concerns, the rise in podcast and screencast courses (for which academic departments do not incur an additional fee, as described later in the chapter) has more than made up for the difference, and Hubbard noted that by the spring of 2010, webcast.berkeley was back to 55 courses per semester (personal communication from Benjamin Hubbard, 3/16/10).

those professors who have been assigned by the registrar to teach in web- or podcast-enabled rooms are invited to participate in the initiative.

Hancock said that the site's content has basically been "un-curated," and Hubbard agreed that "it was never really our goal to just capture specific faculty, specific courses, [or] specific disciplines"; rather, the webcast team captures as many courses as there are willing faculty members teaching in enabled classrooms.[18] An automated invitation is sent to the faculty members who have been scheduled to teach in those classrooms at the beginning of each semester, at which point they can opt into webcasting. Beginning in the fall of 2009, there were 40 classrooms enabled for video or audio capture on the Berkeley campus, but until then the webcast team had been working with about half that.[19] Of all the faculty members who are asked to participate, roughly 20 percent agree to be webcast.

webcast.berkeley's body of courses covers a range of disciplines but skews heavily toward the hard sciences, perhaps because the large lecture halls that tend to house those courses (as seen in Figure 6.1) are also frequently webcast enabled.[20] Hancock said the site focuses on "sciences, computer sciences, [and] engineering," and data compiled by Hubbard confirm that from the fall of 2001 to the fall of 2008, 129 courses were offered in the arts, humanities, and social sciences, compared to 285 in the physical sciences.[21] Faculty do not receive payment or special incentives to participate in webcast.berkeley, but the barriers to doing so are kept to a minimum. Hancock remarked that in working with faculty, "we try not to interrupt their flow at all," and the amount of extra time that webcasting requires of a faculty member is truly minimal. "One of the great things about it is that it doesn't get in the way of the teaching," Hancock said. "We're just capturing them doing what they do best."[22]

[18]Interviews with Mara Hancock, 8/19/08, and Benjamin Hubbard, 6/8/09.
[19]Interview with Mara Hancock, 6/8/09.
[20]Interview with Christina Maslach, 8/20/08.
[21]Table compiled by Benjamin Hubbard, 6/16/09.
[22]Interview with Mara Hancock, 6/8/09.

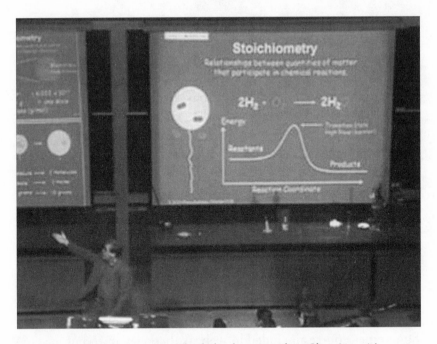

FIGURE 6.1   Still from webcast.berkeley lecture video, Chemistry 1A, session 2, with Professor Heino Nitsche (as taught in fall 2010).

Available at http://webcast.berkeley.edu/course_details_new.php?seriesid=2010-B-11206& semesterid=2010-B. Permission provided courtesy of University of California Berkeley. © 2002–2010 Regents of the University of California. License: Creative Commons BY-NC-ND.

With a full-time staff of only three and a relatively low budget —in 2008 the budget for webcast.berkeley's courses was approximately $700,000—the program must focus on efficiency if it is to, in Hubbard's words, "do a lot with a little."[23] Funding for webcast.berkeley has been provided entirely by the university, without outside foundation money. The initiative is supported by a unique business model that divides the cost burden of roughly $5,000 for creating a video course between the ETS budget, which

[23]Interviews with Mara Hancock and Benjamin Hubbard, 6/8/09. Hubbard noted that while webcast.berkeley has three dedicated full-time employees, the program does "rely a lot on a really large group," including other ETS staffers like classroom technicians in charge of video recording or production, and those who install the cameras and maintain the equipment. As is the case with all online courseware projects profiled here, individuals from around the university devote portions of their time to assisting with the webcasting initiative in addition to their other responsibilities.

comes from the provost-controlled central campus fund, and the budget of the relevant academic department, which must contribute $2,000 toward the development of the course.[24] Berkeley's Director of Strategic Communications Dan Mogulof said that this reliance on partial cost recovery may also contribute to webcast .berkeley's emphasis on the sciences, as this business model "inherently favors the departments that [are] well endowed, which tend to be the hard sciences."[25] But early data indicate that the options to create podcasts of audio-only courses, introduced in 2006, and screencasts, started in 2009, may work to restore some disciplinary balance.[26] While video courses have cost up to $5,000 to produce (excluding the original investments in recording infrastructure), Hubbard said that ETS can create an audio recording for around $800, eliminating the need to charge the departments to underwrite the overall cost.[27] The more cost-effective audio-only model (and now the recently added screencasting option as well) has brought about an "uptick" in the number of arts and humanities courses included in webcast.berkeley in recent years.[28]

Each element of Berkeley's production process contributes to the initiative's goal of "video at scale"—webcast.berkeley's main value proposition and a key feature distinguishing it from other efforts in this space. Whereas programs like OYC have placed a premium on high production values and maintaining rigorous standards of excellence in the look and feel of course videos and podcasts,

---

[24]Interview with Mara Hancock, 6/8/09. Hancock said that very rare exceptions are made to this cost-sharing model. For example, Berkeley physics professor Rich Muller expressed interest in participating but "his department doesn't want to pay for it, and he's a big star, so we said we would cover it. He gets a lot of publicity for the program . . . so we didn't want to lose that—he's the kind of advocate you want to have out there and visible. So it's a small investment for long-term gain."

[25]Interview with Dan Mogulof, 6/18/09. Hancock agreed with this reasoning but offered additional explanations for the science-heavy nature of webcasting, pointing out that "it originated in EECS [electrical engineering and computer science] with Larry [Rowe], and they're not afraid of technology, so in the early days they weren't afraid of going that way." She also said that there tend to be fewer intellectual property concerns with introductory science courses than their counterparts in the humanities (interview with Mara Hancock, 6/8/09).

[26]Ibid.

[27]Interview with Benjamin Hubbard, 6/9/09. The webcast program concentrates much of its costs up front, including the one-time purchase of the recording devices to equip classrooms.

[28]Interview with Benjamin Hubbard, 6/8/09.

webcast.berkeley has tended to prioritize the quantity of courses it is able to publish over their appearance. Hancock has acknowledged this trade-off, saying that "our program came out of [the desire to] have a really high impact on a lot of people, and that means that sometimes you're not really top quality, but opt for good-enough quality."[29]

The webcast.berkeley and OYC staffs are in frequent communication and acknowledge one another as leaders in the field of open online video lectures, while also recognizing the differences in their approaches and resource bases. As Hancock said, "the Yale stuff is incredibly beautiful, but it's just higher end and we can't afford to do that." Berkeley does, however, create more video courses in a semester than OYC has produced over eight semesters to date. Hancock cited some complaints Berkeley has received regarding the quality of the webcast lectures, such as difficulty in following the professor's point if the camera is on him or her when it should be on the blackboard, but she responded that webcast.berkeley is more focused on "the breadth of what we're trying to capture."[30] Hubbard also related the issue of webcast.berkeley's production values to the project's ability to serve its most important audience —Berkeley students. "We were very conscious of the benefit of this content to the world and the visibility that that provided the university," he said, but that did not strongly influence the production process. "Production value was not one of the primary drivers for the project; it was really about [creating] a study tool for the students."[31]

Several other aspects of the project's design make it clear that, as webcast.berkeley staff member Richard Bloom said, "[our] students are driving our course casting initiative."[32] Focus groups conducted by the webcast team have indicated high demand for the service, and a 2007 study of incoming Berkeley freshmen "revealed that students ranked podcasting to be just as important as

[29]Interview with Mara Hancock, 6/8/09.
[30]Ibid.
[31]Interview with Benjamin Hubbard, 6/8/09.
[32]Riismandel, Paul, "How to Manage Video Content in Higher Education," *Streaming Media Magazine*, online edition, February–March 2008.

wireless Internet and access to email."[33] To ensure that the site can be an effective study tool, lectures are made available on webcast .berkeley within 24 hours after they are delivered in the classroom. Hubbard emphasized that it is essential to upload the content lecture by lecture as the semester progresses—rather than waiting to publish the complete course, as MIT OCW and OYC do—because "it wouldn't be valuable to our students to have this content available for review after their midterms."[34]

webcast.berkeley is also willing to frequently rerecord the same courses. MIT OCW does occasionally create new versions of courses to ensure that its content remains timely and accurate, but such updates occur on a three-year cycle. In contrast, the webcast.berkeley course Biology 1A has been recorded and webcast 11 times in as many semesters. According to Hubbard, "the current student experience is important," as a subject covered in this year's lectures may not have been included in last year's. An initiative primarily geared toward providing a window into the university for external audiences might consider this an unnecessary duplication of effort, but webcast.berkeley clearly caters to enrolled students who use the recordings in the course of their studies. Hubbard also explained that due to the occasional professor's preference that his or her class not be publicly broadcast, there is a group of "very few" webcast .berkeley courses—about three per semester—that are behind authentication and cannot be accessed by non-enrolled learners without Berkeley student logins and passwords. Hubbard acknowledges that such courses cannot serve the mission of opening up Berkeley to the world, but he said that the webcast team's willingness to record such courses anyway is "another demonstration of how student-centered we are—we're here to serve them, and if faculty and students determine there's value in webcasting but for whatever reason it can't be made public, we still want to do that."[35]

[33]"Cisco Prepares Higher Education Market to Seize Two Leading Tech Trends: Web 2.0 and Interoperable Communications," press release, *Market News Publishing*, October 24, 2007.
[34]Interview with Benjamin Hubbard, 6/9/09.
[35]Ibid.

Though many aspects of the project's design are focused on students, the inclusion of recordings of campus special events alongside course content in webcast.berkeley seems designed to appeal to an external viewership.[36] Nearly all of the universities profiled here record events like performances, speeches, and panels that take place on campus, and often these recordings are freely available, in whole or in part, somewhere on the university's website. But the webcast program is unique in its decision to combine the course content and events on a single platform (Figure 6.2).

The BIBS program had included a few special events, but that portion of the project was not formalized until 2002 at the behest of a former associate vice chancellor for public affairs, resulting in the launch of a linked but distinct webcast.berkeley/events site. The cost of capturing and disseminating events is not subsidized by the ETS budget; the sponsoring organization in charge of the specific event covers the cost of webcasting it. Hancock said that while the webcast team does not hand-pick professors or courses for webcasting, "we do target events when we know something big is going to be happening," specifically referencing the team's recent pursuit of the Dalai Lama when he visited Berkeley.[37] Provost George Breslauer explained the decision to combine courses and events based on the similarities of the two content types, saying that "both perform the function of bringing to a humungous audience things that are happening at Berkeley, whether it's in the classroom or extracurricular."[38]

webcast.berkeley has also catered to external audiences through its use of secondary distribution channels for all content, including events and courses. Berkeley was among the first universities to launch channels on iTunes U, in April 2006, as well as the first university to offer full video courses to the public on YouTube.[39]

---

[36]According to Hubbard, students "are probably not the primary audience for events—the motivations for putting that [event] content up are specific to each individual sponsor" (ibid.).

[37]Interview with Mara Hancock, 6/8/09.

[38]Interview with George Breslauer, 6/9/09.

[39]Lee, Ellen, "Full Cal Courses Are on YouTube," *San Francisco Chronicle,* October 4, 2007, C1.

FIGURE 6.2 webcast.berkeley's landing page (as it appeared on April 29, 2010).

Hancock said that the webcast team was interested in these venues' potential to expand access to the material: "While we were doing a great thing in providing this content, people had to find us. We thought with these distribution channels, we would go where the people were."[40]

Impact of webcast.berkeley

webcast.berkeley did not begin as a strategically planned effort at the institutional level. Nevertheless, the initiative has since taken

---

[40]Interview with Mara Hancock, 8/19/08. Hubbard noted that these platforms are also familiar to Berkeley students and therefore help ETS reach its core student audience as well (interview with Benjamin Hubbard, 6/8/09).

on strategic significance, as it occurred to administrators early on that webcasting could be a relatively low-cost means of furthering some of Berkeley's institutional objectives, and factors like garnering goodwill or press attention became additional motivators for continuing and expanding the project.

webcast.berkeley has had a variety of internal impacts, both intended and unanticipated. The webcast team has learned that the site's core audience—enrolled Berkeley students—considers the recorded courses a useful tool for study and review. The BIBS report submitted in 2001 included data from surveys and focus groups of Berkeley students enrolled in the webcasted courses. A majority of those surveyed agreed or strongly agreed that webcasts allowed them to learn at their own pace and "enabled them to better juggle coursework with other work and/or home responsibilities" by allowing them to time-shift their schedules.[41] Berkeley researchers also learned that nonnative English speakers particularly appreciated the service, as it allowed them to slow down and repeat the lecture at their convenience.[42] The 2001 report also stated that 90 percent of students surveyed "felt that webcasts improved their learning experience."[43]

Maslach, Hancock, and Hubbard confirmed that students still use webcast content for those purposes, and that student reactions in more recent focus groups have been similarly positive. Provost Breslauer pointed out that one motivation for recording and disseminating courses may be simply to keep pace with student expectations for technological support. He noted that features like webcasting are becoming an expected facet of the student experience: "That's what they grew up with, that's what they're comfortable with." In his view, the internal impact of webcast.berkeley is simple: "It makes our students happier; that's a strategic goal. It augments the channels through which they can learn."[44]

[41]Rowe et al., *BIBS: A Lecture Webcasting System*, 15.

[42]Harley, Diane, Jonathan Henke, Shannon Lawrence, Flora McMartin, Michael Maher, Marytza Gawlik, and Parisa Muller, *Cost, Culture, and Complexity: An Analysis of Technology Enhancements in a Large Lecture Course at UC Berkeley*, March 2003, http://cshe .berkeley.edu/publications/docs/cost_culture_and_complexity.pdf, 25.

[43]Rowe et al., *BIBS: A Lecture Webcasting System*, 15.

[44]Interview with George Breslauer, 6/9/09.

Berkeley professors have also reported that participating in the webcast program has enhanced their lecturing ability and improved the dynamic of the lectures, as students need not copy furiously when they know they can review lectures at their own pace. As Hubbard put it, "For students, it changes the way they engage in class—and faculty have told us that now they see faces, not the tops of people's heads" during lectures.[45] Professor Marian Diamond, who teaches a popular introductory anatomy course, said that she watches her own webcasts to "improve future lectures—because no one else will give you that feedback; you just keep making the same mistakes."[46] Some concern has been expressed among faculty that lecture attendance might decline significantly, but Professor Diamond estimated that about 75–80 percent of her students are still showing up to lectures—a number that is not far off the pre-webcast attendance figures.[47]

Such impacts on the key teaching and learning components of the university experience are crucial for an internally supported project. Hancock said that students remain at the core of webcast .berkeley's self-conception, partially due to the historical fact that serving local students was the basis of Rowe's initial vision, and also "because of funding issues. . . . It's unlikely that we'd be doing what we do if the students weren't impacted by it in a really positive way—and also driving it. Students really want it, so we need their support in order to keep it going."[48]

Perhaps the most significant unforeseen internal impact of the webcast program has been the press attention it has garnered for the university. According to Rowe, webcasting has "create[d] amazingly positive worldwide publicity for the University of California at Berkeley."[49] Gray agreed, emphasizing that the visibility the webcast program has afforded the university has "really helped our self-image." He said that despite UC Berkeley's already sterling reputation and strong name recognition, fresh

[45]Interview with Benjamin Hubbard, 6/9/09.
[46]Interview with Marian Diamond, 6/9/09.
[47]Harley et al., *Cost, Culture, and Complexity;* interview with Marian Diamond, 6/9/09.
[48]Interview with Mara Hancock, 6/8/09.
[49]Interview with Lawrence Rowe, 6/8/09.

positive press attention can still be meaningful. "We get the press we get largely because we have famous scientists that are big-time research people. But the people of California value the teaching side over the research side," Gray said, "so [webcast.berkeley] is a chance to get some public recognition for the educational role and teaching." [50]

It is instructive to consider the webcast.berkeley project within the context of the primary mandate for California's public colleges and universities: to expand access to higher education within the state. The California Master Plan for Higher Education, proposed in 1960, guarantees admissions consideration for the top one-eighth of high school graduates to the UC system and the top one-third to the California State University (CSU) system; the rest are to be admitted to the state's community colleges. [51] Each tier of the system has its own mission and its own student populations from which to draw; the plan is intended both to maintain excellence—with few exceptions, the UC system is legally limited to drawing from the top 12.5 percent of applicants—and to ensure widespread access to higher education for California residents through the CSU and community college tracks. [52] The plan has undergone revision each subsequent decade and has since mandated that all applicants in the top one-eighth be offered a place somewhere in the UC system. [53]

The master plan, an unfunded mandate to guarantee access to all the state's high school graduates, was put in place in an era when the system was well financed and the state's population considerably smaller. [54] In 2004 the UC system was forced to turn down qualified applicants for the first time since the plan's adoption, as the state's rising population coupled with the system's budget

---

[50]Interview with Paul Gray, 6/9/09.

[51]University of California Office of the President, "Major Features of the California Master Plan for Higher Education," http://www.ucop.edu/acadinit/mastplan/mpsummary.htm.

[52]University of California Office of the President, "The California Master Plan for Higher Education in Perspective," http://www.ucop.edu/acadinit/mastplan/mpperspective.htm.

[53]University of California Office of the President, "Access Provisions of the California Master Plan for Higher Education," http://www.ucop.edu/acadinit/mastplan/mpaccess.htm.

[54]Keller, Josh, "California's 'Gold Standard' for Higher Education Falls upon Hard Times," *Chronicle of Higher Education*, online edition, June 11, 2009.

cutbacks caused demand to outstrip supply.[55] The situation had righted itself by 2006, but it recurred in 2008.[56] Thus the webcast .berkeley project has developed against a backdrop of anxiety about the system's ability to educate the students who are eligible for it, as well as to provide value to the vast majority of California residents who are not.

The exposure that webcast.berkeley has afforded the university allows the institution to demonstrate its return on the public's investment. Discussing why Berkeley continued to support—indeed, to expand—webcasting under ETS after the BMRC closed, Gray said that "it just seemed obvious that at a public university like this, if you can dramatically increase access to the knowledge base with almost no incremental cost, it would help us, because we could buy taxpayer support, we could buy public support, we could do good for the state. There were a lot of good reasons to recommend it."[57] Given the current economic situation, that need to demonstrate value is more pressing than ever. Mogulof said that through webcast.berkeley, the university is "perceived to be and actually [is] sharing with the public, whose financial support is vital to our survival, and creating a sense of shared ownership and shared benefit" of public higher education.[58]

Provost Breslauer agreed, saying that "you could think of [webcast.berkeley] as a builder of goodwill toward UC Berkeley, which is a nontrivial consideration. Given the crisis in public higher education in state funding, we need all the goodwill we can get. So that you might say it performs a political function." He added that the initiative has not yet directly been used to appeal to legislators for funding, "but showing a legislator a 15-minute clip of a course by Richard Muller on 'Physics for Future Presidents' could be a good political strategy. I don't know that we've even begun to tap the potential . . . of webcast for purposes of political lobbying."[59]

[55]Trounson, Rebecca, "UC System Accepts Record 55,242 Calif. Applicants for Fall Term," *Los Angeles Times,* online edition, April 20, 2006.

[56]Gordon, Larry, "UC Might Limit Freshmen Enrollment," *Los Angeles Times,* November 20, 2008.

[57]Interview with Paul Gray, 6/9/09.

[58]Interview with Dan Mogulof, 6/18/09.

[59]Interview with George Breslauer, 6/9/09.

Closer to home, webcasting has also become one element of Berkeley's campus disaster preparedness planning, as some feel it would offer a way to resume teaching quickly following an earthquake or other incident. Maslach pointed out that webcast .berkeley was not originally developed for this purpose, but it has been discussed as an aspect of Berkeley's approach to "being a disaster-resistant institution."[60] She spoke of the need for an archive of courses on hand should classes have to be suspended—logic that seems to be gaining traction at other schools as well. A September 2009 item in *Inside Higher Ed* reported that multiple public university systems are looking into strengthening online learning options as a way to continue instruction for students who may be quarantined due to outbreaks like pandemic flu.[61] Hancock added that the cache of webcasted courses is considered valuable for its potential "to help with what we call instructional continuity: getting back to teaching as soon as possible."[62]

All involved confirm that enrolled Berkeley students were the project's original audience and remain foremost in the minds of the webcast team. In Hancock's words: "MIT OpenCourseWare had this grand vision and an influx of capital to make it happen," but Berkeley's initiative was different. "We weren't focused on being OpenCourseWare, we were focused on providing a basic community service and a service to our students. So I think we really started from different places."[63] But it quickly became apparent that the material had a global viewership, and the importance of that secondary audience has increased over time.

The webcast team has never had a concrete target for the project's level of usage, but all involved are satisfied and even pleasantly surprised with the traffic the materials have received. Viewership started off small and mostly confined to the Berkeley community. In a 1999 story on the BIBS program, Berkeley's student newspaper, the *Daily Californian,* reported that "at one point Wednesday afternoon, there were 70 people throughout the world watch-

[60]Interview with Christina Maslach, 8/20/08.
[61]Kolowich, Steve, "Dodging Swine Online," *Inside Higher Ed,* September 18, 2009.
[62]Interview with Mara Hancock, 6/8/09.
[63]Ibid.

ing one of three UC Berkeley classes broadcast over the Internet. Rowe said he was stunned by the program's popularity."[64] The BIBS project saw incremental increases in usage; in the spring of 2000 the lectures had 10,892 plays per month, and in the spring of 2002 they had 44,184 plays per month.[65]

But in recent years the addition of Berkeley's iTunes and YouTube channels has caused usage to increase dramatically, and webcast .berkeley's non-enrolled viewing population now greatly outnumbers the number of enrolled students using the materials. ETS project manager Adam Hochman said in 2007 that "since we launched [podcasting] in 2006, overall we saw 2 million downloads of our podcasts in the first year alone from our iTunes U channel. We have had 650,000 views in the first two weeks of our YouTube channel launch. Interest in our content has exploded."[66] More recent statistics compiled by Hubbard corroborate this trend: as of the spring of 2010, webcast.berkeley content on iTunes has been downloaded over 13 million times (since the service was introduced in April 2006), content on YouTube has been downloaded over 9 million times (since the service was introduced in October 2007), and the webcast.berkeley site has received over 80 million streams and downloads since it launched in 2001.[67]

Other than gathering simple web analytics, webcast.berkeley has not conducted any overall usage studies, so the external impact of the current effort has not yet been systematically quantified or analyzed.[68] But all involved are confident that the project is having

[64]Yaffe, Jonathan, "Online Lectures Get Mixed Reviews," *Daily Californian*, online edition, October 4, 1999.

[65]Rowe, Lawrence A., Diane Harley, Peter Pletcher, and Shannon Lawrence, "BIBS: Usage Statistics," *BIBS Report Executive Summary*, July 2002, http://bmrc.berkeley.edu/research/publications/2001/160/bibs-stats.html.

[66]Quoted in "Cisco Prepares Higher Education Market."

[67]Personal communication with Benjamin Hubbard, 3/16/10. Rowe cautioned that "the statistics that the folks at Berkeley get [now], I'm a little skeptical about, to be very honest. They do the kind of easy analysis of the logs; I just don't trust the way they're getting the data" (interview with Lawrence Rowe, 6/8/09). Indeed, Hubbard indicated that the webcast team is currently reassessing their methods of evaluating and reporting usage data.

[68]Exceptions came during the BIBS phase—for instance, an in-depth two-year analysis (2000–2) funded by the Mellon Foundation's Cost-Effective Uses of Technology in Teaching program. The study examined the economic and pedagogical consequences of using an online version of Chemistry 1A, a major Berkeley gateway course enrolling approximately

an impact, based on the anecdotal feedback that Berkeley receives from viewers around the world. Hancock admitted that "we continue to be challenged because of the openness aspect" when it comes to "*really* knowing how this content is being used."[69] Hubbard confirmed that the webcast team has not undertaken public usage or impact studies: "We've had a lot of anecdotal conversations with people and received love letters from users," but not much more than that. "We'd like to do more of that sort of thing, but we're doing what we can when we can, and that's producing the content and making it available."[70]

Hancock said, "I don't know if it's had a huge external impact on the world, but it has certainly had an impact on individuals, and that is how you change the world. I really believe that."[71] Professor Marian Diamond, whose webcasted course on anatomy is one of the initiative's most popular, feels that the project has had great significance for her and her global classroom: "I just love being on . . . YouTube because I get letters from [people] all over the world saying they love the anatomy class, and I correspond with every one." Diamond recalled that going in, she didn't think about the world audience, so that kind of attention was a pleasant surprise. But it is that external audience's reaction that has really

---

2,000 students per year. The online version in the study utilized webcast lectures created via the BIBS project, as well as other elements not otherwise included in BIBS or webcast .berkeley, like "on-line quizzes and pre-laboratory assignments" and "conversion of the lecture chalkboard content to digital slides." The study found measurable cost savings in the second year of the project and no significant difference in learning outcomes between the students using the online version and a control group (see Harley et al., "Cost, Culture, and Complexity"). But the study's principal investigator, Diane Harley, said that these results "were generally ignored by the campus, which was not ready to reengineer large lecture/ laboratory courses to reduce costs and/or serve more students" (personal communication with Diane Harley, 1/19/10).

[69]Interview with Mara Hancock, 6/8/09.

[70]Interview with Benjamin Hubbard, 6/8/09. Hubbard added that "we've made conscious choices about where we're placing our priorities," and that "we feel like there's enough anecdotal evidence or momentum that it would be great, but supplemental, to have that kind of [evaluation] effort. Our core focus needed to be producing the content or improving the system or expanding to new classrooms, so that's where we focused our energies." Discussing the effort's external impact, Breslauer reported hearing encouraging anecdotes related to use of webcast.berkeley, "but those are anecdotes, I don't really know what to make of it except to feel good about that one story" (interview with George Breslauer, 6/9/09).

[71]Interview with Mara Hancock, 6/8/09.

captivated her: "It's just opened a world for people, and that's why I'm enthusiastic. You don't get that with your students here, who have paid to be there and are thinking about what they're going to eat for dinner" during lectures.[72]

webcast.berkeley and Sustainability

As with other aspects of the program, webcast.berkeley's budget and funding were not meticulously planned from the start but have evolved naturally over time. Gray said that the business or resource allocation model was not formally developed at the outset: "I don't think there ever was a process. It was subterranean; it was an incremental, 'well, why not?' sort of thing"—he would increase the budget if the BMRC asked.[73] Hancock also does not know how the project's budget was originally determined. "There was not solid data around this, and in fact this program has continued to grow without really solid data around capacity planning"; though she also noted that due to the initiative's focus on automation, as the number of courses webcast has scaled up, the project's staffing costs have remained stable. Hancock is also unsure of the program's total costs to date, saying that "some of the decisions weren't even made strategically in the early days"—choices as to which vendors to work with and agreements reached could very much have been related to the personalities involved.[74] But despite the lack of complete transparency as to costs, those involved share a sense that the project is quite inexpensive. Rowe said that the original BIBS program "didn't cost us much to produce it; we were really efficient in what we were doing. We did it for $50,000 per semester for 15 courses," or $3,000–$4,000 per course.[75] Gray also perceived the budget as quite low during his tenure as provost: in

[72]Interview with Marian Diamond, 6/9/09.

[73]Interview with Paul Gray, 6/9/09.

[74]Interview with Mara Hancock, 6/8/09.

[75]Interview with Lawrence Rowe, 6/8/09; Rowe et al., "BIBS: A Lecture Webcasting System—Executive Summary." Rowe did point out that that figure excludes the hardware costs.

both its BIBS and webcast.berkeley incarnations, the project "was a pretty cheap thing."[76]

Currently, webcast.berkeley does not have a discrete budget of its own; it draws its funding from the overall ETS budget.[77] According to Hancock, the initiative's annual budget allocation fluctuates, as different numbers of courses and events are captured each semester, but she estimated that the course component of webcast .berkeley cost about $700,000 for the 2008–9 school year.[78] The webcast team makes a substantial upfront investment in hardware for particular classrooms: each outfitted room contains recording hardware—a Mac Mini computer—as well as additional equipment to enable either podcasting or screencasting, at a total cost of $2,300–$2,800.[79] The ongoing costs of creating video amount to about $5,000 per course, while audio podcasts and screencast courses cost about $800 to produce.[80]

Because the webcast project was launched as an experiment, not much attention was paid to long-term sustainability in the initiative's early phases. Rowe recalled that when he started the project, "it was purely a question of can we do this, and if so, how do we make it work?"[81] Gray agreed, but ventured that "it would have been good to have those discussions. I think we figured that it was sustainable when it started in the early 2000s because it wasn't that expensive and we had plenty of money. We didn't sit around and say . . . 'what are we going to do when tough times hit?'"[82]

Webcasting was not originally conceived as an institution-wide program, and consequently it developed with a low degree of administrative involvement. The senior university leadership was not

[76]Interview with Paul Gray, 6/9/09.

[77]Interview with Christina Maslach, 8/20/08.

[78]Interview with Mara Hancock, 6/8/09.

[79]Personal communication with Benjamin Hubbard, 3/27/10.

[80]Interview with Benjamin Hubbard, 6/9/09. The hardware needed for podcasting is substantially less expensive than that required to record video lectures. "Each audio recording room is outfitted with an Instreamer—a device that takes recordings from lecture-hall sound systems and converts them into Web-ready MP3 files" and retails for $395 (Read, Brock, "How to Podcast Campus Lectures," *Chronicle of Higher Education,* online edition, January 26, 2007).

[81]Interview with Lawrence Rowe, 6/8/09.

[82]Interview with Paul Gray, 6/9/09.

consulted about the particulars of the BIBS project. Gray remarked that decisions to develop new initiatives "typically get made in a chancellor's cabinet meeting, but I don't remember anything like that [related to webcast.berkeley]. I think it just sort of grew."[83] The Carnegie Mellon provost had concerns about the funding mechanism for the OLI at the outset, but he was present for the initial meetings with the Hewlett Foundation, whereas the Berkeley administration was not directly engaged in developing webcast .berkeley. Provost Breslauer confirmed that this is still the case today: discussing the administration's role in the project, he explained that "annually they ask for money and annually I give it, and we get occasional updates on how it's going through the vice provost for teaching and learning. But there's not a great deal of interaction, because I know it's in good hands."[84]

The vast majority of the decisions regarding webcast.berkeley are made at ETS's level, and Hancock said that at such a large institution, keeping the project visible to the university president and provost can be "quite challenging."[85] She feels confident that webcast.berkeley is a good fit with the chancellor's overall vision of Access and Excellence for the university,[86] but she said that her team has had to demonstrate that connection: "He hasn't picked it up himself. It's not like MIT, where you had the president going whole hog with this vision." Rather, it has been ETS's responsibility to articulate the importance of the webcast project.[87] Hubbard agreed, noting that the Berkeley leadership does not take a "proactive" approach to promoting webcast.berkeley on campus.[88]

Gray pointed out that when webcast.berkeley began in earnest under ETS in 2001, the university was in a solid financial position: "2000, 2001, and the start of 2002 were really good times; there was lots of money," and in webcast.berkeley's case, "it wasn't [asking for] much money, so it was easy." In years past, the financial

[83]Ibid.

[84]Interview with George Breslauer, 6/9/09.

[85]Interview with Mara Hancock, 6/8/09.

[86]Birgeneau, Robert J., "Access and Excellence," Fall 2008, http://newcenter.berkeley .edu/news/chancellor/access/access.shtml.

[87]Interview with Mara Hancock, 6/8/09.

[88]Interview with Benjamin Hubbard, 6/9/09.

threshold for university support and participation was fairly low, but Gray added that he is not sure what the university will do about webcasting in the near future: "times are really a lot tougher now than they were then."[89]

In July 2009, the president of the UC system issued a "Declaration of Extreme Financial Emergency, effective September 1, 2009 to August 31, 2010" and approved a salary reduction plan to furlough all university employees paid by the state, among other measures.[90] Across the UC system, incoming first-year classes have been reduced by 6 percent while tuition has been raised by 9 percent, in addition to reducing individual campus budgets by over $300 million.[91] Decreased budgets have resulted in extreme cutbacks on hiring—"at Berkeley . . . faculty searches are expected to fall from about 100 a year to 10 in 2009–10"—and there is a serious risk of losing current faculty to wealthier institutions.[92] The upshot of all this is that UC schools have been forced to accept a 20 percent across-the-board budget cut. In a speech on August 20, 2009, University of California President Mark Yudof predicted further cutbacks, stating that "when the stimulus package disappears next year, that's when our budget will go back into the hole again,"[93] indicating that there are no signs of recovery in the near future. In the current economic climate, nearly all university activities are facing unprecedented pressure to prove their return on investment. As Hancock sees it, the question regarding webcast.berkeley now becomes "Is this just a nice-to-have? Or is it a strategic imperative?"[94]

The new economic realities pose a series of challenges to webcast .berkeley's current business model. The video portion of the program has been funded to date by cost-sharing with the departments, but Gray has concerns about the continuing viability of this

[89]Interview with Paul Gray, 6/9/09.

[90]University of California Office of the President, "Recommendation for Declaration of Financial Emergency and Approval of Budget Reduction Actions," for meeting of July 15, 2009, of the committees on finance and compensation, http://www.universityofcalifornia .edu/regents/regmeet/jul09/j2.pdf, 1.

[91]Young, Samantha, "University Leader Warns of More Steep Budget Cuts," *Mercury News,* online edition, 8/20/09.

[92]Stripling, Jack, "Tarnished Jewel," *Inside Higher Ed,* July 13, 2009.

[93]Quoted in Young, "University Leader Warns of More Steep Budget Cuts."

[94]Interview with Mara Hancock, 6/8/09.

system: "We're in really bad shape right now budget-wise, and the departments are the ones that are really getting killed. So I would guess that model is under severe stress. . . . A lot of these departments are laying people off right now, and this is a nice add-on, but if it's a choice between doing [webcast.berkeley] and laying someone off, you're not going to do it."[95] In Mogulof's view, "I think [webcast. berkeley], like a lot of other programs, could be on the bubble. This is something really unprecedented; the leadership of this institution have never seen anything like this in their academic careers. They're facing some tough choices, and it remains to be seen" whether the program will retain its funding. Mogulof said that losing the initiative would deprive students of a resource they have become accustomed to, and "it would put a chink in our ability to communicate what we want to communicate to the public about what's great and good about this place. . . . [But] can the university maintain their standard of excellence without webcast? The answer is probably yes."[96]

This difficult budgetary scenario may pose challenges for webcast .berkeley's planned expansion, which according to Hubbard includes increasing the number of equipped classrooms from the current 40 to 70 by 2011. Budgetary considerations may also prompt Berkeley to evaluate monetization options for the project that might not have otherwise been contemplated. To date, offering credits for webcast.berkeley courses has not been seriously considered, though in this economy many interviewees envision that possibility in the future. Hancock said that at the moment, "we are not talking about credit. People are hostile to the idea that we would simply take a webcast and provide credit; you have to build opportunities for student engagement, assessments, and the additional material around it."[97] Gray recounted that at Berkeley,

[95]Interview with Paul Gray, 6/9/09.

[96]Interview with Dan Mogulof, 6/18/09. In 2009 ETS proposed levying a course materials fee on Berkeley students to cover the costs of the webcast program. Despite positive feedback on the issue from a few early student focus groups, the approving subcommittee (composed of students, faculty, and administrators) ultimately rejected the proposed fee. According to Hancock, "there was a sentiment that we couldn't charge students for something that we gave away for free" to the broader public (interview with Mara Hancock, 4/16/10).

[97]Interview with Mara Hancock, 6/8/09.

"we've been talking about a remote-access for-credit program for a long time, and the faculty have resisted it every time . . . the reason is quality: when we turn out a masters student or a PhD, it's someone who's been here on the campus, in this building, rubbing shoulders with professors here . . . so a Berkeley degree has that threshold to it, and the faculty here has never wanted to produce a student that didn't have that."[98]

But signs are beginning to emerge of a willingness, born out of financial necessity, to fundamentally rethink the way things are done in the UC system. In the summer of 2009, the chairman of the UC Board of Regents, along with UC President Yudof, committed to establishing "a commission to examine fundamental questions about the university's future," including foundational issues related to its institutional structure, methods of teaching, and business model.[99] To that end, several bold proposals have been made to move into the online space. The dean of the Berkeley campus's law school, Christopher Edley, wrote in a 2009 *Los Angeles Times* opinion piece that the UC system should develop an eleventh campus, on par with the current ten but entirely online.[100] It is conceivable that the webcasting begun at Berkeley could provide an interesting bridge to such a program, though Edley told the *Chronicle* that for a UC "cybercampus" to be successful, it would be imperative to "use the best teachers and very high production values in the video offerings, not just setting up a camera in the back of the room while somebody delivers their lecture."[101] More recently, the University of California has approved a pilot project

[98]Interview with Paul Gray, 6/9/09.

[99]Stripling, "Tarnished Jewel."

[100]Edley, Christopher J., "Building a New UC—In Cyberspace," *Los Angeles Times,* online edition, July 1, 2009.

[101]Quoted in Beja, Marc, "Online Campus Could Solve Many U. of California Problems, a Dean Says," *Chronicle of Higher Education,* online edition, July 22, 2009. Clearly, Edley envisions something beyond webcast.berkeley's current capabilities. Along those lines, Hancock reported that, as of the spring of 2010, webcast.berkeley was working with the chemistry department on a project to create higher-quality videos of Chemistry 1A. The professor will deliver the lectures in a recording studio, allowing for improved quality, and ETS has upgraded some of its recording equipment to high definition to accommodate the project. This is a small pilot initiated by the academic department itself (which secured outside grant funding to cover the costs), so it is uncertain whether other webcast.berkeley courses will receive similar upgrades in the near future (interview with Mara Hancock, 4/16/10).

to create and evaluate fully online courses, which could be offered for credit either to enrolled UC students or, eventually, as part of full online undergraduate degrees.[102]

Other aspects of online education intrigue Provost Breslauer—namely, the revenue possibilities that charging for an expanded program of online courses might offer. "There's a huge, huge untapped market out there." He said that particularly in the university extension area, Berkeley is interested in developing webcast technology "for extracurricular revenue enhancement." But while the Berkeley administration certainly "see[s] potential for leveraging their webcasting *ability*," he is not sure if the webcast.berkeley program per se will be involved in a potentially monetized online course program.[103]

••••••••••••••

It has always been imperative that the UC system provide value to California taxpayers. But the financial insolvency that has gripped the state government (and with it the university) since 2008 has jeopardized all non-essential projects, necessitating a renewed demonstration of the value that higher education brings to the state. Depending on how a small media program like webcast .berkeley is viewed by university leadership in the coming years, it may be considered either a prime target for budget cuts or an essential tool for outreach and community relations.

The way forward is unclear, as there are competing notions of how webcast.berkeley can best make a case for itself in changing times. Daniel Greenstein, the University of California's vice provost

[102]University of California, University Committee on Educational Policy, "Online Undergraduate Instruction at a Selective University: An Intensive, Faculty-Led Evaluation of Opportunities, Challenges, Quality, Cost, and Viability," draft prospectus, version 12, March 30, 2010, http://ccfit.ucdavis.edu/calendar/2009-10/docs/ucep%20project%20description%20 final.pdf.

[103]Interview with George Breslauer, 6/9/09. Breslauer said that for future online money-making ventures, "I think we ought to be concentrating our attention on UC Berkeley extension degrees, because they are the real big potential moneymakers." He noted that the extension has been profitable lately, "and we're now planning on its becoming a cash cow for the campus, while at the same time offering extension degrees and masters degrees to the world." Such a plan still must be approved by the regents, but Breslauer commented that "There's a huge upside potential for leveraging the university extension."

for academic planning, programs and coordination, has argued that projects deemed truly essential to the university's core teaching and learning mission may have the best chance of survival: "Where we can demonstrate that the things that we're doing aren't just sort of public goods, but they actually help [the university] as well . . . they'll have a better chance" of retaining their funding.[104] This potential turn inward stems from a key characteristic of the webcast program—the student-centric nature of its initial design—that has set it apart from others in this space.

But there is also an argument to be made for focusing on the project's outreach component by emphasizing its impact beyond Berkeley. Discussing the university's financial state in the summer of 2009, Hancock said, "It's dire right now. And one of the issues that comes up [among California residents] is 'what is this big, hefty, expensive institution doing for us?' And if we all live in our ivory tower, nobody can really understand what we do and where the value is, and this is a way of exposing that work."[105] Provost Breslauer echoed this sentiment, suggesting that Berkeley's investments in acts of intellectual philanthropy may eventually pay dividends. "It's sort of an act of faith that the more things you're willing to give away for free, the more goodwill you'll generate," he said. "We need all the friends in the state of California we can possibly get."[106]

[104]Interview with Daniel Greenstein, 6/8/09.
[105]Interview with Mara Hancock, 6/8/09.
[106]Interview with George Breslauer, 6/9/09.

7

CLOSING THE GAP IN INDIA: THE NATIONAL PROGRAMME ON TECHNOLOGY ENHANCED LEARNING

India's National Programme on Technology Enhanced Learning (NPTEL) is a large-scale, freely available online educational effort, the product of a partnership between government and higher education with a mandate to serve the nation. Launched with funding from the Indian government and executed by seven of the prestigious Indian Institutes of Technology (IITs) and the Indian Institute of Science (IISc), NPTEL responds to a specific problem in Indian higher education: the widening gap in quality and resources between top universities like the IITs and the remainder of the country's engineering education system.[1]

NPTEL was conceived in 1999, and funding for the project's first phase became available in 2003. Phase I—which saw the establishment of the project's leadership and committee structure, as well as the creation of courseware related to several hundred IIT courses—was completed in June 2007, and the second phase—which will focus more on publicity and evaluation, in addition to creating new content—is proceeding from mid-2009 to 2012.

With over 250 web and video courses and more in development, NPTEL's extensive offerings are rivaled in scale by few other

---

[1]When the NPTEL project was founded, there were seven IITs; eight new ones were established in 2008. Just one testament to the prestige of these institutions is the fact that two of them (IIT Bombay and IIT Delhi) were the only Indian universities to be included in the 2009 *Times Higher Education Supplement* international rankings of the top 200 universities ("Top 200 World Universities," *Times Higher Education Supplement 2009,* online edition, http://www.timeshighereducation.co.uk/Rankings2009-Top200.html).

online courseware programs.[2] Though each initiative profiled here approaches the task of creating courseware from a unique perspective, this project differs from the others in several key respects, providing interesting points of comparison and contrast with its peers around the world.

Origins and Development of NPTEL

To address the underlying motivations behind the NPTEL project, it is helpful to begin with a brief overview of engineering instruction in India. A series of structural issues have long beset India's system of engineering education—chief among them the disparities in quality between the country's relatively tiny elite sector, typified by the IITs, and a much larger group of less prestigious institutions.

Created by an act of Parliament following Indian independence, the IITs were designed to stand for excellence, and much of the country's teaching and student talent is concentrated in these flagships.[3] Professor Anup Ray, the head of IIT Kharagpur's Center for Educational Technology, referred to the IITs as "the temple of modern India," and NPTEL's national video coordinator Kushal Sen said that "the government of India has decided to look after these institutions, so whatever maximum support can be offered to them is. There is a pride in these institutions—among faculty, students, and staff—that gives fuel to running these as well as we can."[4] But the same cannot be said of engineering education more broadly; Mangala Sunder Krishnan, NPTEL's national web co-

[2]Dan Colman, director and associate dean of Stanford's continuing studies program, wrote on his blog OpenCulture that, with the launch of NPTEL, "suddenly MIT is not the only tech powerhouse getting into the business of providing free educational resources" (Colman, Dan, "India's Answer to MIT Presents Free Courses on YouTube (in English)," May 27, 2008, http://www.openculture.com/2008/05/indias_answer_to_mit_presents_free_courses_on_youtube_in_english.html, cited in Bonk, Curtis J., *The World Is Open: How Web Technology Is Revolutionizing Education,* San Francisco: Jossey-Bass, 2009, 177).
[3]The official act defining the IITs is dated 1961, though the earliest IITs (Kharagpur, Bombay, Kanpur, and Madras) were established in the 1950s ("The Institutes of Technology Act, 1961," http://www.iitb.ac.in/legal/IITsAct.pdf).
[4]Interviews with Anup Ray, 4/3/09, and Kushal Sen, 4/6/09.

ordinator and a professor of chemistry at IIT Madras, emphasized
that "Indian engineering education is not uniform, and the gap
between the rich and poor institutions is enormous."[5]

With an acceptance rate of approximately 2–3 percent—lower
than that of any U.S. university—IIT admission is highly competitive.[6] That acceptance rate has only been declining in recent
years—a major source of frustration and concern for officials at
the IITs and observers of Indian higher education in general, who
regret that more of the country's undergraduates cannot access
the IITs' resources. M. S. Vijay Kumar, a senior associate dean at
MIT who has advised the Indian government on higher-education
policy, said that a robust tutoring industry has grown up in India
to prepare students for the rigorous IIT entrance examinations,
and that the process requires the IITs to turn away many qualified
students—a circumstance which he called "a tremendous national
waste."[7]

Compared to the IITs, conditions at other institutions, where
the majority of Indian higher education takes place, are far less
favorable. A 2009 item in *The Hindu* describing the current state
of engineering education in India said that "while several colleges
have imposing buildings and state-of-the-art lab equipment to
boast about, the appointment of inexperienced and undergraduate degree holders as teachers leaves a yawning gap between the
desired level and the current level of expertise available among the
faculty."[8] A 2008 report similarly declared that "one of the biggest
constraints for the development of engineering education in the
country is the shortage of quality faculty."[9] The IITs have much

[5]Interview with Mangala Sunder Krishnan, 2/23/09.
[6]In April 2008 "a record 320,000 applicants took the entrance exam for fewer than
7,000 seats," about a 2 percent acceptance rate (Neelakantan, Shailaja, "Elite Technology
Institutes in India Double Their Tuition," *Chronicle of Higher Education*, online edition,
May 16, 2008).
[7]Interview with M. S. Vijay Kumar, 12/11/08.
[8]Rangarajan, A. D., "NPTEL Streaming Knowledge to All," *The Hindu*, English edition,
online edition, March 9, 2009.
[9]Banerjee, Rangan, and Vinayak P. Muley, "Engineering Education in India," sponsored
by the Observer Research Foundation, December 16, 2008. Even the IITs are unable to
fill over a quarter of their available faculty slots due to a shortage of qualified candidates

more favorable teacher-student ratios than the national average, and they employ instructors with PhDs to teach undergraduates, as is the case in American universities.[10] In contrast, many of the private colleges boast very few PhDs on the faculty, and they allow instructors holding masters or even bachelors degrees to conduct most of the teaching.[11] Researchers also find cause for concern in the fact that insufficient numbers of PhDs are awarded in India each year, which perpetuates the cycle of a shortage of trained teachers for the next generation of engineers.[12] These factors have led to the fear, articulated by Vijay Kumar to the *Chronicle of Higher Education,* that for the vast majority of students not admitted to the competitive IITs, "the likelihood of them going to institutions where there are good faculty is slim."[13]

The options in Indian higher education have also expanded enormously in recent years, eliciting reservations over the quality of these numerous new institutions. A 2006 *New York Times* article reports that "the number of technical schools in India, including engineering colleges, has more than tripled in the last 10 years."[14] Most of the growth in Indian higher education has been

---

(Neelakantan, Shailaja, "India Plans New Elite Institutes," *Chronicle of Higher Education,* online edition, September 7, 2007).

[10] Krishnan said that the average teacher/student ratio in Indian higher education is 1:200 or 1:250, while at the IITs it is significantly lower (interview with Mangala Sunder Krishnan, 3/31/09).

[11] "Almost all engineering colleges and . . . universities face an acute shortage of teachers with adequate subject knowledge and teaching experience. The Master's programmes in engineering are too weak and small in number to meet the demand for qualified teachers. Most of the persons employed as teachers for the Bachelor's programmes are young B. Tech. or MCA graduates who themselves graduated from the same indifferent engineering education system" (Mahadevan, G., "A Seamless Hi-Tech Learning System," *The Hindu,* English edition, online edition, June 8, 2009).

[12] "India awarded about 2.3 lakhs [230,000] engineering degrees, 20,000 engineering masters degrees and about 1,000 engineering Ph.D.s in 2006. India's doctorate degrees are less than 1% of graduate engineering degrees," whereas in the United States, doctoral degrees make up 10 percent of all engineering degrees awarded (Banerjee and Muley, "Engineering Education in India," i).

[13] Aujla, Simmi, and Ben Terris, "Around the World, Varied Approaches to Open Online Learning," *Chronicle of Higher Education,* online edition, October 11, 2009.

[14] Sengupta, Somini, "Skills Gap Hurts Technology Boom in India," *New York Times,* online edition, October 17, 2006.

in the proliferation of privately run colleges that are now responsible for educating the vast majority of Indian engineers.[15] And despite the recent mushrooming of new colleges, the expansion in the higher-education sector continues: the Indian National Knowledge Commission "has recommended the creation of 1,500 universities in India by 2015."[16] Regulation of these institutions is far from uniform, a problem recognized by India's current minister of human resource development, Kapil Sibal, who has "reportedly threatened to toss out India's alphabet soup of higher-education regulators and replace them with a single body." Sibal, elected in 2009, wants to begin the process of creating a National Council for Higher Education "to oversee India's myriad higher-education regulatory bodies."[17]

This combination of factors—inadequately prepared faculty, burgeoning numbers of subpar private institutions, poor regulation —has contributed to mounting concern that India will not be able to supply sufficient skilled labor to meet demand for it. The recent building boom in private higher education reflects increasing demand for engineering instruction, but the brick-and-mortar institutions built to do the job are of insufficient quality to make their graduates employable. A *New York Times* article describing the problem stated that "India is bumping up against an improbable challenge. In a country once regarded as a bottomless well of low-cost, ready-to-work, English-speaking engineers, a shortage looms. India still produces plenty of engineers, nearly 400,000 a year at last count. But their competence has become the issue."[18] Indeed,

[15]"Higher education has seen an impressive growth since India's independence in 1947. Overall, the number of universities has increased from 25 in 1950 to 371 in 2006, [and] the number of colleges has increased from 700 to 18,064. . . . Growth of financially independent private institutions has been the most significant development over the past few decades" (Agarwal, Pawan, *Indian Higher Education: Envisioning the Future*, New Delhi: Sage India, 2009, 17, 22). "About 75% of the engineering graduates are taught at the private engineering colleges" (Banerjee and Muley, "Engineering Education in India").

[16]Vaidhyasubramaniam, S., "Funding Higher Education," *Hindu Business Line*, online edition, September 30, 2009.

[17]Neelakatan, Shailaja, and Karin Fischer, "News Analysis: What Recent Moves in India Could Mean for American Higher Education," *Chronicle of Higher Education*, online edition, June 17, 2009.

[18]Sengupta, Somini, "Skills Gap Hurts Technology Boom in India," *New York Times*, online edition, October 17, 2006. The article goes on to say that "with the number of tech-

a 2005 report by the McKinsey Global Institute found that of the engineers working in India, only 25 percent "would be suitable . . . to work for multinational companies." The report went on to recommend that "countries seeking to play a role in the emerging global labor market should concentrate on improving the *quality* of their talent, not just the *quantity* of educated workers."[19]

Members of the Indian governmental and educational establishment also understand this, lamenting the lack of qualified applicants for highly skilled domestic jobs as well as foreign ones. A month before his 2009 retirement from the post "after an illustrious career," the chairman of the Indian Space Research Organization (ISRO), G. Mahavan Nair, was reported to "bemoan that the country's higher education system is not up to the mark, churning out graduates only for routine jobs." Of India's technical colleges, Nair said that "instead of concentrating on quantity, these institutions should concentrate on quality. . . . I am not happy with the system in the country. The bulk of applicants [who applied for scientific and engineering jobs at the ISRO this year] . . . are not able to get even 50 percent marks on our entrance tests."[20]

The motivations that participants ascribe to NPTEL stem directly from these perennial concerns over the state of higher education in India. Krishnan told *The Hindu* that there are simply not enough resources or trained faculty to accommodate the demand for IIT-level education in a residential format.[21] And since they can educate so few students in person, Krishnan explained that the IITs wished to find some way to expose all who are interested to aspects of the educational experience they offer.[22] As his colleague Anup Ray put

---

nology jobs expected to nearly double to 1.7 million in the next four years, companies are scrambling to find fresh engineering talent and to upgrade the schools that produce it."

[19]McKinsey Global Institute, "The Emerging Global Labor Market: Part II—The Supply of Offshore Talent in Services," June 2005, http://www.mckinsey.com/mgi/publications/emergingglobballabormarket/part2/index.asp, 7, 13.

[20]"Nair Set to Retire: Bemoans Poor Quality of Higher Education," *Press Trust of India/Bangalore*, October 16, 2009, *Business Standard,* http://www.business-standard.com/india/news/nair-set-to-retire-bemoans-poor-quality-higher-education/76136/on.

[21]Jebaraj, Priscilla, "IIT Online Learning Courses Gaining Momentum," *The Hindu*, English edition, online edition, July 28, 2008.

[22]Interview with Mangala Sunder Krishnan, 4/1/09.

it, the IITs found themselves in a position to conclude "If we can't support more students, how can we reach out? Electronically."[23]

NPTEL seeks to digitally capture IIT courses for the use of students and faculty from the country's other (non-IIT) science and engineering colleges. The NPTEL courses are "meant to enhance learning of basic science and engineering concepts at the undergraduate level," and the initiative's leadership is practical and outcome-oriented in its goals.[24] As program director M. S. Ananth said, "the broad aim of the NPTEL project is to facilitate the competitiveness of Indian industry in the global markets through improving the quality and reach of engineering education."[25] In short, the project team—in conjunction with its funding partner, the Ministry of Human Resource Development (MHRD), the government body charged with understanding the nation's sector-wide higher-education needs—designed something it thought the thousands of other engineering colleges in India would find useful.[26] Summarizing his colleagues' intentions for the project, Kushal Sen said that with NPTEL, "the plan is only to help, to give back in some way to our community."[27] Though descriptions of the project acknowledge the many links between NPTEL's mission and that of MIT OCW, Ananth cited a key difference between the two. In his opinion, the MIT model aims to provide its student users with "the icing on the cake of education"—a supplement to what is already a relatively strong education for U.S. students—while in India NPTEL needs to be "the cake itself."[28]

[23]Interview with Anup Ray, 4/3/09.

[24]Naha, Abdul Latheef, "NPTEL Set for Second Phase," *The Hindu,* English edition, online edition, November 27, 2007.

[25]National Programme on Technology Enhanced Learning, "Project Document: July 2003–June 2006," July 2006, http://nptel.iitk.ac.in/NPTELBooklet.pdf, 5.

[26]Interview with M. S. Ananth, 4/2/09.

[27]Interview with Kushal Sen, 4/6/09.

[28]Interview with M. S. Ananth, 4/2/09. In Ananth's view, MIT OCW could be effective for users who are already educated, but in India, colleges are so lacking in qualified teachers that they need the basics, not enrichment; NPTEL is perhaps the only means by which many Indian students could be exposed to faculty with PhDs. While some technology-enhanced educational opportunity "is really a necessity in India, it's not a matter of enhancement in the quality of education, it's just providing the education. There's a real thirst for learning, and I think that's characteristic of developing countries."

The IITs also had internal motivations for starting a program like NPTEL, but even these relate back to systemic concerns. Krishnan expressed anxiety over what he described as deteriorating overall quality of graduate applicants to the IITs, which he attributes to the declining standards of instruction in most of the higher-education system.[29] So R. K. Shevgaonkar, IIT Bombay's NPTEL institutional coordinator, admitted that in addition to attempting to help students and faculty outside the IITs, "we have a second sort of selfish motive in this": the hope of increasing the overall quality of applicants for graduate study by providing access to higher-quality materials during their earlier education.[30] Ananth agreed, saying that "in the long run it's selfish, because if the overall quality of education rises, the quality of input to our graduate programs will improve."[31] Deepak B. Phatak, a professor of computer science and engineering at IIT Bombay, added an additional rationale for investing in a content creation program like NPTEL: the desire—shared by other project leaders of open-education initiatives based in the developing world—to be considered an active producer of online resources.[32] According to Phatak, India now downloads far more from the web than it uploads, and he would like to see the country become a net producer of digital educational content in the next decade.[33]

The process of translating these goals into a concrete initiative began with a series of conversations in the 1990s among several Indian universities, an American university, and the Indian gov-

[29]Interview with Mangala Sunder Krishnan, 2/23/09. According to Krishnan, the construction of new private colleges has increased the pool of college graduates eligible to apply to graduate school, but given the questionable quality of those undergraduate institutions, the overall quality of graduates has declined even as their numbers have increased.

[30]Interview with R. K. Shevgaonkar, 4/9/09.

[31]Interview with M. S. Ananth, 4/2/09. Ananth acknowledged that the current IIT undergraduates might also benefit from NPTEL content as a study tool, though not all interviewees cited that kind of internal use as an initial motivation for the project.

[32]Catherine Ngugi, the director of the Hewlett-funded OER Africa initiative, has similarly expressed the importance of Africa becoming a producer of content for its own population and for the world at large, rather than merely consuming Western education (Ngugi, Catherine, keynote address, 2009 Open Education Conference, Vancouver, August 12, 2009).

[33]Interview with Deepak B. Phatak, 4/8/09.

ernment, all of which shared an interest in technology's potential to improve education in India. The directors of some of the IITs (as well as the MHRD) were intrigued by the possibilities of technology-enhanced learning, and a group of Indian representatives visited Carnegie Mellon University in 1998 to share perspectives on this issue.[34] Carnegie Mellon had a long history of institutional involvement with instructional technology, as well as multiple ties to India through personal relationships forged over generations.[35] Paul Goodman, a professor of organizational psychology at Carnegie Mellon and the director of its Office of Educational Innovation and Technology, had experience setting up networks for technology-enhanced learning to aid underserved populations in Latin America, and he received a small grant from the Ford Foundation to conduct workshops in India. According to Krishnan, one such workshop was attended by representatives from five IITs, as well as four Indian Institutes of Management.[36]

The ideas that emerged from that workshop were legion, including a shared digital library model, online PhD programs, a virtual university that could grant degrees, and a project aimed at "developing interactive and electronic resources for core courses for undergraduates."[37] These potential directions coalesced into a single effort, originally called the Virtual Center for Technology Enhanced Learning. The group drafted a memorandum of understanding to work together and submitted a proposal to the Indian government outlining the four possible avenues along which they might proceed. The proposal was revised several times. Its original scope was deemed too broad to pursue in its entirety, and the ministry and IIT representatives decided to take a pragmatic and phased approach to achieving their goals. This decision resulted in a project limited to the online undergraduate course compo-

[34]Interview with Mangala Sunder Krishnan, 2/23/09; Vencatesan, Jayshree, "Recent Initiatives in Distance Education," *Current Science* 91, no. 7 (October 10, 2006), 891–93.
[35]Interview with Paul Goodman, 3/19/09.
[36]Interview with Mangala Sunder Krishnan, 4/1/09. Carnegie Mellon's discussions with the IITs that resulted in NPTEL predated the Open Learning Initiative (OLI) by several years; the two are unconnected, and Goodman has not been involved with the OLI project.
[37]National Programme on Technology Enhanced Learning, "Project Document: July 2003– June 2006," 5.

nent. On the advice of the ministry, the group of participants was also reconstituted to include each of the seven then-extant IITs and the IISc at Bangalore (the IIMs left the partnership at this time).[38]

The final proposal "for creating contents for 100 courses as web based supplements and 100 complete video courses, for forty hours of duration per course" was drafted in 1999 and submitted to the MHRD.[39] But turnover in the government caused the project to stall at that point, and funding to initiate NPTEL was not available until 2003, when the project received 20.47 crores (204.7 million rupees, or about $4.4 million U.S. dollars) for its first phase, to be used over three years.[40] The initiative—the name of which was changed to the current National Programme on Technology Enhanced Learning—was launched in July 2003 upon receipt of the first round of funding.[41] The next three years were spent on course creation, and the NPTEL website "was launched officially on September 3rd [2006] by the Honourable Minister for HRD, Shri. Arjun Singh in a function held in IIT Madras."[42] Phase I was completed in the summer of 2007, and funding for the project's second phase was formally granted in March 2009.

NPTEL's Content and Organization

Perhaps the most striking feature of NPTEL is its consortial structure. The IITs, a federation of universities with shared missions but otherwise independent governance, have traditionally contended

---

[38]Interview with Paul Goodman, 3/19/09. Carnegie Mellon ceased official involvement at that point and continued to play only an informal advisory role in the project. As Goodman said of NPTEL, "It's their project, and they run it, but they also acknowledge that it came about because of our relationship."

[39]National Programme on Technology Enhanced Learning, "Frequently Asked Questions," http://nptel.iitm.ac.in/faq.php.

[40]National Programme on Technology Enhanced Learning, "Project Document: July 2003–June 2006," 5.

[41]Special Correspondent, "Quota Bill Will Not Face Opposition," *The Hindu,* English edition, online edition, September 4, 2006.

[42]National Programme on Technology Enhanced Learning, "Project Document: July 2003–June 2006," 32.

for the country's best faculty and students.[43] So as Paul Goodman noted, "implementing NPTEL and getting all these other schools to collaborate and to produce is nontrivial. They're all called IITs, but they're independent, they compete with each other, and it's no small thing that they got everyone involved."[44] The IITs have worked together to some extent since their founding. They share a source of funding (the MHRD) and have long conducted joint entrance examinations. Various centers and discipline-specific projects, such as an earthquake engineering center based at IIT Kharagpur, also involve multiple campuses. But NPTEL marks the IITs' deepest and most high-profile collaboration to date, as it requires all parties to build consensus on fundamental curricular issues (Figure 7.1). Professor Ray noted that NPTEL "is the first time that the combined experience and talent of faculty across the IITs has been able to reach out to a much larger population."[45]

The decision to collaborate arose from the IITs' determination that, in this case, more could be accomplished together than apart —though both the MHRD and the IITs themselves viewed this partnership as an experiment. Shevgaonkar remarked that designing and running a multi-institutional project "has really been a tremendous task, and [the MHRD] thought we wouldn't be able to do it because there would be coordination problems." In his opinion the MHRD's initial skepticism was evidenced by the fact that the original allocation was "pretty meager."[46]

NPTEL has a different consortial structure than those attempted by Fathom and AllLearn. Though university partners initiated and developed the concepts for all three efforts, Fathom and AllLearn both created strong central governing structures and hired professional CEOs to run the initiatives. In contrast, NPTEL's organizational leadership is drawn entirely from the IITs' faculty and administrative ranks and lacks a central, physical space. Every

---

[43]Kushal Sen explained that a pan-IIT counsel works with the MHRD to set policy at the highest level, but "after that these institutions are autonomous bodies: they give their own degrees, they decide what they want to teach, they decide which ways they want to grow." Each IIT has a great deal of curricular freedom (interview with Kushal Sen, 4/6/09).

[44]Interview with Paul Goodman, 3/19/09.

[45]Interview with Anup Ray, 4/3/09.

[46]Interview with R. K. Shevgaonkar, 4/9/09.

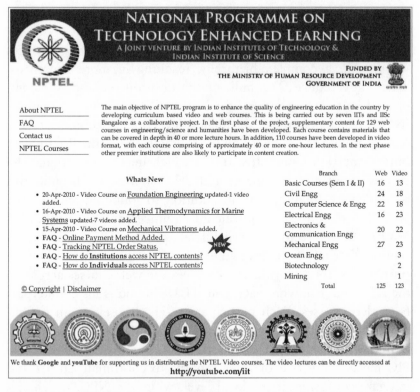

NATIONAL PROGRAMME ON TECHNOLOGY ENHANCED LEARNING
A JOINT VENTURE BY INDIAN INSTITUTES OF TECHNOLOGY & INDIAN INSTITUTE OF SCIENCE

NPTEL

FUNDED BY THE MINISTRY OF HUMAN RESOURCE DEVELOPMENT GOVERNMENT OF INDIA

About NPTEL

FAQ

Contact us

NPTEL Courses

The main objective of NPTEL program is to enhance the quality of engineering education in the country by developing curriculum based video and web courses. This is being carried out by seven IITs and IISc Bangalore as a collaborative project. In the first phase of the project, supplementary content for 129 web courses in engineering/science and humanities have been developed. Each course contains materials that can be covered in depth in 40 or more lecture hours. In addition, 110 courses have been developed in video format, with each course comprising of approximately 40 or more one-hour lectures. In the next phase other premier institutions are also likely to participate in content creation.

Whats New

- 20-Apr-2010 - Video Course on Foundation Engineering updated-1 video added.
- 16-Apr-2010 - Video Course on Applied Thermodynamics for Marine Systems updated-7 videos added.
- 15-Apr-2010 - Video Course on Mechanical Vibrations added.
- **FAQ** - Online Payment Method Added.
- **FAQ** - Tracking NPTEL Order Status.
- **FAQ** - How do **Institutions** access NPTEL contents?
- **FAQ** - How do **Individuals** access NPTEL contents?

Branch	Web	Video
Basic Courses (Sem I & II)	16	13
Civil Engg	24	18
Computer Science & Engg	22	18
Electrical Engg	16	23
Electronics & Communication Engg	20	22
Mechanical Engg	27	23
Ocean Engg		3
Biotechnology		2
Mining		1
Total	125	123

© Copyright | Disclaimer

We thank **Google** and **youTube** for supporting us in distributing the NPTEL Video courses. The video lectures can be directly accessed at **http://youtube.com/iit**

FIGURE 7.1   NPTEL's landing page (as it appeared on April 29, 2010).

Available at http://nptel.iitm.ac.in/. © 2006–2010 Indian Institute of Technology. All rights reserved.

NPTEL coordinator is a tenured IIT faculty member, as the initiative does not want to burden those still working to earn tenure with extra tasks.[47] Coordinators receive an honorarium for their administrative efforts, but only after they have devoted three years to NPTEL to ensure their commitment to the organization; accord-

[47]Interview with Mangala Sunder Krishnan, 3/31/09. Programs like MIT OCW and the OLI are run by full-time professionals who are not professors, and Ray believes that approach is preferable to NPTEL's reliance on tenured faculty to do the bulk of the work. In his opinion, the project coordinators should be outsiders, because running the effort is such a strain on professors' time (interview with Anup Ray, 4/3/09). Ananth said that he had originally hoped that someone from the business world would administer NPTEL, because that skill set would be useful for project management. When the creation of content for NPTEL's Phase II is complete, he wants to revisit the idea of having industry operate the program (interview with M. S. Ananth, 4/2/09).

ing to Krishnan, "the intention should be . . . to contribute rather than to treat this as a position for hire."[48]

The program is administered by a tiered system of committees working in a complex hierarchy, resulting in more consensus-driven governance. The bulk of the decision making is accomplished by two committees: the National Programme Committee (NPC), which determines the highest-level policy decisions and coordinates with the ministry on funding issues, and the Programme Implementation Committee (PIC), which makes operational decisions about course content and delivery modes. The initiative is headed by Ananth, who in addition to founding and leading NPTEL is the director (equivalent to a university president) of IIT Madras. The director of each IIT sits on the NPC, and this executive body also includes two national coordinators: Krishnan, a professor at IIT Madras, who oversees the web courses across all the IITs, and Sen, who teaches at IIT Delhi and is his counterpart for video courses. Each participating IIT also selects an institutional coordinator to administer all day-to-day NPTEL activities at that IIT; as a group, these coordinators comprise the PIC.[49] The PIC meets every two or three months to coordinate efforts and mitigate confusion at the local level, while the NPC, which sets the vision and scope for the overall project, meets less frequently.[50]

NPTEL seeks to build a curriculum in science and engineering, capturing and packaging IIT content for an audience of students and faculty outside the IITs. Content creation is a collaborative effort, with faculty from each institution contributing courses in five major disciplinary areas: civil engineering, computer science and engineering, electrical engineering, electronics and communication engineering, and mechanical engineering. In determining which subject areas to focus on in Phase I, the NPTEL team looked to

[48]Interview with Mangala Sunder Krishnan, 3/31/09.

[49]At IIT Madras and IIT Delhi, Krishnan and Sen, respectively, serve this role in addition to their system-wide responsibilities, but each of the other IITs selects an individual for this specific task.

[50]National Programme on Technology Enhanced Learning, "Frequently Asked Questions." The location of the meetings shifts from one IIT to the next to ensure that each director has a chance to host and the travel burden is equitably distributed (interview with Mangala Sunder Krishnan, 4/1/09).

the subjects most commonly taught at other engineering colleges throughout India and consulted with the government-led All India Council on Technical Education (AICTE) to establish which subjects were most in demand nationwide. After choosing the disciplines "that most institutions would offer," the NPTEL team set out to create digital versions of all of the courses required for a bachelors degree in those fields.[51] The curricular standards established by the AICTE, as well as syllabi from some of India's largest public universities, were helpful in ensuring that NPTEL courses covered the rubric and requirements adhered to by most Indian engineering colleges.[52] Phase II will see the project expand to include a broader range of disciplines, as well as graduate-level courses.

Unlike efforts like MIT OCW or webcast.berkeley, NPTEL does not exactly mirror the curriculum of any one institution, but instead aims to convey a useful and comprehensive curriculum to other institutions. Shevgaonkar said that NPTEL does not intend to eventually capture every course at every IIT, but to create a collection of all the key engineering course materials that the majority of Indian students need.[53] Because the content is designed to be useful to students and teachers at the regional colleges, maintaining course quality is a priority for the NPTEL team. To that end, each NPTEL course created by a given faculty member is reviewed by a colleague at a peer institution before it is posted on the web. The peer-review process is intended to minimize mistakes and ensure that the courseware is factually correct and fulfills its curricular objectives.[54]

NPTEL courses take two forms, web and video. The web courses contain faculty bios, syllabi, and descriptions of course objectives. Unlike MIT OCW, whose web-only courses often consist only of handouts or slides that were originally supplements to live lectures,

---

[51]Ibid.

[52]Interview with M. S. Ananth, 4/2/09.

[53]Interview with R. K. Shevgaonkar, 4/9/09.

[54]Interview with Anup Ray, 4/3/09. He explained that reviewers are paid for their efforts. Fathom, another initiative that collected content created at multiple independent institutions, also instituted a review method, although one carried out by a central board (headed by then–Columbia Provost Jonathan Cole) as opposed to the distributed peer-review process deployed by NPTEL.

NPTEL web courses have been specifically redesigned to accurately and completely impart course knowledge over the web. Though lacking the interactive features and structured feedback to users offered by Carnegie Mellon's OLI, many NPTEL web courses verge on the OLI's level of completeness in the depth and breadth of material covered.

The initial plan for NPTEL was to focus only on web courses, but in early discussions the MHRD suggested that video would be another important direction for the project. Video courses are recorded in studios housed at each partner institution. In contrast to MIT OCW's video content, Open Yale Courses (OYC), and webcast .berkeley, which capture professors delivering their lectures to actual students, NPTEL courses are often recorded without an audience. By bringing professors into the recording studio to deliver their lectures exclusively for NPTEL, the video team can ask that they look directly into the camera when they speak (Figure 7.2). Shevgaonkar said that when delivering electronic content, "it is very important to establish that link, or the audience loses interest very quickly," and he thinks this is best achieved by creating a somewhat different lecture experience for the home user than that of the IIT students hearing the material in a lecture hall.[55] This approach to video differs most markedly from that of OYC, which seeks to provide a window into the Yale classroom experience and therefore values the naturalism of "hidden camera"–style lecture videos. A goal of NPTEL is to impart some of "the IIT training, flavour and rigour" to those who could not otherwise receive an IIT-caliber education.[56] For NPTEL, that goal is accomplished by simply delivering the lecture content, while OYC wants to capture the ambience of the lecture hall along with the information.

The scope of the NPTEL effort is significant, resulting in a great deal of content so far and more to come. Between the site's launch in 2006 and the completion of Phase I in the summer of 2007,

---

[55]Interview with R. K. Shevgaonkar, 4/9/09. In some cases, students are brought into the studio so that the professor delivering the lecture has someone to talk to, but many professors prefer to record alone.

[56]National Programme on Technology Enhanced Learning, "Frequently Asked Questions."

FIGURE 7.2   Still from NPTEL lecture video, "Artificial Intelligence," session 1, with Professor Anupam Basu of IIT Kharagpur (© 2004).

Available at http://nptel.iitm.ac.in/video.php?courseId=1080. Permission provided courtesy of Indian Institute of Technology. © 2006–2010 Indian Institute of Technology. All rights reserved.

NPTEL produced 239 courses, 110 of which have full video.[57] The project plan outlines the goal of creating 600 more engineering and science courses in Phase II, 400 of which will be video courses (containing about 16,000 hours of lectures).[58] Additional content creation is envisioned beyond the completion of Phase II, leading to the claim that "when this is completed, this will be the *largest video repository of technical lecture-courses in the world* in the streaming video format."[59] In addition to making the courses available via its website, NPTEL airs the video content on the Indian public television station Eklavya and offers it through an

---

[57]Ibid. Each video course contains at least 40 hours of video.

[58]Ananth, M. S., and Mangala Sunder Krishnan, "Proposal under the National Mission on Education through ICT: NPTEL Phases II and III, July 2007 to June 2012," submitted to Higher Education, Ministry of Human Resource Development, Government of India, New Delhi, 2.

[59]National Programme on Technology Enhanced Learning, "Frequently Asked Questions." Emphasis in original.

NPTEL YouTube channel. To enhance local accessibility in parts of India with low connectivity or limited bandwidth, NPTEL also distributes video content on hard drives and DVDs for a small fee (to cover its costs).

In parallel to the project management committees, five discipline coordinators drawn from across the IITs work to ensure comprehensiveness, set pedagogical standards for each discipline, and identify faculty as potential instructors for NPTEL.[60] The discipline coordinators are themselves IIT professors, and in consort with the institutional coordinators they decide which faculty in their subject areas should create which courses. Covering the necessary courses in each discipline is the primary concern, but Usha Nagarajan, IIT Madras's web studio project manager, said the coordinators also highlight the various IITs' strengths in particular subfields and consider individual professors' skills as lecturers.[61]

According to Sen, almost 350 faculty are involved in creating content for NPTEL, so "it's not easy to decide who will do what," and coordinating the faculty effort has been a successful "experiment in cooperation."[62] Ananth said that "we've tried to keep the redundancy to a minimum because we want to cover as much ground as possible"; about half the NPTEL courses have been created by two professors working together, occasionally from different institutions.[63] Several interviewees recalled early difficulties in convincing faculty to participate, but Krishnan reported that faculty have since warmed to the idea and have begun to approach the NPTEL staff about contributing courses. Faculty receive an honorarium of $2,000–$5,000—a policy that the ministry at first resisted. But Krishnan explained that the IITs "wanted an 'in principle' recognition that those who do extra work should be paid for it."[64]

[60]The PIC chose the five discipline coordinators at its first meeting in July 2003.

[61]Interview with Usha Nagarajan, 4/1/09. She explained that IIT professors are rated by their students at the end of each semester, and the highest-rated professors are chosen for NPTEL first.

[62]Interview with Kushal Sen, 4/6/09.

[63]Interviews with M. S. Ananth, 4/2/09, and Mangala Sunder Krishnan, 3/31/09.

[64]Interview with Mangala Sunder Krishnan, 3/31/09.

At each IIT, NPTEL funds a staff of temporary employees to liaise with the faculty and see to the technical aspects of producing courses at each campus. These project administrators are instructed to collect whatever materials faculty have available and create the courses from those materials, helping with design and simple animations for web courses and with studio recording and editing for video lectures.[65] Krishnan recounted that "in the first phase we hired one project associate for every two courses, and they work[ed] with those faculty. We would never ask faculty to do something they don't want to do—we provide the technology and the human resources." He said that in Phase I 20–30 people at IIT Madras worked on NPTEL at any one time.

NPTEL materials differ from their American counterparts in that they do not carry open licenses; the content is currently copyright protected, with the copyrights jointly owned by the faculty creators and the MHRD.[66] The NPTEL team had initial reservations about Creative Commons and is currently debating its adoption for the Phase II material. According to Krishnan, they entered into the project without much clarity regarding content licenses: "We are moving toward Creative Commons, but we're not there yet."[67] Deepak B. Phatak, of IIT Bombay, started Creative Commons India three years ago and thinks that NPTEL should move in that direction. Creative Commons licenses allow end users to modify content and republish adapted versions, a feature that Phatak sees as key to the materials' utility. But he realizes that there is work to be done in convincing the IIT faculty of the virtues of allowing for remix and reuse, as they still harbor concerns that the integrity of their content may be compromised.[68] The site's FAQ currently states that "barring a few courses, the rest of the materials are likely to be distributed under a Creative Commons license in the future."[69]

[65]Ibid.
[66]Interviews with Mangala Sunder Krishnan, 4/1/09, and Anup Ray, 4/3/09.
[67]Interview with Mangala Sunder Krishnan, 4/1/09.
[68]Interview with Deepak B. Phatak, 4/8/09.
[69]National Programme on Technology Enhanced Learning, "Frequently Asked Questions."

Impact of NPTEL

NPTEL's target audience—students and faculty at other institutions of higher education in India—is built into the very premise of the project. Shevgaonkar said that the "usage goal was that we would like to make content available to the largest number of students and engineering aspirants in the country as possible," creating a situation in which "no one would be deprived because they didn't have access to good teachers—we have the teachers."[70] Though the student users are paramount in NPTEL's envisioned audience, the project's teacher training possibilities were also clear from the beginning. In India, "we have a very small ratio of good to average teachers," Krishnan said, "so we thought we would also use these materials to train" teachers at institutions of lower quality than the IITs.[71]

Although the vast majority of NPTEL's usage comes from India, the next largest group of users is from the United States. Sen noted that "it was basically designed for India . . . so we weren't sure how useful it would be to students outside the country," and Krishnan emphasized that "if people use NPTEL contents outside of India, that's a by-product. That's not our motive. Our motive is to solve a local problem."[72] NPTEL's curricular design attests to this local interest. In the process of consulting with the AICTE to determine which disciplines were most in demand at the national level, it came to the NPTEL team's attention that some concepts considered remedial at the IITs, and thus not covered in their own classes, were part of the standard curriculum at other colleges. The faculty then added modules with more basic content to the NPTEL versions of their courses in order to make them as useful as possible outside the IITs.[73]

---

[70] Interview with R. K. Shevgaonkar, 4/9/09.

[71] Interview with Mangala Sunder Krishnan, 2/23/09.

[72] Interviews with Kushal Sen, 4/6/09, and Mangala Sunder Krishnan, 3/31/09.

[73] Ananth said that in NPTEL courses, "the content is very similar to what we teach in IIT, but our students are typically more mathematically prepared than others, so we have to add some modules." (IIT courses are typically 40 lectures, but an NPTEL course can include as many as 56, to provide remedial help to users who might need it.) He said that the project's leaders wanted to make sure the courses were useful to students who might not be at the IIT level, but he felt strongly that the IITs shouldn't dilute their quality if they

The NPTEL team's ultimate goal is to see the resource used as a study or teacher training aid by students and faculty from all of India's technical colleges. But as Krishnan said, "we know that could not happen in five years."[74] Many involved with NPTEL are not yet satisfied with the level of usage their site has received, though it gets 100,000 visits per month and the NPTEL YouTube channel received over 1.6 million views in its first two years.[75] When the website was launched, free registration was required. According to the project document, "within ten months of its launch date in September [2006], more than 160,000 users have registered and more than 580,000 visits have been recorded" with users coming from "140 countries or more." But the practice of registering users and requiring passwords was ended in November 2007 to encourage greater usage.[76] Describing the site's traffic to date, Shevgaonkar said, "I wouldn't say it is meager, but it certainly could be better." Based on his conversations with colleagues at other institutions, he thinks that faculty at about one in three Indian colleges have heard of NPTEL, but he cautions that that is not a scientific figure.[77] As Krishnan described it, "the usage is less than what we thought, but there is an increase almost every month."[78]

Though awareness of the initiative is not as widespread as the NPTEL team might like, the site has attracted its current users with minimal outreach and very little marketing. According to Krishnan, the team has sent out mailings on NPTEL to about 2,200 Indian colleges on two different occasions, and Ananth has spoken

---

wanted to share the courses with external audiences. He explained that, in order not to appear to condescend, the IITs elected to supplement their core content rather than change it (interview with M. S. Ananth, 4/2/09). The OLI pursued a similar approach in deploying its statistics course in community colleges.

[74]Interview with Mangala Sunder Krishnan, 4/1/09.

[75]A recent NPTEL brochure cites Google Analytics data, stating that the NPTEL site received over 100,000 visitors per month in the fall of 2008. The usage statistics have also revealed that the video courses are far more popular than the web courses—a finding that, according to Ray, makes sense: "Inspiration comes from [the professor's] voice modulation, from the face, from the way he presents the material" (interview with Anup Ray, 4/3/09).

[76]National Programme on Technology Enhanced Learning, "Project Document: July 2003–June 2006," 32, 35.

[77]Interview with R.K. Shevgaonkar, 4/9/09.

[78]Interview with Mangala Sunder Krishnan, 4/1/09.

about it at some international meetings. "We do some talking [on behalf of NPTEL], but probably not as much as we should."[79] Ananth and Kannan M. Moudgalya, a professor of chemical engineering at IIT Bombay who has worked on NPTEL, remarked that the initiative was not interested in drawing attention to itself in Phase I, though all involved realize that more outreach will be necessary in the future to increase awareness of the project.[80] Krishnan added that "people are slowly becoming aware of it, but people are always asking 'how come I didn't know this existed?'" He said NPTEL would like to increase its marketing efforts, but it has no designated staff for those activities. "Advertisement is not a strength of the IITs—they sell themselves. [NPTEL] is run by academics," who are not used to having to think about marketing and may not be well suited to the task.[81] In Phase II, NPTEL's leadership plans to conduct a series of workshops at private colleges to encourage faculty and student adoption and to gather feedback.

Within India, NPTEL has received a fair amount of press attention, and the coverage has positively reinforced the initiative's value propositions. One article begins: "Didn't make it into IIT this year? Don't worry, you can still get an IIT education on YouTube."[82] To quote another, "with this, every student in the country can virtually become a 'product' of acclaimed institutions like IITs or IISc!"[83] And a 2006 item in the *Hindustan Times* called NPTEL "a unique nation-building exercise."[84] The tone of such articles is strikingly similar to the coverage of MIT OCW's launch, with headlines like

[79]Ibid. In addition, the ministry placed ads in several major Indian newspapers announcing the launch of NPTEL (interview with Kushal Sen, 4/6/09).

[80]Interviews with M. S. Ananth, 4/2/09, and Kannan M. Moudgalya, 4/8/09. In Moudgalya's words, "We have not publicized it, because when NPTEL started, it was not clear how successful it would be."

[81]Interview with Mangala Sunder Krishnan, 4/1/09. This is certainly true in the United States as well, but universities like MIT and Yale have recently begun to invest more resources in brand management than the IITs.

[82]Jebaraj, "IIT Online Learning Courses Gaining Momentum."

[83]Rangarajan, "NPTEL Streaming Knowledge to All."

[84]"HRD Ministry Announces National Programme on Technology Enhanced Learning," *Hindustan Times,* online edition, September 19, 2006. At least one article couches NPTEL in decidedly nationalistic terms with the headline "Thanks, But We Don't Need Your Courses: IITs Tell MIT" (*Indian Express,* online edition, December 8, 2007).

"Free Higher Education: MIT's OpenCourseWare Plan Fires the First Real Shot" and "All the World's an MIT Campus."[85]

Reflecting on the project in the spring of 2009, many interviewees claimed it was too soon to properly assess the impact of NPTEL, as courses have only been available on the site for a few years.[86] Discussing NPTEL's impact to date, Krishnan suggested "it is difficult to assess. It's all euphoria now, everyone's happy to see that the materials are free, but it will take three or four years to see what it will really do."[87] From Goodman's perspective, "NPTEL is achieving what it was supposed to do, and the fact that it received good government funding for another five years is not a bad metric for evaluation."[88]

In Phase I, the ministry did not fund or require evaluation, and as a result Sen said that "so far we have not assessed—in formal terms —the impact. We will do it in Phase II; we will take that up."[89] But some preliminary attempts were made at evaluating usage in non-labor-intensive ways. Though the requirement that users register was abandoned after a few months, that policy provided NPTEL with some information about its demographics. According to Krishnan, of the first half million visitors to the site, 40 percent self-identified as students, 10 percent as teachers, and 50 percent as working professionals.[90] NPTEL has since subscribed to Google Analytics to keep track of basic site statistics; beyond that, evaluation of the site's efficacy does not seem be much of a personal priority for Ananth, the project's leader. He said that in his opinion, it is misguided for educational initiatives to make evaluation more important than conveying information, "but others say I'm very old-fashioned."[91]

---

[85]Plotkin, Hal, "Free Higher Education: MIT's OpenCourseWare Plan Fires the First Real Shot," SF Gate (*San Francisco Chronicle*), May 10, 2001, http://www.sfgate.com/cgi-bin/article.cgi?file=/gate/archive/2001/05/10/mit.DTL; Mayfield, Kendra. "All the World's an MIT Campus," *Wired*, online edition, October 4, 2002.

[86]Ananth for one believes "it is too early to calculate the impact" (interview with M. S. Ananth, 4/2/09).

[87]Interview with Mangala Sunder Krishnan, 4/1/09.

[88]Interview with Paul Goodman, 3/19/09.

[89]Interview with Kushal Sen, 4/6/09.

[90]Interview with Mangala Sunder Krishnan, 4/1/09.

[91]Interview with M.S. Ananth, 4/2/09.

Krishnan takes a different view: "This country is spending a lot of money to help us fund these courses, so we owe the responsibility to the government that what comes out of it is actually useful to its citizens."[92] To that end, NPTEL is considering possible methods for more robust evaluation in Phase II, and team members also intend to make research trips to the colleges to gather qualitative evidence of on-the-ground usage. Shevgaonkar said that in the near future, those involved with NPTEL will need to supplement their enthusiasm with objective assessment: "There was a honeymoon period, but now that's over."[93]

Interviewees mentioned several possible impacts NPTEL may have had on the IITs themselves, but the lack of consensus on this point indicates that internal impacts were not a substantial part of the initiative's mission or self-conception. IIT Bombay Director Devang V. Khakhar reported that in his understanding, NPTEL was "different [from other educational technology projects] because it was prepared as a package to be given to somebody outside . . . it wasn't something we did for our own students."[94] The coordinators are not sure if IIT students make significant use of the resource, and several claimed that the project's real internal contribution has simply been to make IIT faculty aware of the role they can play in the broader community.[95] Little is known of the initiative outside India, so it has not yet been of great benefit to the IITs internationally in terms of public relations.[96] Domestically, Moudgalya stressed that publicity is not a priority for the IITs. While some peer initiatives have considered the roles that online courses could play in attracting prospective students, he noted that the IITs are flooded with more applicants than they could ever accept and have no local competition but each other: "We're a to-

[92]Interview with Mangala Sunder Krishnan, 2/23/09.

[93]Interview with R. K. Shevgaonkar, 4/9/09.

[94]Interview with Devang V. Khakhar, 4/9/09.

[95]Interviews with Anup Ray, 4/3/09, Kannan M. Moudgalya, 4/8/09, and R. K. Shevgaonkar, 4/9/09.

[96]While the initiative has received national coverage, press attention for NPTEL outside India has been very limited. (However, an NPTEL course was listed at number 5 in a *New York Times* item on the top ten most popular university course videos on YouTube; see "What They're Watching," *New York Times*, online edition, April 8, 2010.)

tally sellers' market."[97] Any strategic value that NPTEL might have to the IITs is tied to the project's and the ministry's overall goal of improving Indian higher education. As Khakhar put it, "I think it's a strategic plan for the nation more than just for one Institute."[98]

NPTEL and Sustainability

The MHRD funded NPTEL Phase I from 2003 through June 2007, at which point NPTEL submitted a final report to the ministry describing Phase I's achievements and requesting funding for Phase II. At that time, the ministry was in a state of flux and could not immediately grant additional funds.[99] The MHRD offered strong indications that more funding would be forthcoming, as it planned to feature NPTEL prominently in the portion of the National Mission devoted to higher education through information and communication technology. But it asked that the IITs chip in some of their own funds to keep the project going in the meantime.[100] In March 2009, the funding for Phase II was approved. Phase II will be funded through 2012, with a budget closer to $20 million, compared to the first phase's budget of under $5 million.[101] The fourfold increase in the budget corresponds to a threefold increase in the amount of content to be created: 239 courses were created in Phase I, and 600 more are slated for Phase II.[102]

Now that the Phase II grant has been awarded, all interviewees seemed confident that the government's interest in the project will

[97]Interview with Kannan M. Moudgalya, 4/8/09. Khakhar agreed: to the suggestion that perhaps high school students in India might use NPTEL to help decide where to go to college, he replied, "They don't have many other choices" (interview with Devang V. Khakhar, 4/9/09).

[98]Ibid.

[99]India works on five-year plans, and the next plan, which would guide government spending from 2008 through 2012, was being written.

[100]As of early 2009, the IITs had collectively contributed about $1 million toward keeping the project going, with the intention of repaying themselves from the second NPTEL grant once it became available.

[101]The MHRD awarded NPTEL 96 crores for Phase II, or about $20.8 million (Jebaraj, Priscilla, "Learning Material for IIT Courses Goes Online in Phase II," *The Hindu,* English edition, online edition, June 14, 2009).

[102]Interview with Mangala Sunder Krishnan, 3/31/09.

remain steady in the near future. "It was quite clear to the ministry that NPTEL would be its star project," Krishnan said, and Vijay Kumar told the *Chronicle of Higher Education* that it is in the government's interest to support such projects because "it's cheaper than building new universities and hiring more professors."[103]

Several interviewees expressed interest in eventually persuading Indian businesses to take on some of the financial burden of NPTEL, as industry will presumably benefit from receiving better-educated entry-level engineers and information technology professionals. Ananth agreed that in the future it would be wise to diversify the sources of funding for the project, and he believes he can easily convince Indian industry to contribute about 30 percent of its budget once the Phase II content has been created.[104] Krishnan agreed that by the end of Phase II, NPTEL might contemplate the possibility of becoming more self-sustaining, but he still thinks the government will always be an important source of educational support in India. He ventured that in a country where much of the adult population is illiterate, only government will be interested in and capable of addressing systemic educational problems of that magnitude.[105]

As the project progresses into its second phase, NPTEL's leadership wants to improve existing content in addition to creating hundreds of new courses. This will involve adding supplemental components, such as assignments and solutions, to existing courses, as well as reviewing the web courses created in Phase I to ensure that all are complete.[106] The NPTEL team also wants to experiment with added functionality by making the courses more inter-

[103]Ibid.; quoted in Aujla, Simmi, and Ben Terris, "Around the World, Varied Approaches to Open Online Learning," *Chronicle of Higher Education*, online edition, October 11, 2009. Of course, NPTEL does not offer credentialing or feedback, so it is by no means a direct replacement for a traditional university experience.

[104]Interview with M. S. Ananth, 4/2/09.

[105]Interview with Mangala Sunder Krishnan, 3/31/09. UNICEF reports 2000–7 statistics placing India's adult literacy rate at 66 percent (United Nations Children's Fund, "India: Statistics," http://www.unicef.org/infobycountry/india_statistics.html).

[106]The web courses tend to vary in presentation style and quality, but Krishnan said that in Phase II resources will be devoted to filling in any holes and bringing all of the courses up to the same standard (interview with Mangala Sunder Krishnan, 3/31/09).

active. Ananth recalled that the learning potential of pedagogically sophisticated web courses had been part of the IITs' initial discussions and workshops with Carnegie Mellon, but that it was important to him to begin simply by producing content: "I [was] most concerned with reach first."[107]

Currently the NPTEL courses have some rudimentary and little-used discussion forums, but there are plans for enhanced interactivity in Phase II.[108] Krishnan said that a goal of Phase I was "also to learn how to create content for students beyond our own." Phase II has new programs "to really provide an education rather than a content-building exercise—which is much more difficult to do." This "educational process" will include laboratory simulations, as well as the creation of user communities built around the content through discussions with peers and question-and-answer sessions with moderators.[109] NPTEL's proposals for more dynamic elements seem to much more closely resemble the Fathom and AllLearn models of interactivity than the asynchronous learning environments, full of embedded assessment tools, created by the OLI. Krishnan admitted that the "OLI is much more sophisticated" than what NPTEL aims to achieve. He went on to say that "it would be nice if we could design something similar, but to do it at the level of OLI would require an enormous shifting of our priorities" away from adding more courses to focus exclusively on developing and implementing technology solutions. "To do something like that for . . . hundreds of courses in India would be an enormous challenge."[110]

Although generating increased and diversified content remains NPTEL's immediate goal, the ultimate vision for this course material is that it might one day support the first "virtual IIT." The desire to found an IIT-caliber institution entirely online dates back

[107]Interview with M. S. Ananth, 4/2/09.

[108]Interview with Mangala Sunder Krishnan, 4/1/09.

[109]Interview with Mangala Sunder Krishnan, 3/31/09. According to Krishnan, IIT Delhi has been promised significant government funding for a project on virtual laboratories, to be associated with NPTEL content. These would allow students to do the labs at a distance. Krishnan remarked that in India most students in the private colleges do not have access to physical laboratories at all and thus have no way to perform hands-on experiments.

[110]Interview with Mangala Sunder Krishnan, 4/1/09.

to the original planning discussions in 1999; it is mentioned as the project's ultimate objective in its first press release.[111] But Ray said that at the time, the government was willing to fund only content creation (i.e., NPTEL) because "a virtual university in India in 1999 was not very palatable to them." So the IITs were told to prove themselves capable of producing content first, with the understanding that NPTEL might provide a foundation of content for such an institution in the future.[112] To date, NPTEL's leadership has not considered offering credit or certification to users due to concerns about maintaining the IITs' academic standards. As Shevgaonkar puts it, "our entrance is very tight, we don't want to just give a certificate or a degree to anybody."[113] But several members of the project team agreed that credit is an issue that NPTEL must address in the future, and Ananth sees the proposed virtual IIT as a means of eventually credentialing more students than the brick-and-mortar IITs are able to support.[114]

. . . .

NPTEL's ambitions for its next phase of development are considerable, and the project's leadership speculates that if it is to scale up, the IITs will need some help. In its current form, Krishnan described NPTEL as "a limited exercise—it is eight institutions providing something that could be a solution to over 2,000 colleges. We can't forever say to the teachers in [the colleges] 'here, we'll make this and you read it'—so in the second phase of NPTEL, we are looking to have some of these teachers as partners."[115] Two or three courses from Phase I were created in conjunction with professors from outside the IITs, but Krishnan said that outreach to faculty at these other institutions "didn't happen as much as we wanted in the beginning." Yet IIT faculty members know of many colleagues who would be strong potential contributors to NPTEL,

[111]Press Information Bureau, Government of India, "The National Programme on Technology Enhanced Learning (NPTEL)," press release, September 19, 2006, http://pib.nic.in/release/release.asp?relid=20799&kwd.

[112]Interview with M. S. Ananth, 4/2/09.

[113]Interview with R. K. Shevgaonkar, 4/9/09.

[114]Interview with M. S. Ananth, 4/2/09.

[115]Interview with Mangala Sunder Krishnan, 3/31/09.

and they plan to bring them in during Phase II. He said that involving faculty from the initiative's target demographic—those who teach and learn at Indian colleges outside the IIT system—may expand NPTEL's adoption, because "some teachers don't want to use something made by someone else."[116]

Some 350 professors contributed content to NPTEL in its initial phase, but "in the next phase this is likely to increase to well over 1,000 faculty."[117] Diversifying the sources of NPTEL content has implications for the initiative's sustainability, as it would spread out the burden of content creation beyond the IITs, and expanding the project to include a wider range of faculty contributions would also reinforce its national character. In Sen's words, "We want other people to feel like they are a part of it. . . . No egos. Our aim is to make everyone rise."[118]

[116]Interview with Mangala Sunder Krishnan, 4/1/09.
[117]National Programme on Technology Enhanced Learning, "Frequently Asked Questions."
[118]Interview with Kushal Sen, 4/6/09.

8

CONCLUSIONS

Online courseware is a sign that the changes technology has wrought across every sector of society have begun to penetrate even the most elite universities. While the initiatives profiled here are ancillary to these universities' core instructional activities, online courseware is a young and evolving field, and these initiatives may be the first inklings of greater changes to come. This chapter, organized thematically to highlight key findings, takes stock of lessons learned to date from the projects discussed here. The subsequent epilogue takes a more speculative view of the possibilities these initiatives might hold for the higher education sector as a whole.

Trade-offs between breadth and depth indicate vastly different ambitions—and intended audiences—from one project to the next.

A key strategic decision faced by providers of online courseware is whether to steer their initiatives toward depth or breadth. The projects profiled here each confronted the choice between producing as many courses as possible, albeit with more limited content or functionality, or concentrating on a small group of the most popular courses and publishing them in a richer format. Fathom did the latter, favoring courses taught by the celebrity professors considered most marketable to a paying audience. The goals of the program were clear from its content choices: the Fathom team hoped to create a product that would spark general consumer interest, and it focused its attention accordingly. Open Yale Courses

(OYC) has taken a similar approach to content creation, concentrating on a limited, "best-of" selection of courses that often feature star faculty and favor introductory-level content to appeal to a broad public. OYC courses have also emphasized the humanities, reflecting Yale's strengths and perhaps filling gaps in the broader field.[1] A careful steward of its brand, Yale was uninterested in creating online presentations deemed inconsistent with the university's reputation for excellence, and this necessitated its "quality over quantity" approach.[2]

Carnegie Mellon's Open Learning Initiative (OLI) also takes a high-production-value approach to a small number of courses, but in a very different way than OYC. Rather than publishing professors' preexisting teaching materials or capturing lectures on video that were originally designed for face-to-face delivery, the OLI asks faculty to work with a team of experts to redesign their courses. This process is intended to optimize each course for web-based delivery, building complete interactive experiences that help achieve strong learning outcomes. This approach results in a labor-intensive design process, so the OLI must rely on faculty who are

[1]Other courseware projects have adopted this strategy, both to distinguish themselves from one another and to highlight a given university's unique capabilities. Courses from the agricultural sciences department constitute the plurality of Utah State University's open courses, in keeping with its status as a Western land-grant university. The content of the University of Notre Dame's OpenCourseWare has a religious bent, including peace studies and courses from its specifically Catholic theology department. As Notre Dame President Father John Jenkins has said, "I am pleased that the University of Notre Dame will be contributing a set of distinctive courses to the opencourseware [sic] collection. It is our privilege to share freely with the worldwide community an intellectual and ethical framework for viewing, confronting, and reflecting upon some of the most complex issues facing our society" ("Welcome to Notre Dame OpenCourseWare," http://ocw.nd.edu/). For its part, Harvard recently entered the open courseware arena through an arrangement to broadcast philosophy professor Michael Sandel's popular "Justice" course on public television. The university thus chose to focus its efforts on one star course in an entirely different medium than that employed by the peer institutions profiled here. Airing university content via public television is not uncommon in other countries: as described in Chapter 7, NPTEL courses are available on the web but are also shown on the government-owned educational TV channel Eklavya. Yet Sandel's course "is the first time that public broadcasters [in the United Sates] can remember a regular college course's being presented on television" (Cohen, Patricia, "Morals Class Is Starting; Please Pass the Popcorn," *New York Times*, online edition, September 25, 2009).

[2]OYC offers only 25 courses, but all contain highly produced, "hidden camera"–style videos, complete with clean transcription for the remote user's convenience. Given the expense of the enterprise, OYC cannot easily be scaled up, but its creators' priority has been to disseminate a few stand-out courses that they feel best capture the Yale student experience.

particularly committed to the idea. Furthermore, the expense of developing a single course has limited the number of courses the OLI has been able to produce thus far to about a dozen.

In contrast to these highly curated initiatives that select only a small portion of the university's courses for publication, MIT OpenCourseWare (OCW) is notable for its comprehensiveness. Virtually all of MIT's curriculum is represented, with about 2,000 courses at the time of writing. MIT opted for a comprehensive model to demonstrate the range and depth of the university's departments, to avoid picking favorites among the faculty, and to achieve the greatest possible impact—in the process creating a sensational story that captured the public's attention.[3] The program's exhaustive nature was announced before a single OCW course had been produced, and faculty participation was voluntary (though certainly encouraged at the highest levels of the Institute). To encourage participation, OCW had to minimize its impact on faculty time. It did so by repurposing existing content wherever possible and setting relatively low thresholds for the amount of content that must be incorporated into OCW courses. Though these measures have contributed to impressive participation rates, they have also led to inconsistency among the courses: while many have complete lectures with student notes, readings, and rich media features, others are little more than course syllabi.[4]

---

[3] OCW officials also contend that the arrangement of its content according to a course's position within the overall curriculum adds value in itself, as a user can always find out what comes before a course and what follows it in the sequence pursued by an MIT student. The Institute's willingness to publish the contents of the entire curriculum also reflects a great deal of confidence in the school's brand: decision makers assumed that anything produced by MIT faculty would be strong enough to project to the world, as they did not choose only their strongest content in the way that Fathom and OYC did.

[4] At a minimum, each OCW course should have a syllabus or calendar, subject matter content like course notes or a reading list, and learning activities like homework problems (interview with Steve Carson, 10/27/08). Although MIT has begun to incorporate more video lectures into its courseware in recent years, at its core the OCW project consists of text-based web material for each course. This content is not that different from the internal websites that many universities have established using course management systems like Blackboard. (Indeed, the policy of the University of California at Los Angeles requiring that a website be established for each of its arts and sciences courses dates back to 1997–98; see http://www.college.ucla.edu/iei/.) The most innovative aspect of MIT's program is not the technology behind it or its content, but rather the university's willingness to expose that content to the general public.

Publishing preexisting materials on the web—which can require that professors merely forward documents to a project staffer or allow their lectures to be recorded—places a relatively light burden on the faculty.[5] By contrast, developing pedagogically effective courses for online delivery requires significant commitments of professors' time. The OLI asks much more of its participating faculty members than do the other programs, as they are required to work with a team of experts to completely re-envision their courses. These divergent approaches to content creation are reflected in vastly different costs per course: dividing MIT OCW's budget by the number of courses produced works out to $10,000–$15,000 per course (although costs are closer to $25,000 for the relatively few courses that contain lecture videos), whereas the OLI has spent up to $1 million to develop a single course.[6] Initiatives based on advanced online pedagogy are thus difficult to scale, whereas MIT's simpler approach—relying largely on text-based content, much of which existed prior to the OCW project—enabled it to cover the university's entire curriculum.

Production quality also varies among online courseware projects, as OYC and webcast.berkeley illustrate. Both offer audio and video recordings of faculty lectures, so the differences between the two are in degree, not in kind. Yale Vice President and Secretary Linda Lorimer explained that "our model here was to say 'how do we get as close [as possible] to having a full Yale College course?'"[7]

---

[5]For instance, MIT OCW "has kept the time commitment of publishing a course below five hours for most faculty" (d'Oliveira, Cecelia, and Steven Lerman, "OpenCourseWare: Working through Financial Challenges," *MIT Faculty Newsletter*, online edition, 22, no. 1 [September–October 2009], http://web.mit.edu/fnl/volume/221/d%27oliveira_lerman .html). And, as David Wiley and colleagues have recognized, "minimizing the time required of faculty to create an OCW course increases the likelihood that faculty will choose to participate" (Caswell, Tom, Shelley Henson, Marion Jensen, and David Wiley, "Open Content and Open Educational Resources: Enabling Universal Education," *International Review of Research in Open and Distance Learning* 9, no. 1 [2008], article 9.1.1, http://www.irrodl .org/index.php/irrodl/article/view/469).

[6]For OCW, see MIT OpenCourseWare, "About OCW," http://ocw.mit.edu/OcwWeb/ web/about/about/index.htm, and interview with Steve Carson, 12/9/09. More recent OLI versions of Carnegie Mellon courses have cost around $500,000 to develop, but according to project co-director Joel Smith, "when we were first starting . . . [the cost per course] was closer to $1 million" (interview with Joel Smith, 8/6/09).

[7]Interview with Linda Lorimer, 3/6/09.

In addition to including syllabi, reading lists, and problem sets alongside the recorded content, Yale attempts to convey a sense of "being there" to viewers through high production values. Two camera operators film each course session, and professional recording and thorough editing give OYC's courses a polished look and feel (Figure 8.1). An article in *Inside Higher Ed* commented that "unlike the static cameras and uneven quality of lectures on the University of California at Berkeley's YouTube portal, for example, Yale's appear professionally produced."[8]

The Berkeley team does not deny the differences between the two approaches. Webcast manger Benjamin Hubbard characterizes their production process as "focus[ed] on automation and efficiency and economies of scale." In contrast to the 25 courses OYC has produced to date, webcast.berkeley has captured nearly 550 courses without the support of outside foundation money. Given the project's ambitions and available funding, Hubbard concluded that for Berkeley, "having a really high-touch production process didn't seem feasible, practical, reasonable."[9] The relative emphasis placed on production quality by Yale on the one hand and Berkeley (and the National Programme on Technology Enhanced Learning [NPTEL]) on the other is aligned with the programs' different goals and intended audiences. Yale wants to represent the institution at its best on a world stage, necessitating a sophisticated look and feel for the courses, whereas Berkeley and NPTEL consider themselves primarily student services (Berkeley to its own students, NPTEL to engineering students throughout India), so the level of polish seems to be less important.[10]

Online courseware initiatives also vary in their approaches to intellectual property (IP) issues that arise when content originally intended for classroom delivery to a live, enrolled student audience is published on the web. MIT places a premium on creating a fully vetted and compliant publication, staffing its IP clearance operation with two full-time employees. The bulk of OCW's IP concerns

---

[8]Guess, Andy, "Open Courses Open Wider," *Inside Higher Ed*, December 12, 2007.

[9]Interview with Benjamin Hubbard, 6/8/09.

[10]In other words, OYC cares about keeping the average user engaged because each user's experience will affect his or her perception of Yale. The NPTEL team has a different attitude toward essentially similar content, as it does not want to waste effort on entertaining users (interview with M. S. Ananth, 2/14/09).

FIGURE 8.1   Still from Open Yale Courses lecture video, MUSI 112, "Listening to Music," session 5, with Craig Wright, Henry L. and Lucy G. Moses Professor of Music (as taught in fall 2008). In OYC's "Listening to Music" course, the camera follows Professor Wright as he moves from the blackboard to the piano and back, focusing in as he plays and then panning out to show the backs of students' heads in the front row—a "reality effect" that re-creates the view of a student in the lecture hall for those accessing the course video online.

Available at http://openmedia.yale.edu/projects/media_viewer/video_viewer2.php?window_size=large &type=mov&title=MUSI%20112%20-%20Lecture%205%20-%20Prof.%20Craig%20Wright&path=% 2Fcourses%2Ffall08%2Fmusi112%2Fmov%2Fmusi112_05_091808.mov. Permission provided courtesy of Yale University. © 2008 Yale University. License: Creative Commons BY-NC-SA.

arose from the inclusion of third-party materials—diagrams and images from copyrighted sources, practice problems from textbooks, excerpts of work by other authors. The production process was designed to thoroughly scrub the online versions of any content that might constitute a copyright infringement. This has often meant excising that content from the OCW course if the proper permissions cannot be obtained.[11] Conversely, Yale's approach to IP has frequently relied on the legal concept of fair use—which allows limited amounts of copyrighted content to be used for educa-

[11]Interview with Cecelia d'Oliveira, 10/29/08.

tional purposes without the need to secure permission—to justify retaining third-party content in its video lectures. This strategy fits OYC's overall goal of simulating the Yale classroom experience for the home user—an illusion that would be shattered if materials were redacted from the online courses.[12]

The efficiency that characterizes webcast.berkeley's production process carries over to its comparatively less intense approach to editing and vetting its content. Rowe said that when he began webcasting lectures through the Berkeley Internet Broadcasting System (BIBS) project, he "turned a blind eye" to copyright but awaited objections from the rights holders. None came.[13] Since then, webcast .berkeley's approach to IP issues has changed little. Hancock attributed Berkeley's IP procedures to the initiative's budget constraints: "We don't have the resources to do a lot of IP review," she said. "We go through every course and check, but we are willing to take more risk than some of our peers in that area."[14] Members of the NPTEL team take a similar approach: Ananth observed that NPTEL is probably far less concerned with vetting content for IP compliance than some of the other online courseware programs, but that Indian society is also less litigious and therefore thinks far less about IP than the West.[15] Krishnan stated that the burden of removing uncleared third-party content from NPTEL falls to faculty and that, in general, IP issues "are not vetted carefully. OCW has probably done that much more thoroughly."[16]

[12]OYC's second grant proposal, submitted in 2007, states that "to eliminate portions of lectures because they contain copyrighted third-party content—a strategy that has been utilized to avoid permissioning issues—carries unacceptable pedagogical costs, in our view. The Project is committed to presenting course lectures in their entirety, rather than condensed or redacted versions" ("Proposal to the Hewlett Foundation Education Program," Yale University, Diana E. E. Kleiner, principal investigator, April 5, 2007, 7).

[13]Interview with Lawrence Rowe, 6/8/09.

[14]Interview with Mara Hancock, 6/8/09. Both Hubbard and Hancock mentioned webcast .berkeley's liberal take-down policy and said that they have not received a single formal request to remove materials from the site.

[15]Interview with M. S. Ananth, 4/2/09.

[16]Interview with Mangala Sunder Krishnan, 4/1/09. Anup Ray dissented somewhat from the initiative's stance on this issue, noting that he has "been a very strong voice in NPTEL from the beginning that we need to ensure we don't violate anyone's IP. IIT Kharagpur is the only one that has enforced that rule by signing a contract with the faculty before the course is produced—no other IIT has done that" (interview with Anup Ray, 4/3/09).

Despite webcast.berkeley's comparatively lax approach to IP, it has never fielded a single copyright complaint.[17] Yale has not experienced negative ramifications from its liberal deployment of fair use either, leading Sheree Carter-Galvan, an attorney in Yale's Office of the General Counsel who has consulted with OYC on IP issues, to conclude that the considered application of fair use is a sensible solution for online courseware projects: "Universities need to be more confident in their application of fair use."[18] Other members of the OCW community seem to be reaching similar conclusions. Lindsey Weeramuni, MIT OCW's rights manager, described how her team worked with others in the online courseware community, including OYC, to develop a code of best practices for fair use modeled on a similar code compiled by documentary filmmakers.[19] Weeramuni remarked that in the past, "Folks [were] afraid of the idea of getting sued so they haven't even tried [to incorporate fair use], but it's turned out that the actual risk of that happening is just so low."[20] MIT has not yet committed to any actual policy changes, but a shift in IP protocols in the direction pioneered by OYC is being discussed at high levels. Thus, subsequent evidence has indicated that perhaps MIT's initially conservative approach to IP was unwarranted—though as a first mover in an untested field, the Institute's decision to minimize risk in the early years may have been prudent.

In general, the initiatives profiled here have focused on converting existing content that was developed for face-to-face delivery into digital form for web-based delivery—giving their existing content a "digital facelift" by making it accessible online, but not transforming it to take better advantage of the possibilities of this new medium.[21] Some programs, such as MIT OCW, have chosen

---

[17]Nor has NPTEL: Krishnan said that the initiative has a liberal take-down policy, but no removal requests have ever come in (interview with Mangala Sunder Krishnan, 4/1/09).

[18]Interview with Sheree Carter-Galvan, 12/18/08.

[19]The code, a publication of American University's Center for Social Media, can be found at http://www.centerforsocialmedia.org/resources/publications/code_of_best_practices_in_fair_use_for_opencourseware1/.

[20]Interview with Lindsey Weeramuni, 8/12/09.

[21]Clay Shirky, a professor of new media in the Interactive Telecommunications Program at New York University, wrote in a 2009 blog post that newspapers could not effectively

to not prioritize complex redevelopment of materials for the digital environment in order to avoid complicating an already difficult task. "This was going to be a big, big project to get 1,800 courses up, and there were going to be lots of people wanting to attach different types of add-ons to it or other agendas to it," OCW external relations director Steve Carson said. And "*anything* added to it—any bit of drag—was going to really endanger the overall success of the project."[22] This degree of focus in the project's scope can be seen as a virtue, but it has also been recognized as a limit on OCW's potential impact. As former President Charles Vest pointed out, MIT OCW does not provide a true educational experience on the web, because "real education requires interaction, the interaction that is part of American teaching."[23]

Of the initiatives profiled here, the OLI is the only one that has pursued a more interactive educational model focused on learning outcomes, which necessitated a thorough redesign of its course materials for the online environment. The OLI's unique strategy has focused on "the ability to embed assessment mechanisms" within its courseware, a factor that Candace Thille has argued differentiates its approach from that of OCW.[24] The OLI's cognitive tutor technology raises fundamental questions about the very nature of teaching, both at a distance and potentially in on-campus settings as well: it may be, in Provost Mark Kamlet's words, a "game-changer."[25]

---

adapt what had been a successful analog business to the online environment because they did not think it necessary to fundamentally rethink the product for the new delivery platform: "the core assumption . . . was that the organizational form of the newspaper, as a general-purpose vehicle for publishing a variety of news and opinion, was basically sound, and only needed a digital facelift" (Shirky, Clay, "Newspapers and Thinking the Unthinkable," blog post, March 13, 2009, http://www.shirky.com/weblog/2009/03/newspapers-and-thinking-the-unthinkable/, as cited in a talk delivered by Gardner Campbell and Jim Groom, "No Digital Facelifts: Thinking the Unthinkable about Open Educational Experiences," 2009 Open Education Conference, Vancouver, August 13, 2009).

[22]Interview with Steve Carson, 10/27/08.

[23]"MIT to Make Nearly All Course Materials Available Free on the World Wide Web," press release, MIT News, April 4, 2001.

[24]Thille said that "OLI and OCW share the belief that knowledge is a public good, and that making it free and open improves the world and doesn't hurt [the parent institution]. The differences lie in where we see the power in the technology. OCW sees the power in online distribution. We do that too, but I see the most power in the ability to embed assessment mechanisms. And that's a distinction I don't want to lose" (interview with Candace Thille, 8/18/08).

[25]Interview with Mark Kamlet, 9/11/08.

These initiatives were motivated by the availability of intellectual resources at the respective universities more than by an identified, specific need on the part of external constituencies. In other words, these projects have been driven primarily by supply, not demand.

In a 2009 article in *Science,* former Hewlett Foundation education program director Marshall "Mike" Smith wrote that "we do not know what the demand is for [Open Educational Resources (OER)], how to use supply to increase demand, how to make use more probable, how best to measure use, or what we might consider to be little or great amounts of use."[26] As Smith's article implies, demand for free enrichment materials from these institutions was assumed but not clearly identified. Use cases were imagined, but knowledge of potential users was vague.

The online courseware projects profiled here were launched because the universities involved had confidence in the value of the content they could provide. The rhetoric associated with these initiatives often suggests that giving away the material would constitute an enormous contribution to society. MIT's Charles Vest has written that one motivation behind OCW was the conviction that "MIT had something special to offer."[27] Discussing the demand for OYC materials, Linda Lorimer of Yale said that "when you think about what need existed in the world, you can turn it on its head and say 'how might we . . . take our intellectual treasury, which is manifested in classroom teaching, and have more people benefit from it?'"[28] And the director of IIT Bombay, Devang V. Khakar, described the IITs' interest in developing an initiative like NPTEL in similar terms: "IITs get very generous funding for all kinds of facilities, and there's been a lot of expertise built up over the years, so this comes from an interest in sharing what we have with places that are not as well endowed."[29]

---

[26]Smith, Marshall, "Opening Education," *Science* 323 (January 2, 2009), 93. Victor Vuchic of the Hewlett Foundation attributed this to the experimental attitude with which Hewlett entered into early grants in this area: "We weren't so focused on the demand audience; it was more just 'let's create this and see where it goes'" (interview with Victor Vuchic, 8/20/08).

[27]Vest, Charles M., "Why MIT Decided to Give Away All Its Course Materials via the Internet," *Chronicle of Higher Education,* online edition, January 30, 2004.

[28]Interview with Linda Lorimer, 3/6/09.

[29]Interview with Devang V. Khakhar, 4/9/09.

Each of these initiatives is predicated on the assumption that content from these universities will be valuable to audiences outside the academy. Elite institutions, however, do not necessarily have expertise in educating the general or global public. Most of these projects offer a window into the universities' existing individual courses and perhaps the overall design of their curricula.[30] But making something transparent does not necessarily make it useful to potential audiences. In some cases external users may derive value from seeing digital versions of materials designed for in-class delivery, but in other cases they may not.[31] The OCW and OYC sites are not overtly geared toward a specific demographic; both initiatives consider their audiences to be teachers, students, and lifelong learners from all over the world—categories into which virtually anyone could fit.[32] NPTEL's approach has been somewhat different, in that it began with a more concrete use case than most other open and free courseware efforts. Its intended audience is composed of Indian college students at other institutions, rather than a general audience of students, educators, and lifelong learners worldwide. Furthermore, in NPTEL's case, the involvement of the Ministry of Human Resource Development (MHRD) formally connects the project to a partner charged with understanding national educational needs.[33]

---

[30]With the clear exception of Carnegie Mellon's OLI, which redevelops courses from the ground up.

[31]MIT OCW's Steve Carson admitted that the burden of actually learning something is passed on to the user: "That's why the expectation was early on that it would mostly be useful for faculty members [at other institutions], because there was the sense that you needed some level of mediation on the other end in order for [the OCW content] to make sense" (interview with Steve Carson, 10/27/08). The authors of a 2008 paper on open courseware also point out that information literacy "goes well beyond merely accessing information, in that it focuses on a person's ability to strategically employ that information for specific purposes. While access to information is relatively easy to provide, the strategic use of that information requires particular skills that need to be taught, which is much more difficult to achieve in an OCW environment" (Huijser, Henk, Tas Bedford, and David Bull, "OpenCourseWare, Global Access and the Right to Education: Real Access or Marketing Ploy?" *International Review of Research in Open and Distance Learning* 9, no. 1 [February 2008], 4, http://www.irrodl.org/index.php/irrodl/article/view/446/1002).

[32]As Casserly said of Hewlett's grantees in OER, "We are very stretched as a program— our target area is the world, the audience is cradle to grave" (interview with Catherine Casserly, 8/19/08).

[33]The MHRD oversees Indian primary, secondary, and higher education, as well as adult literacy. Grants from the MHRD have supported NPTEL since its inception.

Most online courseware initiatives received funding and launched their operations without presenting much evidence of direct public demand for free course materials from elite universities.[34] Fathom and AllLearn found that demand for non-credit-bearing enrichment courses from elite universities was insufficient to cover these projects' costs. By contrast, the remarkable financial success of for-profits like the University of Phoenix indicates that there is high demand for some types of credit-bearing online courses. But free and open initiatives launched in the wake of Fathom and AllLearn's failures have not encountered signals of success in the marketplace, suggesting that the level of demand for materials provided by MIT OCW and similar initiatives may be quite high, but is also very difficult to gauge.

To date, the market research and data-driven assessments of online courseware offerings have been relatively circumscribed, limiting these initiatives' ability to determine their overall impact.

A profit-seeking project like Fathom had a bottom line: its balance sheet determined its failure. But many university activities do not interact directly with the market and must therefore rely on other metrics to gauge success or failure. In *Shakespeare, Einstein, and the Bottom Line,* David Kirp writes that "embedded in the very idea of the university . . . are values that the market does not honor: the belief in a community of scholars and not a confederacy of self-seekers; in the idea of openness and not ownership; in the professor as a pursuer of truth and not an entrepreneur."[35] Yet while the value of something like an academic department cannot always be clearly assessed in financial terms, success can be evaluated to

---

[34] As Diane Harley has noted, "A 'build it and they will come' approach to many university digitization initiatives has precluded systematic investigations of the demand for these resources" (Harley, Diane, *Use and Users of Digital Resources: A Focus on Undergraduate Education in the Humanities and Social Sciences,* April 5, 2006, http://cshe.berkeley.edu/research/digitalresourcestudy/report/digitalresourcestudy_final_report.pdf, 1-1).

[35] Kirp, David L., *Shakespeare, Einstein, and the Bottom Line: The Marketing of Higher Education,* Cambridge, Mass.: Harvard University Press, 2003, 7.

some degree based on well-understood metrics like faculty publishing records, number of undergraduate majors, and faculty and graduate student recruiting—all measured against similar departments elsewhere or different departments within the same university.

The free and open courseware programs profiled here—and many others like them—face the challenge of developing sound and relevant metrics in the absence of clear market signals. Even in an altruistic endeavor, efficiency and effectiveness should be a priority. For the majority of the free and open initiatives, success has been defined by positive impact on the world—a worthy goal, but one that is ambiguous and difficult to measure. If these projects are to determine what sort of outcome would constitute a solid return on investment, more work must be done to clearly define benchmarks and develop better metrics to articulate objectives and reliably judge success.

One challenge in project evaluation in this field stems from the fact that, when it came to desired levels of usage for these resources, few tangible markers of success were established at the outset or required by funders. For the Hewlett Foundation and its grantees, this was intentional. At least in the early years of the OER program, Hewlett felt that, as former program officer Catherine Casserly said, "you have to have enough content out there before you can study use." Seeding the nascent field by supporting content projects was the Foundation's first priority, and serious study of usage was largely tabled for the future.[36] Casserly added that the Foundation also opted not to press for metrics early on so as not to discourage projects from innovating and taking risks in terms of content.

These projects have nevertheless made consistent efforts to tabulate and analyze the traffic on their websites—which often reaches tens or hundreds of thousands of visitors per month—and have also conducted surveys that reveal their users to be globally dispersed and generally quite satisfied with the content. Through content partnerships with other universities around the world, Carnegie Mellon, MIT, and Yale know that their materials are being incorporated into curricula elsewhere, and MIT OCW courses

---

[36]Interviews with Catherine Casserly, 8/19/08 and 4/20/10.

have now been translated into at least ten languages.[37] In addition, voluminous anecdotal feedback—often in the form of grateful emails pouring in from users all over the world—provides impressive and often emotional testimonials from users describing the impact the courseware has had on their lives or classrooms.

Around 2008, the Hewlett Foundation began to encourage grantees to adopt Google Analytics, which provides a first set of comparable data between online courseware projects.[38] As is evident from Figure 8.2, MIT OCW's traffic far outpaces that of the other initiatives. Analytics data applies only to visits to these projects' primary sites; MIT OCW, OYC, and webcast.berkeley courses are also available through secondary distribution sites such as YouTube and iTunes U, so their content is viewed in some format more frequently than these numbers reflect. These data are consistent with MIT OCW's position as the most established, comprehensive, and widely known of the initiatives profiled here.

Beyond counting visits and pageviews, usage data can provide insight into the sources of traffic and allow project leaders to get a better idea of how users find their site (directly or via search engines), as well as users' locations. Benchmarking different aspects of these projects against one another is revealing. Figure 8.3 shows that, in addition to receiving more traffic than the other three initiatives, MIT OCW also attracts the highest percentage of users from around the world—a strong indicator of international awareness of the site (even without taking into account usage of mirror or translation sites carrying OCW content). A more granular breakdown of visits by city is also available; as might be expected for an initiative conceived primarily as a student service, 12 percent of webcast.berkeley's traffic

---

[37]There has been a great deal of translation activity in this space over the past decade, particularly in translating MIT OCW content into Spanish (through the international Universia effort led by a consortium of universities in Spain and Latin America) and Chinese (through China Open Resources for Education). Official translations of MIT OCW materials are available in three additional languages (Persian, Portuguese, and Thai), and independent translation efforts exist as well (MIT OpenCourseWare, "Translated Courses," http://ocw.mit.edu/OcwWeb/web/courses/lang/index.htm).

[38]webcast.berkeley has been independently using Google Analytics since 2006; those data are included in Figure 8.2, along with data from the three Hewlett grantees profiled. NPTEL has also been collecting usage data through Google Analytics in recent years, but those figures were not available for inclusion.

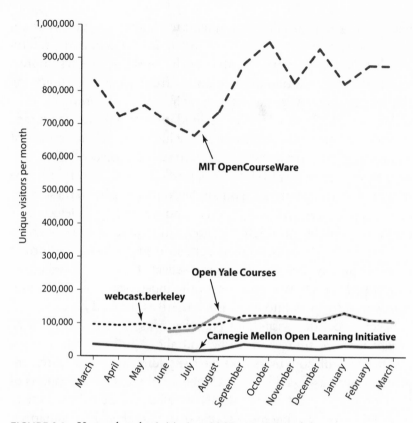

FIGURE 8.2   Usage data by initiative, 2009–10. Four of the projects profiled here granted permission to view their Google Analytics data. This graph shows the number of unique visitors per month to each site from March 2009 to March 2010. OYC's data begin in June 2009 (the first full month of data available, as this initiative was the last of the four to adopt Google Analytics).

in 2009 came from Berkeley, while 2 percent of MIT OCW's (considerably higher) visits came from Cambridge. Usage patterns are reflective of the differing goals that these initiatives have set for themselves, and they may have implications for specific outreach and marketing strategies if increasing traffic is an objective.

Ideally, usage analysis would empower these initiatives to understand the full range and depth of uses to which their materials are put. But while raw analytics are helpful in gauging the traffic websites attract, this method does not offer insight into how ex-

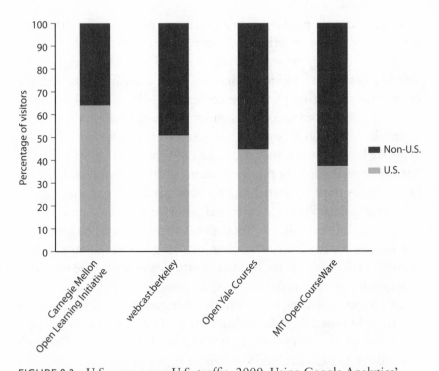

FIGURE 8.3   U.S. versus non-U.S. traffic, 2009. Using Google Analytics'
breakdown of visits by country, this graph shows the percentages of U.S.
versus non-U.S. visitors from January 1, 2009, to December 31, 2009.
OYC's data include only the period May 8, 2009–December 31, 2009
(the only available data for that project, the last of the four to adopt
Google Analytics).

actly the materials, once accessed, are used, or how effective they
are for learning.[39] Anecdotal feedback and voluntary user surveys
generate more qualitative data than mere hit counts can provide,
but reliance on these methods also biases results toward the most
opinionated and invested users, without indicating what percentage of the overall user population this group constitutes.[40]

[39]As Casserly put it, "All data is good—it tells part of the story. Still, we have a lot of
challenges with being unaware of what happens when content gets distributed freely" (interview with Catherine Casserly, 4/20/10).

[40]For a general discussion of these problems, see Harley, Diane, and Jonathan Henke,
"Toward an Effective Understanding of Website Users," *D-Lib Magazine* 13, no. 3–4
(March–April 2007), http://www.dlib.org/dlib/march07/harley/03harley.html.

Stakeholders in public-facing educational projects will in the long term want to know whether end users are actually learning anything from these online course materials. The OLI project is uniquely designed to enable that kind of analysis, as its asynchronous learning environments not only provide constant feedback to the students but also embed assessments of the user experience within the courses themselves. The OLI's stated goal is to create courseware that can generate learning outcomes equivalent to those of enrolled Carnegie Mellon students taking the equivalent course on campus; head-to-head studies have indicated that students studying statistics via the OLI course learn the material as well as or better than their counterparts in traditional courses. But the other projects profiled here were not designed with built-in mechanisms to generate empirical data on students' comprehension, and thus they cannot provide their creators with concrete information on learning outcomes.

Of course, any usage that online courseware projects receive is positive. Summarizing the attitude of OYC and many of its peer initiatives toward usage goals, OYC's Diana Kleiner said, "This isn't a numbers game, since we're not making money off this; this is a gift we're giving to the world, so we want to see if we can bring that to as many people as possible."[41] But it is also important to establish mechanisms for evaluating outcomes relative to the resources invested and the opportunity costs incurred by pursuing these projects. Now that nearly a decade has passed since the first grants were made in the open courseware field, impact can be considered in the context of the investments made in the creation and ongoing maintenance of these resources. This issue might also be approached by more strictly articulating the user populations that these initiatives can realistically expect to reach and measuring usage against them. For instance, if an initiative like OCW or the OLI feels it could and should be of great use to any undergraduate in the United States, then website hits from that demographic might be productively considered relative to the size of that defined user population.

These projects could also do more to understand not only figures like how many unique visitors they receive, but also how important users consider the resources to be. Online courseware sites

[41]Interview with Diana Kleiner, 2/25/09.

like MIT OCW have surveyed users extensively; 80 percent of respondents rate OCW's impact as extremely positive or positive and 96 percent of respondents would recommend it.[42] That said, respondents to a voluntary survey posted on a site may be among its most enthusiastic users. And while these users may rate OCW highly, there is more information to uncover about how they value that resource relative to others. A survey of 3,000 faculty at U.S. four-year colleges and universities conducted by Ithaka S+R found that 18 percent of respondents consider "free web-based educational resources such as iTunes U, YouTube EDU and OpenCourseWare" to be very important to their research and teaching; respondents ranked online courseware tenth most valuable of the eleven types of digital resources listed.[43] An earlier study by Diane Harley found that faculty at research universities, liberal arts colleges, and community colleges used "curricular materials and Web sites created by other faculty and/or other institutions" at much lower rates than they reported using other types of digital resources.[44] It is worth noting that both these surveys focused only on university faculty, who of course make up only a portion of the audience for online courseware; but the approach is one that might be extended to other target populations.

As such outside studies indicate, an expanded usage analysis program would also benefit from paying considerable attention to those who are *not* currently using the content. Harley points out that creators of digital resources like open courseware do not measure nonuse. If online courseware sites continue to consult and report only raw usage numbers, there will be no way to gauge market penetration by determining if the number of users is significant relative to the overall potential user population, the factors that differentiate a nonuser from a user, or the reasons for nonuse.[45] Victor Vuchic of

[42]MIT OpenCourseWare, "2009 Program Evaluation Findings Summary," November 6, 2009, http://ocw.mit.edu/ans7870/global/09_Eval_Summary.pdf.

[43]Schonfeld, Roger C., and Ross Housewright, "2009 Faculty Survey: Key Strategic Insights for Libraries, Publishers and Societies," April 7, 2010, http://ithaka.org/ithaka-s-r/research/faculty-surveys-2000-2009/Faculty%20Study%202009.pdf, 23.

[44]For a summary of this study, based on surveys conducted in 2004–5, see Harley, Diane, "Use and Users of Digital Resources: A Survey Explored Scholars' Attitudes about Educational Technology Environments in the Humanities," *Educause Quarterly*, no. 4 (2007), 15.

[45]Harley writes: "We suggest that, in any study interested in assessing user demand, one

the Hewlett Foundation said in 2008 that usage of open courseware projects "is growing rapidly, but is still only a drop in the bucket compared to how many people could be using it."[46]

These initiatives have certainly done much good, but it is impossible with currently available data to determine *how* much good they have done. The Hewlett Foundation acknowledges that there is "a clear research gap in OER development" and that "while high-quality content is now openly accessible, evidence is needed of its impact."[47] Survey data provide these initiatives with a sense of who uses their materials—people from all over the world and all walks of life, including teachers, students, and lifelong learners. But there has yet to be a systematic and data-driven evaluation of the character and significance of that use across courseware projects. And while enthusiasts in the field are confident that these initiatives will have broad-based or even system-wide impacts on global education, evidence of such disruptive change has not been quantified, nor have research designs for doing so been developed.[48] Such a study would be of great value to university leaders in determining whether the goals of their projects are being realized by users, as well as to funders in calculating the impacts of their investments.

Though founded as altruistic gestures toward the outside world, some of the free and open courseware projects have yielded significant reputational benefits to the universities that developed them.

Although many of these initiatives were designed for the betterment of the world at large, universities can realize a variety of ben-

---

key group to include is individuals who do *not* currently use digital resources, especially if the aim is to increase demand" (Harley, Diane, "Why Understanding Use and Users of Open Education Matters," in *Opening Up Education: The Collective Advancement of Education through Open Technology, Open Content, and Open Knowledge,* ed. M. S. Vijay Kumar and Toru Iiyoshi, Cambridge, Mass.: MIT Press, 2008, 208).

[46]Interview with Victor Vuchic, 8/20/08.

[47]William and Flora Hewlett Foundation, "2009 Budget Memorandum: Education Program," November 17, 2008, http://www.hewlett.org/programs/education-program, 14.

[48]As Casserly said, "we need to demonstrate the added value of OER to teaching and

efits from their involvement with online courseware. Burnishing the parent institution's reputation is rarely an explicit component of open courseware projects' stated missions, but some of the free digital courseware initiatives have nevertheless delivered substantive branded content to broad audiences—and generated considerable media coverage in the process. The effects of these initiatives on perceptions of their parent institutions—in the eyes of the press, of funding agencies, and of the broader university community—are worthy of exploration.

By exposing classroom teaching to the public, these projects have allowed universities to attract attention—and even acclaim—for activities that have always been of central importance but that have historically been difficult to communicate. Berkeley's former provost emphasized the importance of highlighting the university's teaching function, particularly for a land-grant institution. "We get the press we get largely because we have famous scientists that are big-time research people. But the people of California value the teaching side over the research side," former Provost Paul Gray said, "so [webcast.berkeley] is a chance to get some public recognition for the educational role and teaching."[49]

The media attention that these initiatives generate can be an important asset to their hosts, and participating universities are able to leverage their online courseware efforts to varying degrees, depending on the particulars of each program. For example, the impact an initiative has on public perceptions of its parent university can be linked to the extent of institutional branding on the site. The OYC site makes extensive use of the Yale name, logo, and even colors, rendering the site's institutional affiliation unambiguous—so good press for OYC is good press for Yale. In contrast, Carnegie Mellon has consciously elected not to incorporate the university's name into that of the initiative, and it has not made extensive use of its imprimatur past the landing page of the OLI site. The decision to downplay the university's brand was an

---

learning. . . . Essentially it's an untested market. We need to step in and prove its effectiveness if it's there—and we believe it's there, but we need to really demonstrate that" (interview with Catherine Casserly, 8/19/08).

[49]Interview with Paul Gray, 6/9/09.

effort to encourage adoption.[50] But by doing so, Carnegie Mellon is perhaps missing an opportunity to further mold external perceptions of the university as a locus of innovative teaching on the forefront of human-computer interaction.

Furthermore, when a consortial or contributed content model is pursued, branding is sacrificed. Adopting a new name to convey the initiative's joint governance may be a necessary step in founding consortia like AllLearn, Fathom, and NPTEL, in which institution-neutral branding and project names may have helped faculty from different institutions feel comfortable contributing. But this approach dilutes the branding potential for each member institution by subsuming the partners' existing brands under the umbrella of a new, previously unknown brand.[51]

The projects that have done the most proactive marketing outreach have typically generated the most media attention. MIT OCW is a media-savvy project that employs an external relations director, and several individuals involved with the initiative believe that press coverage of OCW has enhanced MIT's overall brand in the eyes of the public. Fathom also allotted staff to market itself and in turn attracted significant media coverage. The Hewlett Foundation did not grant the OLI's request for a marketing budget;[52] perhaps as a result, the project garnered little press attention in its early years. That said, the federal government's interest in funding online courses under the Obama administration has raised the OLI's public profile in recent months.

---

[50]According to Candace Thille, "OLI was designed to contrast to OCW," and one aspect of this contrast is in the approach to branding. "Even though the OLI's content is developed at CMU, I wanted it to be useful at other schools, so once you're inside the learning environment it doesn't scream Carnegie Mellon" (interview with Candace Thille, 8/18/08).

[51]From a branding perspective, universities may also be strategically interested in developing organized online courseware initiatives to hedge against the institution's IP becoming available online without a formal home and branded landing page. The ease and ubiquity of uploading content to the web make it almost inevitable that a university's course materials will leak out, whether through personal faculty websites or student note-sharing services like Harvard's FinalsClub.com (see Parry, Marc, "Free Web Site Helps Harvard Students Cut Class," *Chronicle of Higher Education,* online edition, December 14, 2009). So it may be to the university's advantage to disseminate that content in a centralized, coherent fashion on a site where the institution can exert some control over its presentation (see Bennett, Drake, "FreeHarvardEducation.com: Does Anyone Own What Universities Teach?" *Boston Globe,* online edition, December 13, 2009).

[52]Interview with Candace Thille, 8/18/08.

In all of the better-known initiatives—AllLearn, Fathom, MIT OCW, OYC—the university's president has played a leadership role.[53] An enthusiastic president or provost can personally draw more funds to a project, generate high-profile press releases (as seen in Figure 8.4), or discuss the project in a variety of venues— increasing the attention it receives from the media. Funders may also be influenced by the involvement of high-level administrators. The MIT OCW concept was first raised in a faculty committee convened by the provost, and President Vest personally reached out to leaders of the Mellon and Hewlett Foundations to fund it. This signaled to funders a depth of institutional commitment that Lawrence Rowe, the single professor who founded what became webcast.berkeley, could not—perhaps contributing to the fact that this project did not attract outside foundation money.[54]

Of course, press coverage is not always positive. To mount an online courseware initiative has proven to be a risk, as a failed

---

[53]But a passionate administration does not ensure success: in Fathom's case, this factor alone was not able to trump other problems. From Fathom's cautionary example, it is evident that if an initiative does not deliver on its stated goals (for Fathom, to be a profitable spin-off) or is unpopular among faculty, it may not survive a transition in the university's administration. MIT OCW, on the other hand, was sufficiently institutionalized that it continued to receive support through a change in senior administration, with both a new president and a new provost.

[54]In the early years of the BIBS project, Rowe and Diane Harley shared the concept with some education-oriented foundations, but beyond the Mellon Foundation's funding of one study associated with a webcast course (Chemistry 1A), foundations did not come forward to support the program's operating costs. Rowe recalled that "the Mellon guys were around talking about new learning technologies. We tried to get them to fund the webcast stuff, [but] they weren't interested. We tried to get Sloan to fund it; they didn't think Berkeley was relevant" (interview with Lawrence Rowe, 6/8/09). Harley, who served as executive director of the Berkeley Multimedia Research Center under Rowe, said that she approached the Hewlett Foundation about funding BIBS in the late 1990s but was turned down (interview with Diane Harley, 8/21/08). Hewlett did, however, fund Berkeley professors Alex Pines and Mark Kubinec in the development of extensions to the Chemistry 1A project that had been primarily funded through the Mellon Foundation's Cost-Effective Uses of Technology in Teaching program. Once webcast.berkeley was transferred to Educational Technology Services (ETS) in 2001–2, no further attempts were made to secure grant funding for the operational costs of webcasting. Though webcast.berkeley's relative lack of administrative championing may have hurt its ability to impress outside funders, Martin Trow argues that there is a positive side to launching innovative programs from the bottom up. At least in the early stages of such a project, Trow claims that "some forms of central planning may be counterproductive. . . . A large public university is too big, and its authority too widely dispersed, to make rapid decisions. Individuals and units need to be able to make many small, rapid, risky, and relatively inexpensive decisions from below and have the opportunities and resources to experiment" (Trow, Martin, "The Development of Information Technology in American Higher Education," *Daedalus* 126, no. 4 [Fall 1997], 311).

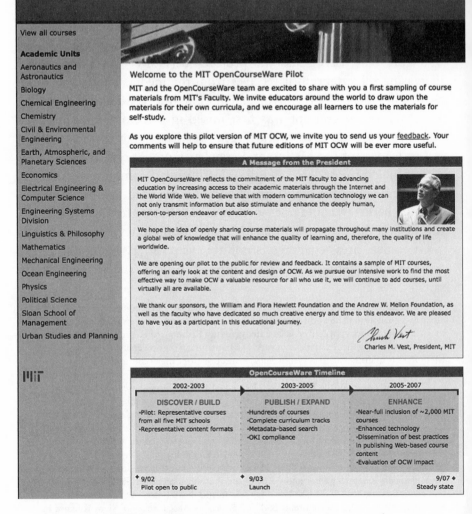

FIGURE 8.4 MIT OpenCourseWare landing page (as it appeared on October 13, 2002). The site's initial webpage announcing the pilot phase of the project featured a prominent message from President Charles Vest, a strong declaration to the public of the institutional support behind OCW.

program can draw negative attention. Multiple postmortems of Fathom, AllLearn, and similar initiatives in the education press made reference to the commercialization of higher education, sometimes portraying the universities behind these initiatives as profit-hungry opportunists—and failed ones at that.[55] The negative light in which a project like Fathom cast its parent university may have made MIT appear all the more altruistic in comparison, perhaps amplifying the positive attention that accompanied OCW's launch.

New entrants to the online courseware field cannot expect to receive the same flood of media attention that MIT did. When asked why other institutions have not launched comprehensive OCW-type efforts, former MIT Provost Robert Brown suggested that "the barrier to entry is enormous for an institution, and the impact of an institution being the second to do it is . . . half as much, maybe even less."[56] The level of press attention that MIT has received relative to similar efforts—as Table 8.1 shows, more press mentions by this measure than all of the other open programs profiled here combined—is evidence of a strong first-mover advantage in this space.[57] In this respect, there are likely to be declining marginal benefits for new entrants if each university mounting an open courseware initiative hopes to appear uniquely generous. In addition to the final tallies, it is worth noting trends over time in the data presented: MIT OCW received its highest number of annual press mentions the year prior to the site's launch, generating buzz that undoubtedly influenced the traffic it received. In contrast, the OLI launched in 2003, but it did not receive heightened attention

---

[55]The 2009 closure of Utah State University's OpenCourseWare project was also covered in the press, and in at least one case has been referenced to raise questions about the sustainability potential of all free and open projects in this space (see Parry, Marc, "Open Courses: Free, but Oh, So Costly," *Chronicle of Higher Education,* online edition, October 11, 2009).

[56]Interview with Robert Brown, 10/27/08.

[57]Naturally this method of counting the raw number of substantive press mentions included in a resource like Nexis has its limitations—for one thing, it cannot convey the quality and reach of the publications in which articles appeared. For instance, Table 8.1 shows the overall number of press mentions for OYC as equal to those of NPTEL, the OLI, and webcast .berkeley. Yet OYC received high-profile press coverage—it was prominently, and quite positively, featured in the *New York Times Magazine* and was the subject of multiple articles and editorials in the education press—within the first two years of the site's launch, while the media have been much slower to take note of some of these other initiatives.

TABLE 8.1

Annual Press Mentions of Online Courseware Initiatives, 2000–10

Initiative	Years Operational	Press coverage (number of substantial mentions)										2010 (through April 20)	Total
		2000	2001	2002	2003	2004	2005	2006	2007	2008	2009		
Fathom	2000-3	44	30	14	12	X	X	X	X	X	X	X	100
Alliance for Lifelong Learning/AllLearn	2001-5	8	8	6	4	2	1	1	X	X	X	X	30
MIT OpenCourseWare (OCW)	2002–	X	54	25	15	5	7	15	19	7	11	7	165
Carnegie Mellon Open Learning Initiative (OLI)	2003–	X	X	X	3	0	1	0	1	0	6	3	14
Open Yale Courses (OYC)	2007–	X	X	X	X	X	X	X	4	4	2	3	13
webcast.berkeley	2001–	X	0	0	0	0	0	5	4	3	0	1	13
National Programme on Technology Enhanced Learning (NPTEL)	2004–	X	X	X	X	0	1	2	2	3	5	0	13

Notes: Shading indicates years non-operational; X indicates no press mentions.

Only substantial mentions and not cursory listings of these selected online courseware projects were counted. "Press coverage" was limited to the following types of U.S. and international print sources: newspapers, magazines, journals, newsletters, press releases, and newswires. Online media, such as blogs, were not included. "Years operational" refers to the years following the launch of the projects' websites (and in the cases of Fathom and AllLearn, the end date is the year the initiatives officially ceased operation); any press mentions in years prior to start dates covered the formation of these programs or impending launch of their official web presences.

Press coverage was retrieved only through news sources available in Nexis (http://www.nexis.com). The 1998–2008 data were collected in March 2009, the 2009 data were retrieved in December 2009, and the 2010 data on April 20, 2010.

This table is not presented as a comprehensive listing of every substantial press mention these projects have received over the past decade; to ensure continuity of search methods, only one database has been queried to produce these data. These numbers should, however, offer an approximation of the level of press attention these efforts have received relative to one another.

Data were prepared by Lisa Bonifacic.

in the press until the start of the Obama administration in 2009, when the initiative became closely linked with the federal government's plans to develop a national clearinghouse of freely available online courses.

In addition to generating positive press attention, open courseware projects can help institutions of higher education communicate their social value to the governments that oversee their budgets or approve their tax-exempt status. Vest discussed the pressure Congress has put on university endowments, which were coming under strict review by the federal government around the time MIT was developing OCW. "So one of the things that I spent a lot of my time on—and not just narrowly for MIT, but for all public and private research universities in general—was promoting here in Washington to anyone who would listen the importance of these institutions and the return to the nation that [they constitute on] investments in science and engineering research and advanced education." Vest explained that the OCW team did not originally plan to use the initiative for federal advocacy, "but once we launched it, I did often point it out as a way that an institution that had been funded very generously was giving back. And I found that I didn't often have to be the one to say it; people said it for me."[58] Berkeley administrators have similarly pointed to their webcast project as a means of demonstrating the university's value to the broader public.

Beyond the media and government funding bodies, online courseware projects can help foster positive perceptions of the university among other important constituencies. For example, publishing a suite of free online course content could help a university attract prospective students by showing off the strength of the faculty; such a benefit would align online courseware efforts with investments that institutions are currently making in recruitment brochures or de-

---

[58]Interview with Charles Vest, 9/30/08. Current MIT President Susan Hockfield also brought up OCW in her testimony before the U.S. Secretary of Education's Commission on the Future of Higher Education—which examined college accessibility, affordability, and accountability—as an example of MIT's efforts to benefit the greater public beyond the Institute's walls (Hockfield, Susan, "Testimony Prepared for the U.S. Department of Education, Secretary of Education's Commission on the Future of Higher Education," public hearing, Boston, March 20, 2006, http://www2.ed.gov/about/bdscomm/list/hiedfuture/2nd-hearing/hockfield.pdf, 4).

tailed admissions websites.[59] If advertised to the university's alumni, those same lecture materials could also help graduates feel more connected to the current life of the institution, as do alumni magazines and reunion weekends. As discussed further in the preceding chapters and the following section, recorded lectures also serve as study aids or expanded course catalogues for enrolled students, and in that sense perform functions similar to those of course management systems and note-taking services.

Based on data collected in user surveys, the MIT OCW team feels confident that the initiative is generating these kinds of returns for the institution. "Over half of incoming freshmen are aware of OCW prior to choosing MIT, and a third of those cite OCW as a significant influence in their choice of school. Ninety-four percent of students at MIT access the site, and half of alumni surveyed use the site."[60] But whether familiarity with OCW—by prospective students, enrolled students, or alumni—translates into tangible gains for the university is difficult to determine.[61] In this sense, online courseware projects face a dilemma similar to that of more explicitly media-focused public relations activities. As a recent *Chronicle of Higher Education* piece by a head of university public relations states, "We have faith that the news-media coverage contributes to the college's overall identity and enhances its image, even if we cannot measure exactly how."[62]

In sum, while the free and open courseware initiatives themselves; the foundations, institutional leaders, and governments that support them; and the press that covers them have emphasized the good that these efforts do for the world at large,[63] the internal im-

---

[59]At least one OCW Consortium member has explicitly revealed the recruiting motivation behind a distance learning project: a University of Southern Queensland press release announcing an international learning network project states that "in addition to the altruistic motives, the University is also excited about the opportunity the agreement creates in relation to student recruitment" (quoted in Huijser, Bedford, and Bull, "OpenCourseWare, Global Access and the Right to Education," 4).

[60]D'Oliveira and Lerman, "OpenCourseWare: Working through Financial Challenges."

[61]And other parent universities have not undertaken the same sort of polling that MIT has conducted in an effort to quantify strategic benefits back to the institution.

[62]Powell, Russell S., "The Productive PR Office," *Chronicle of Higher Education*, online edition, December 11, 2009.

[63]Former MIT Provost Robert Brown pointed out that "when the foundations were fund-

pacts of these initiatives should not be discounted—and may prove just as important (if not more so) to these projects' continued success and sustainability.

Long-term financial sustainability remains an unresolved issue for most of the free and open courseware projects examined in this book.

Discussing free and open online courseware projects for a 2009 *Fast Company* article, Catherine Casserly of the Hewlett Foundation commented that "the advent of the Web brings the ability to disseminate high-quality materials at almost no cost, leveling the playing field."[64] But while the marginal costs of digital distribution of content are much lower than those of print, there are still significant upfront costs associated with the production of courseware. Even after materials have been developed, the server capacity and bandwidth associated with disseminating these materials to users remain ongoing expenses. Furthermore, given the constantly evolving digital environment, courseware initiatives cannot remain static, but must adapt to meet contemporary format standards and user expectations.[65] These projects therefore need to develop strategies to pay not only for recurring operational costs, but also for investments in continuing innovation.[66] Third parties like foundations covered the start-up costs of content development for many initiatives, but they may be reluctant to pay for ongoing opera-

---

ing it, that's what they were funding—they weren't funding the internal piece at all" (interview with Robert Brown, 10/27/08).

[64]Quoted in Kamenetz, Anya, "How Web-Savvy Edupunks are Transforming American Higher Education," *Fast Company*, online edition, for the print edition of September 1, 2009.

[65]Discussing MIT OCW, Catherine Casserly said, "If they don't evolve, they will become outdated, so it's a question of how much they want to continue to lead in this space. And I think they're going to want to, because now their reputation's riding on it to a certain extent" (interview with Catherine Casserly, 8/19/08).

[66]For this reason, a recent Ithaka S+R report defines sustainability as "the ability to generate or gain access to the resources—financial or otherwise—needed to protect and increase the value of the content or service for those who use it" (Maron, Nancy L., K. Kirby Smith, and Matthew Loy, "Sustaining Digital Resources: An On-the-Ground View of Projects Today," Ithaka Case Studies in Sustainability, July 2009, http://www.ithaka.org/ithaka-s-r/strategy/ithaka-case-studies-in-sustainability/report/SCA_Ithaka_SustainingDigitalResources_Report.pdf, 11).

tions, so finding a regular source of funding to offset these costs is a key sustainability challenge facing the field.

With the exception of webcast.berkeley, the open courseware initiatives profiled here were launched using outside funding, with the Hewlett Foundation playing a primary role.[67] Hewlett and Mellon funded most of the start-up costs associated with MIT OCW; Hewlett was the major source of seed capital for the OLI and OYC; and the Indian government has bankrolled the NPTEL start-up costs.[68] Because the field was so new, funders typically did not require projects to have definite business plans to support ongoing operations after initial grants had been spent. According to Marshall "Mike" Smith, former director of Hewlett's education program, Hewlett has asked grantees to "address sustainability," but in the initial grant proposals it did "not ask people to propose a model itself."[69] Hewlett has, however, required that the funded portions of these projects remain openly accessible (i.e., without fees for access or use) in perpetuity. In MIT's case, the Institute pledged to "assume full responsibility for the costs of sustaining OCW as a permanent activity" once the project reached its so-called Steady

[67]The Hewlett Foundation's organizational leadership and funding generosity have been of central importance, both in seeding this terrain and in shaping its open ideology. In fact, it is difficult to imagine how this field would have developed in the absence of Hewlett's support of it. The Foundation's major infusion of capital toward open-education projects—according to personal correspondence with program officer Victor Vuchic, nearly $110 million between 2001 and 2010—and its institutional commitment to free and open online courseware have helped shape the business models and access policies in this space.

Since Hewlett created a division of its education program devoted to funding projects of this kind, the model of providing high-quality content from brand-name universities—underwritten by outside start-up funding and available through open licenses—has dominated this sector and informed university thinking around developing such initiatives. For example, although the design and pedagogy of the OLI reflect Carnegie Mellon's institutional strengths and character, the initiative's access policy responds to Hewlett's "open" objectives for grants in its OER division. And, after attempting a revenue-generating model in AllLearn and observing the trajectory of Hewlett's grant-making in this area, Yale pitched a project aligned with the Foundation's clearly expressed priorities. For more on Hewlett's role, and for an overview of the funding it provided, see Atkins, Daniel E., John Seely Brown, and Allen L. Hammond, "A Review of the Open Educational Resources (OER) Movement: Achievements, Challenges, and New Opportunities," Report to the William and Flora Hewlett Foundation, February 2007, especially page 5.

[68]A variety of foreign efforts besides NPTEL have been funded by national governments. For example, the Dutch and Vietnamese governments have made investment in online courseware a national priority, and the Joint Information Systems Committee (JISC), the funding arm of the British university system, has seeded strategic courseware investments.

[69]Interview with Marshall Smith, 8/19/08.

State phase.[70] But as these start-up grants near completion—and as the Hewlett Foundation's priorities shift away from institution-specific open courseware programs in favor of OER projects like open textbooks, open educational games, and uses of open content in the K-12 sector—Hewlett has begun formulating an "exit strategy" from these initial investments.[71] The need for sustainability models is therefore becoming more immediate.

The availability of significant grant funding has allowed many initiatives the flexibility to experiment with creative approaches to the production of courseware, but it has also meant that long-term sustainability planning has been a lower priority; developing practical sustainability solutions is often supplanted by more immediate concerns.[72] OLI co-director Joel Smith said that in the OER world, members of the community would often "try to have a meeting about sustainability and . . . all dance around it, and that's something we really need to figure out." He added that "when one of these things blinks out, I'm not even sure that's going to be a wakeup call. Lots of powerful but little-used digital environments have just disappeared, and that's something that I fear for all these efforts."[73] At least one free and open courseware project—a Hewlett-funded initiative at Utah State University (USU)—has

---

[70]"MIT OpenCourseWare: A Proposal Submitted to the William and Flora Hewlett Foundation," April 27, 2001, principal investigators Harold Abelson, Robert A. Brown, and Steven R. Lerman, 16. Not all Hewlett grantees have made similar commitments, and the methods by which MIT would sustain the initiative were not specified.

[71]William and Flora Hewlett Foundation, "2009 Budget Memorandum: Education Program," 13. Other foundations that seeded this field have also closed or reorganized grant-making programs in this space. The Alfred P. Sloan Foundation, which had invested over $80 million in online education programs since the early 1990s, discontinued its grant-making program in 2009 (Parry, Marc, "Sloan Foundation Ends Major Grant Program for Online Education," *Chronicle of Higher Education,* online edition, April 6, 2009). In addition, the Andrew W. Mellon Foundation, one of the banner funders of MIT OCW in 2001 and a steady supporter of open-source software, another pillar of OER, drastically reorganized its Research in Information Technology (RIT) program in January 2010 (Parry, Marc, "In Potential Blow to Open-Source Software, Mellon Foundation Closes Grant Program," Wired Campus blog [*Chronicle of Higher Education*], January 5, 2010, http://chronicle.com/blogPost/In-Potential-Blow-to-Open-S/19519/).

[72]Moreover, reliance on foundation money also carries the risk that the initiatives may be out of touch with the needs of specific users. As discussed previously, their sustainability is not dependent on financial contributions from customers, which in more traditional marketplaces serve as a common tool for judging the impact and efficacy of services.

[73]Interview with Joel Smith, 9/10/08.

already shut down.[74] Yet most of the initiatives profiled here have still not developed comprehensive strategies to address sustainability. Former OCW Consortium Director John Dehlin said that "we've been having the same sustainability and the same evaluation conversations for five years, and they're no more advanced."[75]

Hewlett's 2009 education program budget memorandum states that "the issue of sustainability remains complex" and that "clear measures of success are needed for this critical infrastructure dimension."[76] As former Hewlett education program director Marshall "Mike" Smith has acknowledged, generating measurable results "and the sustainability goal are very tightly linked. The more we can make it obvious that the open materials are helping to solve certain educational problems, the more likely we are to move . . . to an overall sustainable system."[77]

University funding may be the most obvious source of support for these initiatives, but there is no guarantee that the parent institutions will be willing to shoulder the burden of funding them in

[74]USU's OpenCourseWare was shuttered in the fall of 2009, when the university and state legislature did not elect to provide funding for ongoing operations beyond the conclusion of the project's grants from the Hewlett Foundation (which totaled $4,585,000 for USU OCW and related projects between 2003 and 2007). The project's charismatic leader, David Wiley, left Utah State for Brigham Young University in the summer of 2008; Utah State OCW's closure may therefore point to leadership stability as another key factor in achieving sustainability for projects of this nature. Ithaka S+R's 2009 "Case Studies in Sustainability" report refers to the "what would happen if we were hit by a bus" scenario that plagues projects whose leaders' personal dedication is crucial to their survival (Maron, Smith, and Loy, "Sustaining Digital Resources," 14). USU OCW has been the only Hewlett-funded open courseware project to close thus far, and leadership turnover and management issues are seen by some as unique challenges that this project faced. But OCW Consortium president Steve Carson told the *Chronicle of Higher Education* that this development "points to the issue of having a diversified set of support for your project. If you've got one way that the project is being supported, then it obviously puts you at some level of risk" (quoted in Parry, Marc, "Utah State U's OpenCourseWare Closes Because of Budget Woes," *Chronicle of Higher Education,* online edition, September 3, 2009). News of this program's closure has prompted some in the education press to postulate that more initiatives could meet a similar fate (see Parry, "Open Courses: Free, but Oh So Costly").

[75]Interview with John Dehlin, 3/4/09.

[76]William and Flora Hewlett Foundation, "2009 Budget Memorandum: Education Program," 12.

[77]Interview with Marshall Smith, 8/19/08. Smith added that "you can only operate on goodwill and positive motives for so long; at some point you have to make the business case that this thing really is having an effect. It may not be a business case based on dollars, but a business case based on positive results."

perpetuity. Open courseware initiatives have always received some degree of in-kind support from their affiliated institutions in order to minimize direct costs. But if that support must increase to cover the costs of staffing and operating these resources when foundation capital expires, project leaders may feel additional pressure to demonstrate their initiatives' value to the parent institutions, their connection to the universities' overall strategic priorities, and the degree to which they have taken root within the university communities. Two examples illustrate the importance of these factors: while the OLI reflects Carnegie Mellon's interdisciplinary and data-driven ethos, it involves relatively few faculty members, and the university's provost has expressed strong reservations at the prospect of committing to fund this project indefinitely. In contrast, MIT OCW engages virtually every faculty member on campus and has been championed by university leaders from the beginning; the Institute has subsequently committed to providing a portion of the program's operating budget on a permanent basis.

Of course, the fact that open courseware projects have not been self-supporting and may well require long-term institutional subvention is not inherently problematic. Many university activities—from libraries to English departments—are budgeted as cost centers that rely on continuing institutional subsidy. The university funds them in large part due to their direct benefit to enrolled students and to local faculty. But issues of sustainability and institutional funding are much more pressing when it comes to public goods such as OER, as these resources are often designed primarily to benefit audiences outside the university community. So the question is not only whether the parent institution *can* sustain an open courseware project in this economic climate, but rather why it should.

Leaders of several participating universities have described online courseware activities as natural offshoots of the university's mission—to create and disseminate knowledge and to educate the next generation—in the digital age.[78] Sharing faculty research and

---

[78]For instance, the webcast.berkeley team feels that the project directly contributes to UC Berkeley's public mission as a land-grant university to provide broad access to education. As ETS director Mara Hancock said, "our mission as a public institution—and [particularly] at this institution, being the flagship university for the UC system as well as one

discoveries externally has long been the main vehicle for elite universities to reach a wider public; the host institutions profiled here have traditionally fulfilled the educational component of their missions by providing courses to a relatively small number of enrolled students. To assert that the mass distribution of the university's instructional content to nonstudents directly contributes to its mission is to view that mission as radically more expansive than it has been historically. Interviews with academic leaders (especially at some private institutions) have shown that, in the context of free and open online courseware projects, leading universities are beginning to explore the boundaries of such an amplified instructional responsibility.[79]

Beyond their fit with institutional missions, continuing internal support for these projects might also be justified by more concrete demonstrations of their local value, as previously discussed. For instance, freely available, open-access online courseware may also prove advantageous in recruiting new students and faculty. Just as universities have increasingly elaborate websites—which have quickly become necessary components of every university's outreach to prospective freshmen or faculty hires—soon posted syllabi or lecture videos might regularly provide a valuable window into the institution for those interested in formally joining it someday.[80] Usage by enrolled students, as a study aid or expanded course

---

of the preeminent public institutions—is to bring that knowledge to the community. We're funded in large part by the community with public dollars, and this is a way we can give back" (interview with Mara Hancock, 6/8/09).

[79]MIT president Susan Hockfield sees OCW as compatible with the Institute's broader mission of "intellectual transfer—moving the things we do on campus out into the world" (interview with Susan Hockfield, 10/30/08). At a speech on the internationalization of the university in Athens in 2008, Yale President Richard C. Levin discussed OYC as an example of his institution exploiting technology to increase access to education: "The Internet offers a whole new range of possibilities for universities seeking to expand and redefine their traditional mission of disseminating knowledge through publication" (Levin, Richard C., "The Internationalization of the University," speech delivered May 6, 2008, Athens, Greece, http://opa.yale.edu/president/message.aspx?id=7).

[80]In 2007 David Wiley stated that "about five years from now, everyone's going to have one of these. It's going to be part of their Web site, just like when you go to a university Web site now you expect to find information about admissions, registration, tuition and fees" (quoted in Chute, Eleanor, "How to Take a Course at MIT Free—At Home," *Pittsburgh Post-Gazette*, online edition, November 18, 2007).

catalogue, is another plausible justification for ongoing internal support of these resources. Institutional investments in similar student support services are not uncommon: many universities staff a writing center, support course management systems to maintain course materials for enrolled students, facilitate tutoring networks, and encourage students to take advantage of research assistance from librarians. If university decision makers come to view online courseware projects as sufficiently aligned with any or all of these other common efforts, support for such projects might eventually be folded into the university's general cost of doing business.[81]

Some projects have begun to pursue sources of financial support other than institutional funding. For example, several years ago OCW began seeking private donations to cover the portion of its operating budget not provided by central university funding. It succeeded in receiving a $6 million gift from a company founded by an MIT alumna, and in one year generated $150,000 in small donations through direct fundraising appeals.[82] Since 2005 OCW has also embedded links to Amazon.com in course syllabi through the

[81]It is worth noting that if usage by enrolled students is an institution's sole justification for investment in online courseware, whether the resource is offered openly and freely to the world or hosted on an internal platform is immaterial. Converting preexisting online courseware materials designed for internal usage to open-access versions would require an additional investment of time and money; universities will likely want their course materials to appear more polished if they are posted in public view, and there are IP issues to consider when opening up a university's course content to the wider world. (Yet webcast.berkeley's more lenient approach to vetting content for possible IP violations has demonstrated that initiatives which devote relatively few resources to this issue have not faced negative consequences.) But if an institution has already invested in creating this content as a student service and can afford a modest additional investment in preparing the materials for public view, this book has shown that there are important branding opportunities to be realized that may well outweigh such costs—with the added benefit of creating materials that may be of use to the world at large.

[82]D'Oliveira and Lerman, "OpenCourseWare: Working through Financial Challenges." OCW is interested in finding more corporate donors in order to explore what it calls "NPR-style underwriting" of content in the future—an approach that emerged from a sustainability planning process in which it engaged consultants from Bain & Company, working pro bono. Bain conducted surveys of stakeholders inside and outside MIT and presented OCW with a slate of possible ideas for generating revenue; Carson said that seeking underwriting funds seemed to be the appropriate course of action because it would not strain the faculty and, unlike more commercial options, would fit with MIT's institutional values (interview with Steve Carson, 3/18/10).

Amazon Associates Program, and it receives 10 percent of the price of any purchases originating from the OCW page.[83]

The OLI has gone in a different direction. Its strategic advantages derive largely from its technological and pedagogical approach, which can be applied to many different educational scenarios. As funding agencies have shifted their focus to K-12 education and community colleges, the OLI has reoriented itself toward content of interest to the community college population. The OLI team, with funding from the Gates, Hewlett, and Lumina Foundations, is now at work on the Community College Open Learning Initiative (CC-OLI), in which Carnegie Mellon learning experts and course developers will partner with community college faculty to develop course content for this sector.[84] The $4 million in additional funds awarded for the CC-OLI effort will allow the project to remain operational but has required it to change course, as the new content it supports will no longer be based directly on Carnegie Mellon courses.[85] This may be a prudent adaptation to changing circumstances, but it also underscores the challenges Carnegie Mellon has faced in achieving long-term sustainability for its initial offerings.

[83]OCW derives "about $30,000 per year" from these Amazon referrals (d'Oliveira and Lerman, "OpenCourseWare: Working through Financial Challenges"), so as Carson has noted, it "doesn't generate enough income—even at our traffic levels—to make much difference" (personal communication with Steve Carson, 3/11/10), though the arrangement also requires minimal effort on OCW's part. According to Carson, MIT faculty are allowed to opt out of the Amazon linking from their OCW courses.

[84]Fishman, Josh, "Community Colleges Get Gift of Millions for Online Education," Wired Campus blog (*Chronicle of Higher Education*), December 3, 2009, http://chronicle .com/blogPost/Community-Colleges-Get-Gift/9067/. Also see Carnegie Mellon University, "Three Foundations Grant $4 Million in Awards to Carnegie Mellon's Open Learning Initiative,"pressrelease,December15,2009,http://www.cmu.edu/news/archive/2009/December/ dec15_openlearninggrants.shtml.

[85]Interview with Candace Thille, 10/28/09. In addition to the $4 million awarded for CC-OLI, Carnegie Mellon received funding from the Kresge Foundation in 2010 to support the creation of an OLI "Concepts of Computer Science" course, created with the help of Carnegie Mellon computer science faculty and aimed at undergraduates with non-technical backgrounds (Kresge Foundation, "Foundation Center: Grant Details," http://maps .foundationcenter.org/grantmakers/grant_profile_page.php?nonp=1&nof=1&id=1690208 3&gmkey=KRES002; interview with Candace Thille, 8/11/09). This grant is a positive sign that funds to convert Carnegie Mellon content to OLI format may continue to materialize, though it also illustrates the piecemeal fashion in which the initiative must go about obtaining such funding in the absence of grants the size of Hewlett's or permanent operational support from the university.

Free and open courseware projects might also find paths to sustainability by earning revenue directly. This might include a "freemium" approach—offering the core content freely, as is a common stipulation of grant funding, while also creating enhanced versions that might be sold to users for a fee. The OLI was the first of the projects profiled here to attempt a freemium business model through its Academic Version, which is targeted to faculty using the OLI in the classroom. However, according to project co-director Joel Smith, the fees that the OLI has been able to collect have not been "at a level that provides us with income for sustainability."[86] The Hewlett Foundation has expressed support for the exploration of advertising models, but elite universities have thus far opted not to pursue them. "I can understand why some of the higher ed institutions [are] hesitant," observed Casserly. "Something like advertising is such a cultural shift for academics that it's going to take time."[87]

Universities with entirely different approaches to the production of open courseware may be better positioned to achieve long-term sustainability. One model that has shown strong progress toward becoming self-sustaining is that of the Open University (OU) in the United Kingdom. Founded in 1969, the OU UK is a public institution geared toward distance education. With the support of the Hewlett Foundation, the OU UK's OpenLearn project has made over 5,400 hours of the university's course content available for free.[88] Project director Andy Lane has said that links to the paid content on the free and open site have resulted in at least 9,000 new customers for the university's distance education courses.[89]

[86]Interview with Joel Smith, 8/6/09. As stated in Chapter 4, student fees from sales of the Academic Version of OLI courses generated only about $25,000 in the 2007–8 academic year—not nearly enough to cover the costs of a program with an annual operating budget of nearly $1 million. Another Hewlett grantee, the National Repository of Online Courses, has fared better in its efforts to offer its (mostly K-12) content freely and openly for individual use while charging a subscription fee to member institutions that use the materials as part of their regular curricula for enrolled students (see Kolowich, Steve, "Open Courses for Community Colleges," *Inside Higher Ed*, April 28, 2010).

[87]Interview with Catherine Casserly, 4/20/10.

[88]This figure applies to the period between the project's start date in 2005 and April 2008 ("About Us: Our Story," OpenLearn, http://www.open.ac.uk/openlearn/about-us/our-story.php).

[89]Interview with Andy Lane, 3/3/09.

For OU UK, continued institutional support for OpenLearn could therefore be justified as a loss leader for the university's traditional, credit-bearing distance education model.[90]

But OU UK has always been a distance-based institution, and OpenLearn differs from the projects profiled here in that its courses were born digital and always intended for online delivery to the OU's enrolled students.[91] Institutions like MIT and Yale, which have required a great deal of upfront investment to convert courses designed for face-to-face delivery into digital format but do not offer online credit, would not be able to replicate this model directly. The OU is also a nonselective institution in which nearly anyone can enroll, in contrast to the highly selective residential universities profiled here.[92] In essence, the OU has added an open and free component on top of an existing, sustainable online business model. The reverse sequence—building the online courseware first and then attempting to find a sustainability model to support it, as the initiatives profiled in this book have done—is proving to be much more challenging.

More radically, open-education enthusiasts like David Wiley and Christopher Mackie have suggested that if universities entrusted enrolled students to create online courseware themselves, with light supervision from tenured faculty or professional staff, the operating costs of such programs could decrease dramatically. The premise of this proposal is that enrolled students would receive university credit for creating high-quality digital materials associ-

[90]This could be considered a "freemium" model, with the open courses offered for free to drive business to the premium product—the enrolled credit-bearing courses. Relatedly, research on a pilot project conducted by Brigham Young University's Independent Study program—a financially self-sustaining distance learning program that has recently created open versions of its otherwise credit-bearing extension courses—has shown that opening up versions of these courses does not cause paid enrollments to drop (Johansen, Justin K., "The Impact of OpenCourseWare on Paid Enrollment in Distance Learning Courses," doctoral dissertation, Brigham Young University, October 2009, http://contentdm.lib.byu.edu/ETD/image/etd3317.pdf).

[91]Of the OpenLearn content, Andy Lane said, "it's all legacy materials; it already existed" (interview with Andy Lane, 3/3/09).

[92]"The Open University was established to be 'open', with no entry requirements. Nearly all of our courses continue to have no entry requirements" other than that matriculating students must be at least 16 years old ("About the OU: Open Admissions," http://www.open.ac.uk/about/ou/p7.shtml).

ated with courses they are taking—and so would not need to be paid.[93] Such a cost-saving approach to producing online courseware would obviously constitute a sharp departure from the highly authoritative, faculty-centered content creation model outlined in this book.

By offering content only, without human interaction or university credit, online courseware allows parent universities to explore the opportunities afforded them by the internet without threatening their core value proposition.

Opening up versions of elite university courses to a mass audience can be seen as a radically populist gesture, in that it enables a significantly wider audience to share in some aspects of the university experience. But these activities do nothing to increase accessibility to the most valuable aspect of a university education—the credential or degree. Though they are exposing some course content for public view, by not offering credits associated with their online courseware initiatives, participating universities retain a significant portion of the value they provide only for enrolled students.[94] Many subsequent factors dictating the shape these projects have taken can be understood in light of that decision.

Declining to offer university credit to online users mitigates the risk of devaluing the traditional degree, maintaining the prestige associated with selectivity (traditional admission) and the on-campus experience (traditional enrollment). By decoupling the traditionally "bundled" aspects of the courses they offer—providing

[93]Interview with David Wiley, 8/18/09; Mackie, Christopher J., "A Modest Proposal for Utterly Transforming Higher Education Pedagogy and Intellectual Property Generation on the Way to Achieving Sustainable OER—And Why Your Campus Might Want to Try It," presentation, Open Education Conference 2009, Vancouver, August 13, 2009. Mackie was formerly with the Mellon Foundation's RIT program.

[94]Some of the institutions involved in this study do offer forms of university credit online: for instance, Stanford University has a long-standing online masters program in engineering, and the UC Berkeley Extension offers credits to local and online students (see http://extension.berkeley.edu/online/). But these programs are not pathways to credit for the universities' core undergraduate offerings, which remain limited to traditional, on-campus students.

digital versions of course content for enrichment purposes only, yet reserving credit for enrolled students—these universities maintain the scarcity that has defined their business model by limiting access, ensuring that admissions rates stay competitively low.

MIT's example is instructive, as the university has strived to maintain a sharp distinction between OCW and its enrolled student experience. Members of the OCW team recalled that when the question of offering credits was raised in early discussions, "there was sort of a philosophical resistance to it" among the faculty; MIT alumni also expressed concerns at the thought of granting credit to online users.[95] Former MIT Provost Robert Brown recounted that in planning the OCW effort, the faculty subcommittee realized that "we're not trying to devalue the brand, we're trying to increase the brand. . . . So whatever you do, it can't be MIT, it can't quite be us."[96] Preserving that distinction between MIT's online offerings and the university's degrees required that OCW's offerings remain strictly recreational and not for credit. As faculty committee member Shigeru Miyagawa said, "We would not offer any kind of MIT credit or degree—we decided that we would not do anything to dilute the MIT brand."[97] Clearly MIT and other institutions have determined that giving away their course content does not undercut the value of the traditional university experience, but giving away the credit might—suggesting that universities view their credit-granting role as an essential source of their value.

By declining to offer credits for online courseware ventures, these universities have also saved themselves the logistical complication associated with a highly involved form of e-commerce. Credit-bearing distance programs would require administrative infrastructure—admissions and remote tuition collection processes that would operate on a course-by-course basis, remote evaluations, and so forth—for which traditional universities like Berkeley and Carnegie Mellon are simply not set up. (And, as AllLearn found,

[95]Interviews with Anne Margulies, 10/28/08, and Steve Carson, 10/27/08. Carson said that MIT's unwillingness to give credit partly stems from "the concerns the alumni had: their degree is worth something, and they want to protect the value of that degree."

[96]Interview with Robert Brown, 10/27/08.

[97]Interview with Shigeru Miyagawa, 10/29/08.

attempting to sidestep some of these obstacles by obtaining separate accreditation for an independent spin-off is no easy task.)[98] By not offering fee-based credit for completion of online courses, these universities deny themselves a potentially lucrative revenue stream, but they also save themselves the expense of developing a more sophisticated technological infrastructure.

Former OCW director Anne Margulies said that the idea of offering credit did come up "early and often" in preliminary discussions of OCW, but that in addition to faculty members' principled objections, there was also "no clear, simple, practical way to pull it off."[99] In this respect, Carnegie Mellon's example is telling: unlike many of its peers, the university seems not to harbor a philosophical objection to offering credit to "outsiders," but it struggles with practical considerations like finding the right price point for credit-bearing courses.[100] The provost feels it would be unfair to charge less than the $4,000 that Carnegie Mellon students pay per course, but he is concerned that this price is too high to keep pace with the market rate for online distance education courses.[101]

The content of these initiatives has also been influenced by their enrichment-only status. When courses are offered for credit, a rigorous set of standards must be put in place to ensure that they are pedagogically sound, students are supported, and student learning outcomes are properly assessed. Indeed, the university accreditation process is designed to ensure that an institution's degree reflects an appropriate educational experience, and faculty committees charged with approving changes to programs of study provide additional safeguards to ensure curricular quality. But universities need not hold themselves to the same standards when it comes to non-credit-bearing entities. Once the university has decided that an offering will not be offered for credit, it has much more flexibility—published

[98]As discussed in Chapter 2, under Herbert Allison's leadership, AllLearn explored the possibility of obtaining New York state accreditation so that it might offer credits as a pathway to sustainability without encroaching on individual member universities' credentialing policies. But it found that there were too many obstacles to becoming independently accredited (interviews with Herbert Allison, 3/11/09, and Peter Bernstein, 4/28/09).

[99]Interview with Anne Margulies, 10/28/08.

[100]Interview with Mark Kamlet, 9/11/08.

[101]Interview with Joel Smith, 9/10/08.

course materials need not be complete, and the obligation to provide interactive features or student assessment and feedback is absent. Were MIT OCW courses to be become credit-bearing, they would have to consist of much more than just a syllabus, reading list, minimal lecture notes, and homework problems presented without solutions or the possibility of receiving instructional feedback. But because OCW is designed only for enrichment, MIT need not invest in creating complete online versions of the educational experience its students receive in Cambridge—it can provide course *materials,* not courses. The same holds true for the many other programs taking a similar approach.

....

These fascinating experiments reveal an array of creative endeavors to extend the university's reach. The free and open programs profiled here have many strengths—chief among them that their global accessibility has unlimited potential, enabling free materials to reach a conceivably boundless audience. But this strength comes with considerable challenges. For example, support of openly and freely available courseware raises concerns about ongoing sustainability in a climate of constrained university, foundation, and government budgets. Furthermore, an approach that emphasizes giving away materials to the broadest possible audience may not prioritize rigorous understanding of users and their needs.

This chapter has examined the current state of these projects. But online courseware's story continues to unfold in real time, and numerous directions for its future development can be envisioned. The following chapter considers the transformations these projects may undergo—and the varied impacts that might arise—should online courseware become an increasingly common strategy for universities in the digital age.

EPILOGUE:
IMPLICATIONS FOR THE FUTURE

The previous chapter analyzes various dimensions of online courseware projects in their current forms. But in this evolving field, the terrain is shifting rapidly. With the sustainability of online courseware initiatives in question and evidence of their impact encouraging but inconclusive, it will be critical to demonstrate the concrete value that projects like these can provide—either within their parent institutions or elsewhere in the higher-education sector. University leaders contemplating new courseware investments must not only consider their peers' experiences to date, but also think strategically about the transformative opportunities that online instruction might hold for their institutions in the long run. This final chapter offers insight into where the field might be headed and considers how its ripple effects may be felt throughout higher education.

A number of future trajectories can be imagined for the projects profiled here, with different approaches to content creation—and varying institutional contexts—opening up distinct possibilities. Broadcasting digital audio or video recordings of lectures—as described in this book's chapters on webcast.berkeley, Open Yale Courses (OYC), and the National Programme on Technology Enhanced Learning (NPTEL)—is becoming an increasingly common activity, as is evident from the growing amount of content on iTunes U and YouTube.[1] In addition

[1]This is true even though universities' iTunes U and YouTube channels are often dominated by non-course-related content, such as captured special events, promotional materials, and performances, in addition to or in lieu of lectures (see Young, Jeffrey R., "College 2.0:

to serving as study aids for review purposes, recorded lectures—in particular those, like webcast.berkeley, that are posted within days of live delivery—may also allow students to time-shift a portion of their education and "attend" lectures on demand. Current students, familiar with services like Hulu, TiVo, and streaming Netflix, are increasingly accustomed to receiving content anywhere at any time, and they have mounting expectations of what constitutes standard technological support for their education. Berkeley Provost George Breslauer said that with each generation, students "increasingly expect to have these options available because that's what they grew up with, that's what they're comfortable with. So to some extent, giving them the benefits of those kinds of technologies is just part of the undergraduate experience wherever it's being held."[2]

Should student demand continue to drive selective universities toward lecture capture initiatives, the availability of recorded content might prompt changes in lecture-based pedagogies, even at the elite level. Berkeley's approach to webcasting has established that lecture capture costs can be kept low enough to enable the recording of key courses every time they are taught—a valuable study tool for students that can serve as a welcome supplement to their otherwise traditional, in-person classroom experience.[3] But lecture capture could potentially enable more substantial curricular change. This technology content makes possible the institutional reuse of one set of recorded lectures several semesters in a row, obviating the need for a professor to deliver the same lectures in person year after year. Such an approach could leave faculty members with more time to devote to upper-level seminar teaching, one-on-one student advis-

---

More Professors Could Share Lectures Online: But Should They?" *Chronicle of Higher Education,* online edition, March 7, 2010).

[2]Interview with George Breslauer, 6/9/09.

[3]Berkeley has long been interested in sharing some of its strategies for affordable course recording with others. In 2008 Berkeley and several partner institutions received planning grants from the Hewlett and Mellon Foundations to form the Opencast project, an online community of practice "to explore, define, and document podcasting best practices and technologies" (http://www.opencastproject.org/). According to Mara Hancock, Berkeley's director of Educational Technology Services, the impetus behind Opencast was "enabling others also to scale and grow and make this more financially viable for more people" (interview with Mara Hancock, 6/8/09).

ing, or research. It could also serve as a cost-cutting measure for the institution, allowing a university to spread the costs of instruction over a broader cohort of students and to realize greater benefits from limited resources like classroom space and faculty time.[4]

Steps in this direction are already evident on a smaller scale: at least one professor participating in webcast.berkeley "uses [the webcast] to over-enroll" his highly popular introductory astronomy course, allowing students relegated to the waiting list to keep up with the webcasts for the first few lectures of the semester, until enough students drop the course that seats free up.[5] Especially for public universities—where space is at a premium and students frequently have trouble gaining admission to key courses needed to progress through their majors and maintain normal time-to-degree—the use of prerecorded lectures may generate needed efficiencies. Recorded lectures from one strong course might even be reused across multiple institutions, potentially allowing for sustainability models that distribute costs accordingly.

At universities with greater resources, where cutting costs and scaling up offerings are less critical concerns, lecture capture might lead faculty members in different directions. Once their course lectures are available for on-demand viewing, some faculty members may introduce or further develop differentiating elements of the "live" versions, to ensure that lecture content does not become stale and that attending in person remains beneficial for students. Possibilities include reorganizing lecture time to encourage more exchange and conversation between students and with the instructor, or incorporating technologies such as "clickers" (hand-held devices that allow students to respond immediately to a professor's questions) to heighten opportunities for interaction.[6] The existence

---

[4]Leadership at highly selective public universities that have come under acute fiscal pressure may be more receptive to these changes; leaders of elite private universities have been less likely to view the application of online strategies toward these ends as relevant for them. As public universities build out capacity in this area, it will be interesting to see if their private counterparts eventually follow suit.

[5]Interview with Benjamin Hubbard, 6/9/09.

[6]See, for example, Hammond, Ruth, "Learning with 'Clickers' Gets Better after Peer Discussion, Wired Campus blog (*Chronicle of Higher Education*), January 7, 2009, http://chronicle.com/blogPost/Learning-With-Clickers-/4456.

of recorded versions of lectures can even prompt professors to change the substance of what they teach. An item in *Inside Higher Ed* confirmed that several participating professors no longer teach the OYC version of their course to Yale students: "Some have questioned whether the easy availability of course lectures might lead to lower attendance back at Yale, but [Professor Ramamurti] Shankar and [Professor Langdon] Hammer seem to have found a novel solution. 'I will never teach this course again,' said Shankar. . . . 'I don't know another way to do it.' For similar reasons, Hammer said he will take a break from teaching the modern poetry course" captured on OYC—an internal curricular change that may have been an unintended consequence of a project aimed at external audiences.[7]

While lecture capture initiatives could potentially inspire modifications to elite institutions' instructional models, the approach taken by Carnegie Mellon's Open Learning Initiative (OLI) seems to offer the greatest potential for large-scale transformative change. The other existing courseware initiatives profiled here provide only content; the OLI includes additional aspects of the learning experience, acting as lecture, textbook, and even assessor. The OLI project makes a convincing case that online teaching can achieve learning outcomes at least equal to those in a traditional classroom, improving educational productivity.[8] But thus far, just as the content-only courseware models have not led to a rethinking of their host universities' core curricula, so Carnegie Mellon has not used what it has learned from the OLI to re-engineer its approach to introductory courses for its own students.[9]

Using OLI courses as the sole means of instruction (or with very limited human support) would seem to have remarkable potential for easing bottlenecks in core courses or for cutting costs

[7]Guess, Andy, "Open Courses Open Wider," *Inside Higher Ed*, December 12, 2007.

[8]And teaching with OLI courses in hybrid mode, combining asynchronous digital learning with targeted course sessions (the latter available only to enrolled students), can be even more effective than the traditional method.

[9]Some enrolled Carnegie Mellon students have been taught through substantial use of the OLI (for instance, in the head-to-head and accelerated studies conducted on the OLI statistics course), but the university has not habitually offered its students the option of taking courses in this format.

while preserving strong educational outcomes[10]—though whether the OLI model would prove effective for courses in the social sciences and humanities, or for more advanced courses, remains an open question. But cost savings through the use of online courseware can be realized only if and when institutions begin to fully integrate these resources into their present operations. As we have seen, highly selective universities have served as willing producers of online courseware content, but they have not yet elected to put it to transformative use on their campuses. Should a project like the OLI achieve widespread, transformative usage in formal settings, adoption is likely to come first from other institutions like large public universities or community colleges (where the OLI has already begun to find some traction).[11]

Of course, universities face a series of ingrained cultural obstacles to large-scale changes in their pedagogical models. Thus, the reluctance to date by top-tier institutions—both public and private —to systematically implement OLI-style courseware in their everyday teaching is understandable. In addition to the expense that such an overhaul would involve,[12] there is hesitancy from a branding perspective. Such changes would require the selective univer-

[10]Carnegie Mellon cognitive scientist and OLI assessment expert Marsha Lovett has described a "minimal support" scenario for students affiliated with a college or university taking OLI courses. Under this scenario the OLI system enacts the instruction, but an instructor of record helps pace the student's progress through the course; creates, administers, and grades in-class exams; monitors students' progress; and holds an optional weekly Q&A session for students. (This is the approach taken to the experimental group in the OLI's head-to-head study of student learning in statistics using the OLI; Lovett, Marsha, "Support Models for Teaching with OLI," undated document.)

[11]The OLI statistics course is already being used in some community colleges, and interactions between community college faculty and the OLI production team should become more formalized through the Community College Open Learning Initiative project, which will be designed for a community college student population with cross-institutional development teams (interview with Candace Thille, 8/11/09).

[12]For any single institution, the economics of restructuring a suite of courses to be taught entirely OLI-style makes little sense: the upfront investment is too steep relative to the savings. Courses of this type are expensive to develop—each OLI course has cost roughly $500,000 to $1 million—but could potentially benefit vast numbers of students simultaneously. A collaborative business model to support cross-institutional development of courses may therefore be the solution, but it would require universities to enter into new partnerships. Major public university systems—in which multiple campuses already share some resources and work toward shared missions—may be a logical starting place to explore investments in a major overhaul like transforming introductory courses.

sity to upend—or at least adjust—the high-touch teaching model that has traditionally served its students well and has sustained its prestigious ranking.[13] Furthermore, despite promising early data from projects like OLI, real pedagogical concerns remain for institutions naturally devoted to offering learning experiences of unassailable quality.

Perhaps most importantly, winning over faculty—especially in an area as closely guarded as teaching methods—could be another obstacle to such sweeping change. Generalized anxiety toward online education persists among faculty, particularly at those institutions where online tools and teaching methods are not ubiquitous.[14] Faculty are likely to react with concern to perceived threats to the autonomy they have historically enjoyed over the development and delivery of their courses.[15] David Noble has suggested that, in the most extreme cases, faculty may find that technology has rendered their services redundant—an obvious disincentive to adopting courseware as a central means of teaching.[16]

But while serious integration of online courseware into the primary undergraduate curriculum would be a significant departure for the most selective institutions, online courses are commonly offered

[13]As Bowen notes in his foreword, for the most prestigious institutions, "Presenting some of their own on-campus courses in a strictly online mode could . . . compromise their ability to compete with other elite universities for the very best students—many of whom expect face-to-face contact with professors and regular in-class interactions with talented peers."

[14]Evidence for faculty fears of being replaced by technology have surfaced in the dissolution of the University of Illinois Global Campus, which curtailed its attempt to develop a for-profit, independently accredited online venture partially due to faculty's wariness of such a program's fit with the academic standards to which they were accustomed (Kolowich, Steve, "What Doomed Global Campus?" *Inside Higher Ed,* September 3, 2009).

[15]As Martin Trow has suggested, "the idea of giving any teaching over to self-contained courseware . . . is at odds with the university's traditions; it threatens its jealously defended reputation for a degree reflecting high academic standards" (Trow, Martin, "The Development of Information Technology in American Higher Education," *Daedalus* 126, no. 4 [Fall 1997], 304).

[16]Noble writes that "once the faculty converts its courses to courseware, their services are in the long run no longer required. They become redundant, and when they leave, their work remains behind. . . . The new technology of education, like the automation of other industries, robs faculty of their knowledge and skills, their control over their working lives, the product of their labor, and, ultimately, their means of livelihood" (Noble, David F., "Digital Diploma Mills: The Automation of Higher Education," *First Monday* 3, no. 1 [January 5, 1998], http://firstmonday.org/htbin/cgiwrap/bin/ojs/index.php/fm/article/view/569/490).

for credit outside of this elite sector. According to a Sloan Consortium report on the status of online education, in the fall 2007 semester over 20 percent of U.S. students enrolled in higher education took an online course, a significant increase over the previous year.[17] By 2009 that number had risen to one in four overall.[18] Within the most selective institutions, though, such experiences remain quite rare, indicating the significant split between major research universities' attitudes toward online courses for enrolled undergraduates and the broader trend in higher education toward online instruction.

That said, there have been some recent signs of change among selective institutions, with first movers coming from the more financially strained public university sector. In the fall of 2009 the University of North Carolina (UNC) at Chapel Hill initiated a pilot program to convert its introductory Spanish course to online-only after several years of teaching the course in hybrid mode. For that pilot, the department has eliminated face-to-face instruction in favor of online course videos, interactive modules, and interaction with peers and instructors via virtual communication environments. The department chair and head of the university's Language Resource Center explained that student performance data had shown no significant difference between traditional and hybrid courses in the past, and that the switch to fully online instruction would relieve strains on space and funds in a difficult economic climate.[19] For a selective state flagship like UNC to embrace such

---

[17]Allen, I. Elaine, and Jeff Seaman, "Staying the Course: Online Education in the United States, 2008," report supported by the Sloan Consortium and the Babson Survey Research Group, November 2008, http://www.sloan-c.org/publications/survey/staying_course, 5.

[18]Allen, I. Elaine, and Jeff Seaman, "Learning on Demand: Online Education in the United States, 2009," report supported by the Sloan Consortium and the Babson Survey Research Group, January 2010, http://www.sloan-c.org/publications/survey/learning_on_demand_sr2010, 1.

[19]See Kolowich, Steve, "Adios to Spanish 101 Classroom," *Inside Higher Ed,* October 21, 2009. Performance data on the hybrid version of the course were collected over several years as part of the Pew Program on Course Redesign. In the hybrid version (which is still being used for Spanish 102), two of the course's four contact hours per week were replaced with online independent learning ("Colleagues Committed to Redesign: University of North Carolina at Chapel Hill—Progress Report as of 3/1/08," http://www.thencat.org/RedesignAlliance/C2R/R1/Abstracts/UNCCH_Abstract.htm).

The decision to convert introductory Spanish to online-only was made in the absence of data to shed light on whether this latest change would affect student learning. An indea model for enrolled undergraduates was a bold, newsworthy step. The outcome of this experiment will provide a chance to explore whether faculty concerns about course quality, curricular autonomy, and staff redundancies are warranted.

Dire financial need, coupled with the institutional mandate to provide access for in-state students, is also spurring conversations at the University of California about a pilot project to create and evaluate fully online courses.[20] These proposed courses could be offered for credit either to enrolled UC students or, eventually, as part of full online undergraduate degrees or a virtual campus that could help the system accommodate more students while collecting needed additional revenues. All-too-limited access to world-class higher education in India has similarly motivated the IITs' plans to eventually utilize NPTEL content as the basis for a virtual IIT.[21] When it comes to using technology to unlock the gates both to course content and to credit toward degrees, the elite public universities are leading the charge—perhaps as a natural outgrowth of the access component of their institutional missions.

The prospect of selective higher education using technology to innovate beyond the course level, to the point of granting full-

---

pendent evaluation team from UNC has been following student progress throughout the pilot (both tracking student performance on assessments and surveying student attitudes toward the course), and it will compare online-only students' learning outcomes to those achieved in the past by students taking the course both in hybrid mode and traditionally. For the second semester of the pilot (Fall 2010), the Spanish department plans to tweak the course according to the evaluation committee's recommendations, and it will decide after the completion of the pilot whether to institutionalize this approach to Spanish 101 (interview with Glynis Cowell, 4/30/10).

[20]University of California, University Committee on Educational Policy, "Online Undergraduate Instruction at a Selective University: An Intensive, Faculty-Led Evaluation of Opportunities, Challenges, Quality, Cost, and Viability," draft prospectus, version 12, March 30, 2010, http://ccfit.ucdavis.edu/calendar/2009-10/docs/ucep%20project%20description%20final.pdf.

[21]A virtual university was one element of the IITs' initial proposal to the Ministry of Human Resource Development, but the Ministry directed the IITs to start with the content element only, which became the NPTEL project. In 2008, Dr. Surendra Prasad, director of IIT Delhi, told the *Indian Express* "there is a proposal to set up a virtual university, which is in the planning stage. We want at least 500 courses to be ready and uploaded on NPTEL by then. Universities in their present form may not be able to cope . . . with the increasing number of engineering students" ("IITs Plan to Set Up Virtual Universities, Labs," *Indian Express,* online edition, April 26, 2008).

fledged online degrees, raises a number of questions. For instance, if elite public university systems like the University of California and the IITs were to offer online-only undergraduate programs, would that jeopardize their appeal to their traditional student bodies? Would a student who is qualified to attend an elite university be interested in forgoing the residential experience in favor of an online-only option? How much less expensive would an online degree need to be to attract the best students in the absence of a residential component (or would the flexibility that a distance learning option affords make it more attractive)? And could the same quality standards be maintained, such that the online degrees from these institutions are not viewed as second-tier?[22]

In order to evolve and expand current online courseware endeavors into more ambitious efforts like those proposed by the IITs and the University of California, additional features must be developed: enhanced interaction (presumably with an online system as well as instructors or teaching assistants), application processes, mechanisms for collecting tuition, and metrics for accreditation. When applied to distance education, these roles lie decidedly outside many traditional universities' core competencies, and new entrants may therefore face stiff competition from more established

[22]Various committees of the University of California faculty have been engaged in vigorous debate about online education. Discussions were initiated by the Academic Senate, which convened a Special Committee on Remote and Online Instruction and Residency, and by the university administration, which in the spring of 2010 framed the proposal to pilot and evaluate UC-designed, credit-bearing online undergraduate courses. Concern and skepticism from faculty have pervaded those discussions, particularly regarding the quality of potential online offerings relative to the high standards to which UC campuses have historically held themselves. UC Berkeley's chair of the statewide Senate's Committee on Educational Policy wrote that his Committee "remain[s] unconvinced that this is a desirable direction in which to go, much less that the faculty actually want to go there. . . . Learning material is not to be equated with getting a university degree. The social as well as educational growth of a student are intertwined and facilitated by being physically present on campus for at least a minimum amount of time. Without the student experience of campus life and face-to-face courses, a university degree becomes a commodity driven to the lowest common denominator. We do not believe a UC degree should be so devalued" (Navarrete, Ignacio, Committee on Educational Policy document contributed to "Berkeley Division of the Academic Senate Committee Responses to Remote and Online Instruction at UC," http://academic-senate.berkeley.edu/issues/Senate_Committee_Responses_to_Online _TF_Report.pdf). Nevertheless, the UC Academic Senate appears ready to explore the possibility of developing and evaluating online instruction.

providers. For-profit institutions (like the University of Phoenix)—as well as many state universities (the University of Maryland University College and the Penn State Global Campus are prominent examples)—have been involved with distance education for years. Their experience with online business and course delivery models, coupled with their tendency to offer more professionally oriented courses that have proved popular in the online environment, might offer superior positioning in this market.

Furthermore, a nimble for-profit institution—be it a commercial university or even a commercial textbook publisher[23]—that attempts to productize and scale up online education efforts may have an advantage over a large and storied research university that is not set up for e-commerce.[24] Harold Shapiro, a former president

[23]Commercial textbook publishers may constitute another source of competition for top universities in courseware creation. These experienced, well-capitalized professionals in information delivery have created a number of software options to supplement their textbooks that have much in common with the OLI. One example is MyMathLab, a customizable software suite by Pearson, which includes features designed for both students (such as guided practice problems that provide instant feedback) and teachers (such as course management software that allows them to convert assignments and tests to automatically graded online formats). (MyMathLab, "Frequently Asked Questions," http://www.mymathlab.com/faqs). Other likely competitors include for-profit companies like 2tor, to which universities can outsource the creation of their online curricula (http://2tor.com/about/), and StraighterLine, a for-profit set of courses that students pay to take independently and for which colleges can grant transfer credit (http://www.straighterline.com/). As entities like these proliferate—on the university side and the vendor side—it will be interesting to see if any fruitful synergies arise between courseware products made *by* the higher education community and those made *for* the higher education community by commercial producers.

[24]The traditional universities in which NPTEL and webcast.berkeley have been housed are large and established institutions that are not easily susceptible to change, so it is perhaps no surprise that representatives from these institutions have envisioned online-only degree-granting endeavors as separate entities—an eleventh UC campus rather than an e-Berkeley degree (see Edley, Christopher J., "Building a New UC—In Cyberspace," *Los Angeles Times,* online edition, July 1, 2009) or a virtual IIT rather than an existing IIT awarding distance degrees. As Clayton Christensen has stated, "It is very difficult for a company whose cost structure is tailored to compete in high-end markets to be profitable in low-end markets as well. Creating an independent organization, with a cost structure honed to achieve profitability at the low margins characteristic of most disruptive technologies, is the only viable way for established firms to harness this principle" (Christensen, Clayton M., *The Innovator's Dilemma,* New York: Collins Business Essentials, 2006, xxiv).

This approach has been successful for public universities (the University of Maryland's online degree option is exercised through its separate University College, and Penn State's through its World Campus). Extension schools have also historically been sites for innovation at a slight distance from the main activities of the university, and could be ideal venues

of Princeton, expressed skepticism at a traditional university's capacity to expand seamlessly into other areas. He pointed out that in deciding where to focus institutional resources, a university must consider what will support its public mission. "But you also have to ask yourself, where do we have the talent? You can't just turn around tomorrow and say 'maybe we should start doing something different'—you have to accumulate the talent first."[25] Time will tell whether the historic strengths of these elite universities will be of value in the distance education market.

Should the highly selective institutions discussed here choose to make online education more central to their instructional models —either to better serve their current student body or to expand it—that move would also be a highly visible vote of confidence in online education itself. "Will [online education] continue [to be viewed] as suspect—the provenance of bottom-feeding for-profits?" asks Daniel Greenstein, the University of California's vice provost for academic planning, programs and coordination, wondering if e-learning will perpetually be considered a second-rate option, appropriate for less selective institutions but not for the best of American higher education. "Online ed will not take off in the quality sector unless and until some leading universities integrate [it] into their traditional undergraduate curricula, not just for their enrolled or in-residence students who might benefit by having access to some required courses online, but as fully distance learning options."[26] Describing highly selective institutions' relatively slow adoption of online education to date, Anya Kamenetz writes

---

for migrating online courseware from enrichment-only to credit-bearing programs. Should UC's proposed credit-bearing online courses eventually lead to online degrees from individual campuses—particularly the most prestigious ones like Berkeley and the University of California at Los Angeles—this would constitute a significant break from these universities' traditional approach to core undergraduate teaching.

[25]Interview with Harold Shapiro, 7/24/08. As Diane Harley has written, the best traditional universities may not necessarily be the best or most successful at delivering online courseware: "E-learning programs vary greatly in quality and there is no clear correlation between quality and the prestige of the provider" (Harley, Diane, and Shannon Lawrence, "The Regulation of E-Learning: New National and International Policy Perspectives," summary report on the proceedings of a meeting, September 2006, revised February 2007, http://cshe.berkeley.edu/publications/docs/ROP.Regulation_of_elearning.pdf, 14).

[26]Personal communication with Daniel Greenstein, 2/26/10.

that "There is snobbery at work: the vanguard of online programs are at colleges that offer only associate's degrees. . . . Perhaps as a result, at traditional universities, digital offerings may be treated as an afterthought, a poor relation of what goes on in the classroom."[27] If elite institutions like those profiled in this book were to fully embrace e-learning, that could go a long way toward establishing online courses as an expected and legitimate element of higher education, even at the most prestigious levels.[28]

· · · · · · · · · · · · · · · ·

Elite universities developed online courseware initiatives to share their educational content with a world audience. But these projects' transformative potential *within* the academy should not be discounted. At a time when the general state of the economy has put all nonessential university projects in jeopardy, demonstrating and enhancing the value that such programs provide to the institutions that created them—or to higher education more broadly—will no doubt be of utmost importance to these projects' long-term success. As the attention of private foundations and federal agencies shifts toward open-education projects for or by community colleges rather than those based at elite institutions, existing online courseware initiatives will be presented with both opportunities for growth and new challenges.

The transformative impact of online courseware will vary tremendously by institutional type. Community colleges, small independent colleges, large public universities, and elite research institutions have varying needs, resource bases, and values that will dictate the degree and kind of usage that they choose to make of these materials and pedagogical approaches. But every tier of higher education stands

[27]Kamenetz, Anya, *DIY U: Edupunks, Edupreneurs, and the Coming Transformation of Higher Education,* New York: Chelsea Green, 2010, 95.

[28]Harley writes that "in the global marketplace, there is an underlying sense of risk, especially in terms of reputation and prestige, which has resulted in cautious undertakings. The result is that many 'prestigious' institutions have been very selective of markets that they have entered and the programming that they have made available. As e-learning grows, however, more well-known institutions will likely enter the e-learning marketplace, lending prestige to e-learning in general" (Harley and Lawrence, "The Regulation of E-Learning," 15). Kamenetz makes the point even more forcefully, asserting that "It would just take a few more prestigious institutions getting on board to change the way people feel about online, on-demand education" (Kamenetz, *DIY U,* 128).

to gain from the strategic implementation of some aspect of online courseware. Community colleges (and perhaps less-selective four-year institutions)—where access, efficiency, and affordability of education are central components of their missions—seem the most likely early adopters of online courseware to drive institutional transformation.

Some observers have even suggested that increased access to affordable educational materials via the internet may result in a more dramatic reconfiguration of higher education, as learners use these technologies to assemble their educational experiences from disaggregated parts. It may someday be commonplace, they hypothesize, for students to pick and choose online courses from several providers, seek credit for their learning from a separate source, and even sidestep the traditional student-teacher relationship entirely by finding peer support through online social networks. Recognition that the digital age might enable the unbundling of university functions—and possibly the impending ruination of the traditional university model—dates at least to the early dot-com period, though it has recently been expressed with mounting urgency.[29] But those who envision near-total dissolution of the university model often spare the most selective institutions from their provocative auguries (at least in the near term), conceding that the most elite research universities and liberal arts colleges offer a traditional residential experience and a prestigious degree that seems to have enduring value.[30] For the highly selective tier of higher education

---

[29]See, for example, Brown, John Seely, and Paul Duguid, "Universities in the Digital Age," *Change* 28, no. 4 (August 1996), 10–19, in which the authors reference the view held by some that the brick-and-mortar universities will give way entirely to virtual entities (though they take a more tempered view). More recently, Kevin Carey has gone so far as to say that, if undergraduate education—the tuition fees from which have subsidized other university functions—can be cobbled together more cheaply and easily outside the traditional institution, it "could be the string that, if pulled, unravels the carefully woven financial system on which the modern university depends. Perhaps the higher-education fuse is 25 years long, perhaps 40. But it ends someday, in our lifetimes," and "less-selective private colleges and regional public universities . . . are in real danger" (Carey, Kevin, "What Colleges Should Learn from Newspapers' Decline," *Chronicle of Higher Education,* online edition, April 3, 2009).

[30]For examples in which commentators have identified this trend but included the caveat that the most prestigious, best-resourced institutions will likely be spared from any resulting fallout, see Carey, Kevin, "College for $99 a Month," *Washington Monthly,* online edition, September–October 2009; Kamenetz, *DIY U;* and Teachout, Zephyr, "A Virtual Revolution Is Brewing for Colleges," *Washington Post,* online edition, September 13, 2009.

described in this book, threats to institutional livelihoods as a result of technologically mediated unbundling are far in the future (if present at all).

To date, the selective universities that have been the trailblazers in developing these courseware materials for the general public have been among the most reluctant to use them to reform their own pedagogical approaches. But even if the wealth and prestige of these selective institutions insulate them from the more extreme disaggregation that some predict will drive reform in other sectors, changing student needs and expectations—as well as pressures from the evolving higher-education landscape—may encourage implementation of these innovative methods. New technologies and strategies for disseminating course content could lead to educational experiences that look very different from those currently available at elite universities.

Such changes could result from any number of drivers: As tech-savvy students increasingly expect to access lecture content on demand, universities of any caliber will have to decide whether and how to meet these demands. Should online lectures come to serve as equivalent substitutes for in-person attendance, one might even imagine—perhaps far in the future—students at MIT being permitted to take online courses from Yale for credit toward their own degrees, and vice versa (a scenario close to what is already happening offline through intercollegiate consortial arrangements and study-abroad programs). Alternatively, budget crunches may eventually lead even the best-resourced universities to, as Bowen states in the foreword, "do more with less." They might use online courseware to expand local capacity for key courses, or establish firmer partnerships with public institutions to see their courseware put to transformative use elsewhere. If substantively integrated into universities' basic educational approaches, the lessons learned from the online courseware projects profiled here may alter the way in which higher education is administered and experienced—at the elite level and beyond.

REFERENCES

Abelson, Hal. "The Creation of OpenCourseWare at MIT." *Journal of Science Education and Technology* 17, no. 2 (April 2008), 164–74.

"About Connexions: Philosophy," http://cnx.org/aboutus/index_html.

"About the OU: Open Admissions," http://www.open.ac.uk/about/ou/p7.shtml.

"About UMassOnline," http://www.umassonline.net/AboutUs.html.

"About Us: Our Story." OpenLearn, http://www.open.ac.uk/openlearn/about-us/our-story.php.

"About: What Is CC?" Creative Commons, http://creativecommons.org/about/what-is-cc.

Agarwal, Pawan. *Indian Higher Education: Envisioning the Future*. New Delhi: Sage India, 2009.

Albanese, Andrew. "Another First, as MIT Faculty Adopts 'University-Wide' Open Access Policy." *Library Journal Academic Newswire,* online edition, March 24, 2009.

Allen, I. Elaine, and Jeff Seaman. "Staying the Course: Online Education in the United States, 2008." Report supported by the Sloan Consortium and the Babson Survey Research Group, November 2008, http://www.sloan-c.org/publications/survey/staying_course.

———. "Learning on Demand: Online Education in the United States, 2009." Report supported by the Sloan Consortium and the Babson Survey Research Group, January 2010, http://www.sloan-c.org/publications/survey/learning_on_demand_sr2010.

Alliance for Lifelong Learning 990 form for AllLearn, filed 2003, http://www.guidestar.org/FinDocuments/2003/134/138/2003-134138834-1-9.pdf.

"Alliance with Yale, Stanford, Oxford Paves the Way for Life-Long Learning." *Princeton Weekly Bulletin,* online edition, 90, no. 5 (October 9, 2000).

"America since 1945: The Politics of Anti-Communism," http://web.archive.org/web/20021017143217/fathom.com/fks/catalog/course.jhtml?id=58705023.

Ananth, M. S., and Mangala Sunder Krishnan. "Proposal under the National Mission on Education through ICT: NPTEL Phases II and III, July 2007 to

June 2012." Submitted to Higher Education, Ministry of Human Resource Development, Government of India, New Delhi.

Anderson, Chris. *Free: The Future of a Radical Price.* New York: Hyperion, 2009.

"Apollo Group, Inc. Reports Fiscal 2010 First Quarter Results." Press release, http://phx.corporate-ir.net/phoenix.zhtml?c=79624&p=irol-newsArticle&ID=1372667&highlight=.

Arenson, Karen W. "At Yale, a New Campus Just for Research." *New York Times,* online edition, July 4, 2007.

———. "Columbia Sets Pace in Profiting off Research." *New York Times,* online edition, August 2, 2000.

———. "Responsible Party: Making Education an Online Brand." *New York Times,* online edition, April 23, 2000.

———. "Senate Looking at Endowments as Tuition Rises." *New York Times,* online edition, January 25, 2008.

Arnone, Michael. "Columbia Senate Questions Spending on Fathom." *Chronicle of Higher Education,* online edition, May 10, 2002.

———. "Fathom Adds Training to Distance-Education Offerings." *Chronicle of Higher Education,* online edition, February 22, 2002.

Atkins, Daniel E., John Seely Brown, and Allen L. Hammond. "A Review of the Open Educational Resources (OER) Movement: Achievements, Challenges, and New Opportunities." Report to the William and Flora Hewlett Foundation, February 2007.

Atkinson, Richard C. "The Globalization of the University." Speech delivered at Nagasaki University of Foreign Studies, Japan, May 26, 2001, http://ucop.edu/pres/speeches/japanspc.htm.

Aujla, Simmi, and Ben Terris. "Around the World, Varied Approaches to Open Online Learning." *Chronicle of Higher Education,* online edition, October 11, 2009.

"Background on Fathom," promotional one-sheet. Fathom.com, undated.

Balakrishnan, Angela. "Reading Poetry at Yale . . . in My Sitting Room." *The Guardian,* online edition, April 29, 2008.

Banerjee, Rangan, and Vinayak P. Muley. "Engineering Education in India." Sponsored by the Observer Research Foundation, December 16, 2008.

Baumol, William J., and William G. Bowen. "On the Performing Arts: The Anatomy of Their Economic Problems." *American Economic Review* 55, no. 1–2 (March 1, 1965), 495–502.

Beam, Chris. "Fathom.com Shuts Down as Columbia Withdraws." *Columbia Daily Spectator,* online edition, January 27, 2003.

Beiles, Nancy. "A League of Her Own." *Grok,* October 2000, 39–44.

Beja, Marc. "Online Campus Could Solve Many U. of California Problems, a Dean Says." *Chronicle of Higher Education,* online edition, July 22, 2009.

Benkler, Yochai. "Coase's Penguin, or, Linux and *The Nature of the Firm.*" *Yale Law Journal* 112, no. 3 (December 2002), http://www.yalelawjournal.org/images/pdfs/354.pdf.

Bennett, Drake. "FreeHarvardEducation.com: Does Anyone Own What Universities Teach?" *Boston Globe,* online edition, December 13, 2009.

Bhattacharjee, Yudhijit. "A Personal Tutor for Algebra: Commercial Software Created in the Lab Anticipates Wrong Answers and Reinforces Needed Skills for First-Year Algebra Students." *Science* 323 (January 2, 2009), 64–65.

Bianco, Anthony, and Sonal Rupani. "The Dangerous Wealth of the Ivy League." *Business Week,* online edition, December 3, 2007.

Birgeneau, Robert J. "Access and Excellence," Fall 2008, http://newscenter .berkeley.edu/news/chancellor/access/access.shtml.

Blau, Jessamyn. "Veteran Takes Over at AllLearn." *Yale Daily News,* online edition, February 6, 2003.

Blumenstyk, Goldie. "Knowledge Is 'a Form of Venture Capital' for a Top Columbia Administrator." *Chronicle of Higher Education,* online edition, February 9, 2001.

Bonk, Curtis J. *The World Is Open: How Web Technology Is Revolutionizing Education.* San Francisco: Jossey-Bass, 2009.

Bowen, William G. "At a Slight Angle to the Universe: The University in a Digitized, Commercialized Age." http://www.mellon.org/news_publications/publications/ romanes.pdf/view.

———. "The Economics of the Major Private Universities." Carnegie Commission on the Future of Higher Education, Berkeley, Calif., 1968.

Brooks, Margaret. "The Excellent Inevitability of Online Courses." *Chronicle of Higher Education,* online edition, May 21, 2009.

Brown, John Seely, and Paul Duguid. "Universities in the Digital Age." *Change* 28, no. 4 (August 1996): 10–19.

Brown, Peter. "What Is DRM? Digital Restrictions Management," http://www .defectivebydesign.org/what_is_drm.

Budapest Open Access Initiative, http://www.soros.org/openaccess/read.shtml.

Campbell, Gardner, and Jim Groom. "No Digital Facelifts: Thinking the Unthinkable about Open Educational Experiences." Talk delivered at the 2009 Open Education Conference, Vancouver, August 13, 2009.

"The Cape Town Open Education Declaration: Unlocking the Promise of OpenEducationalResources,"http://www.capetowndeclaration.org/read-the-declaration.

Carey, Kevin. "College for $99 a Month." *Washington Monthly,* online edition, September–October 2009.

———. "What Colleges Should Learn from Newspapers' Demise." *Chronicle of Higher Education,* online edition, April 3, 2009.

Carlson, Scott. "After Losing Millions, Columbia U. Will Close Online-Learning Venture." *Chronicle of Higher Education,* online edition, January 17, 2003.

———. "For-Profit Web Venture Shifts Gears, Hoping to Find a Way to Make a Profit." *Chronicle of Higher Education,* online edition, February 9, 2001.

———. "Going for Profit and Scholarship on the Web: A Woman Who Made the NFL Hot Online Turns Her Attention to Higher Education." *Chronicle of Higher Education,* online edition, May 5, 2000.

Carnegie Learning. "About Carnegie Learning," http://www.carnegielearning.com/company.cfm.

———. "Our Research Based Approach to Mathematical Success," http://www.carnegielearning.com/approach.cfm.

"Carnegie Mellon Technology Will Reshape Curriculum of New Jersey's Centenary College." Press release, *AScribe Newswire,* September 15, 2003.

Carnegie Mellon University. "Three Foundations Grant $4 Million in Awards to Carnegie Mellon's Open Learning Initiative." Press release, December 15, 2009, http://www.cmu.edu/news/archive/2009/December/dec15_openlearninggrants.shtml.

Carnegie Mellon University (Eberly Center for Teaching Excellence). "Learning Principles: Theory and Research-Based Principles of Learning," http://www.cmu.edu/teaching/principles/learning.html.

Carr, Sarah, and Vincent Kiernan. "For-Profit Web Venture Seeks to Replicate the University Experience Online." *Chronicle of Higher Education,* online edition, April 14, 2000.

Carson, Steve. "The Unwalled Garden: Growth of the OpenCourseWare Consortium, 2001–2008." *Open Learning: The Journal of Open and Distance Learning,* online edition, 24, no. 1 (February 2009).

Casper, Gerhard. "Come the Millennium, Where the University?" Speech delivered to the annual meeting of the American Educational Research Association, San Francisco, April 18, 1995, http://www.stanford.edu/dept/pres-provost/president/speeches/950418millennium.html.

Casselman, Ben. "Columbia Committee Reports on Fathom.com's Difficulties." *Columbia Daily Spectator,* reprinted in *University Wire,* online edition, January 29, 2001.

Cassidy, John. *dot.con: The Greatest Story Ever Sold.* New York: HarperCollins, 2002.

Caswell, Tom, Shelley Henson, Marion Jensen, and David Wiley. "Open Content and Open Educational Resources: Enabling Universal Education." *International Review of Research in Open and Distance Learning* 9, no. 1 (2008), article 9.1.1, http://www.irrodl.org/index.php/irrodl/article/view/469.

Christensen, Clayton M. *The Innovator's Dilemma.* New York: Collins Business Essentials, 2006.

Chute, Eleanor. "How to Take a Course at MIT Free—At Home." *Pittsburgh Post-Gazette,* online edition, November 18, 2007.

"Cisco Prepares Higher Education Market to Seize Two Leading Tech Trends: Web 2.0 and Interoperable Communications." Press release, *Market News Publishing,* October 24, 2007.

Cohen, Patricia. "Morals Class Is Starting; Please Pass the Popcorn." *New York Times,* online edition, September 25, 2009.

Cole, Jonathan R. *The Great American University: Its Rise to Preeminence, Its Indispensable National Role, Why It Must Be Protected.* New York: Public Affairs, 2009.

Colman, Dan. "India's Answer to MIT Presents Free Courses on YouTube (in English). May 27, 2008, http://www.openculture.com/2008/05/indias_answer _to_mit_presents_free_courses_on_youtube_in_english.html.

"Colleagues Committed to Redesign: University of North Carolina at Chapel Hill—Progress Report as of 3/1/08," http://www.thencat.org/RedesignAlliance/ C2R/R1/Abstracts/UNCCH_Abstract.htm.

"Coming to Terms: ALN." *Sloan-C View: Perspectives in Quality Online Education* 2, no. 4 (June 2003), http://www.aln.org/publications/view/v2n4/pdf/ v2n4.pdf.

Courant, Paul, James Duderstadt, and Edie Goldenberg. "Needed: A National Strategy to Preserve Public Research Universities." *Chronicle of Higher Education*, online edition, January 3, 2010, http://chronicle.com/article/A-Plan-to-Save-Americas/63358/.

D'Antoni, Susan. "Introduction," in *Open Educational Resources: Conversations in Cyberspace*, ed. S. D'Antoni and C. Savage. Paris: UNESCO, 2009.

Diamond, David. "MIT Everyware." *Wired*, online edition, September 2003.

D'Oliveira, Cecelia, and Steven Lerman. "OpenCourseWare: Working through Financial Challenges." *MIT Faculty Newsletter*, online edition, 22, no. 1 (September–October 2009), http://web.mit.edu/fnl/volume/221/d%27oliveira_lerman.html.

Edley, Christopher J. "Building a New UC—In Cyberspace." *Los Angeles Times*, online edition, July 1, 2009.

Edmonds, Victor. "Video Vision." *Educause Review*, online edition, 43, no. 5 (September–October 2008).

Ehrenberg, Ronald G. *Tuition Rising: Why College Costs So Much*. Cambridge, Mass.: Harvard University Press, 2000.

Fabrikant, Geraldine. "For Yale's Money Man, a Higher Calling." *New York Times*, online edition, February 18, 2007.

Fischman, Josh. "Community Colleges Get Gift of Millions for Online Education." Wired Campus blog (*Chronicle of Higher Education*), December 3, 2009, http://chronicle.com/blogPost/Community-Colleges-Get-Gift/9067/.

———. "Yale U. Puts Complete Courses Online." Wired Campus blog (*Chronicle of Higher Education*), December 11, 2007, http://chronicle.com/blogPost/ Yale-U-Puts-Complete-Courses/3550.

Fisher, Saul. "Teaching and Technology: Promising Directions on Research on Online Learning and Distance Education in the Selective Institutions." Andrew W. Mellon Foundation, http://cshe.berkeley.edu/research/ebusiness/papers/ teaching_and_technology.pdf.

"Four Courses, Millions of Users: Creating a New Paradigm for Online Education: A Proposal from Carnegie Mellon University to The William and Flora Hewlett Foundation." February 22, 2002.

Friedman, Thomas L. "Foreign Affairs: Next, It's E-ducation." *New York Times*, online edition, November 17, 1999.

Frydenberg, Jia, and Gary Matkin. "Open Textbooks: Why? What? How? When?" University of California, Irvine, Distance Learning Center, October 2007.

Gates, Bill. "2010 Annual Letter from Bill Gates," http://www.gatesfoundation .org/annual-letter/2010/Pages/bill-gates-annual-letter.aspx.

Gerrard, David, and Jacob Kurlander. "Columbia U. Enters Distance Education Territory." *Columbia Daily Spectator,* reprinted in *University Wire,* online edition, April 3, 2000.

Goldberg, Carey. "Auditing Classes at M.I.T., on the Web and Free." *New York Times,* online edition, April 4, 2001.

Goldstein, Michael. "A Capital Innovation for Making a Profit." *Times Higher Education,* online edition, December 17, 1999.

Gootman, Elissa. "An Intricate Bond: New Haven's Past and Future Are So Tied to Yale, But It Took 300 Years for the Two to Get Along." *New York Times,* online edition, February 18, 2001.

Gordon, Larry. "UC Might Limit Freshmen Enrollment." *Los Angeles Times,* November 20, 2008.

Guess, Andy. "Open Courses Open Wider." *Inside Higher Ed,* December 12, 2007.

Hafner, Katie. "Lessons Learned at Dot-Com U." *New York Times,* online edition, May 2, 2002.

Hammond, Ruth. "Learning with 'Clickers' Gets Better after Peer Discussion." Wired Campus blog (*Chronicle of Higher Education*), January 7, 2009, http:// chronicle.com/blogPost/Learning-With-Clickers-/4456.

Hane, Paula J. "Columbia University to Close Fathom.com." *Information Today, Inc.,* January 13, 2003, http://newsbreaks.infotoday.com/nbreader.asp? ArticleID=16813.

Harley, Diane. *Use and Users of Digital Resources: A Focus on Undergraduate Education in the Humanities and Social Sciences,* April 5, 2006, http://cshe .berkeley.edu/research/digitalresourcestudy/report/digitalresourcestudy_final_ report.pdf.

———. "Use and Users of Digital Resources: A Survey Explored Scholars' Attitudes about Educational Technology Environments in the Humanities." *Educause Quarterly,* no. 4 (2007), 12–20.

———. "Why Understanding Use and Users of Open Education Matters," in *Opening Up Education: The Collective Advancement of Education through Open Technology, Open Content, and Open Knowledge,* ed. M. S. Vijay Kumar and Toru Iiyoshi. Cambridge, Mass.: MIT Press, 2008.

Harley, Diane, and Jonathan Henke. "Toward an Effective Understanding of Website Users." *D-Lib Magazine* 13, no. 3–4 (March–April 2007), http://www .dlib.org/dlib/march07/harley/03harley.html.

Harley, Diane, and Shannon Lawrence. "The Regulation of E-Learning: New National and International Policy Perspectives." Summary report on the proceedings of a meeting, September 2006, revised February 2007, http://cshe .berkeley.edu/publications/docs/ROP.Regulation_of_elearning.pdf.

Harley, Diane, Jonathan Henke, Shannon Lawrence, Flora McMartin, Michael Maher, Marytza Gawlik, and Parisa Muller, *Cost, Culture, and Complexity:*

An Analysis of Technology Enhancements in a Large Lecture Course at UC Berkeley, March 2003, http://cshe.berkeley.edu/publications/docs/cost_culture _and_complexity.pdf.

Hebel, Sara. "State Cuts Are Pushing Public Colleges into Peril." *Chronicle of Higher Education,* online edition, March 14, 2010.

Heffernan, Virginia. "The Camera-Friendly, Perfectly Pixelated, Easily Downloadable Celebrity Academic." *New York Times Magazine,* online edition, September 21, 2008.

William and Flora Hewlett Foundation. "Education: Open Educational Resources." http://www.hewlett.org/oer.

―――. "News: The Hewlett Foundation's Role in Advancing Open Educational Resources," http://www.hewlett.org/news/hewlett-foundations-role-in-oer.

―――. *Hewlett Foundation Annual Report—2003,* http://www.hewlett.org/ news/2003-annual-report.

―――. *Hewlett Foundation Annual Report—2005,* http://www.hewlett.org/ news/2005-annual-report.

―――. "2005 Budget Memorandum: Education Program."

―――. "2009 Budget Memorandum: Education Program." November 17, 2008, http://www.hewlett.org/programs/education-program.

Hockfield, Susan. "Testimony Prepared for the U.S. Department of Education, Secretary of Education's Commission on the Future of Higher Education." Public hearing, Boston, March 20, 2006, http://www2.ed.gov/about/bdscomm/ list/hiedfuture/2nd-hearing/hockfield.pdf.

Hoxby, Caroline M. "The Changing Selectivity of American Colleges." National Bureau of Economic Research Working Paper 15446, 2009, http://www.nber .org/papers/w15446.

"HRD Ministry Announces National Programme on Technology Enhanced Learning." *Hindustan Times,* online edition, September 19, 2006.

Huijser, Henk, Tas Bedford, and David Bull. "OpenCourseWare, Global Access and the Right to Education: Real Access or Marketing Ploy?" *International Review of Research in Open and Distance Learning 9,* no. 1 (February 2008), 4, http://www.irrodl.org/index.php/irrodl/article/view/446/1002.

"IITs Plan to Set Up Virtual Universities, Labs." *Indian Express,* online edition, April 26, 2008.

Institute of International Education. "Open Doors 2009 Report on International Educational Exchange," http://opendoors.iienetwork.org/page/150807/;jsessionid =ueknj8vvfjy5.

"The Institutes of Technology Act, 1961," http://www.iitb.ac.in/legal/IITsAct.pdf.

"Interim Status Report on Carnegie Mellon Open Learning Initiative," March 2008.

Jaschik, Scott. "The Evidence on Online Education." *Inside Higher Ed,* June 29, 2009.

―――. "U.S. Push for Free Online Courses." *Inside Higher Ed,* June 29, 2009.

Jebaraj, Priscilla. "IIT Online Learning Courses Gaining Momentum." *The Hindu,* English edition, online edition, July 28, 2008.

———. "Learning Material for IIT Courses Goes Online in Phase II." *The Hindu,* English edition, online edition, June 14, 2009.

Johansen, Justin K. "The Impact of OpenCourseWare on Paid Enrollment in Distance Learning Courses." Doctoral dissertation, Brigham Young University, October 2009, http://contentdm.lib.byu.edu/ETD/image/etd3317.pdf.

Johnstone, Sally M. "Importing and Exporting Online Courses." *Change 35,* no. 4 (July 1, 2003), 49–50.

Jokivirta, Lisa. "What Went Wrong with AllLearn?" *University Business,* online edition, June 2006.

Kamenetz, Anya. *DIY U: Edupunks, Edupreneurs, and the Coming Transformation of Higher Education.* New York: Chelsea Green, 2010.

———. "How Web-Savvy Edupunks Are Transforming American Higher Education." *Fast Company,* online edition, for the print edition of September 1, 2009.

Kamlet, Mark. Keynote address, Open Education Symposium, Carnegie Mellon University, March 10, 2008, http://telstar.ote.cmu.edu/groups/olisymposium2008/wiki/15495/I_Keynote_Opening_Learning.html.

Keller, Josh. "California's 'Gold Standard' for Higher Education Falls upon Hard Times." *Chronicle of Higher Education,* online edition, June 11, 2009.

Kingsbury, Alex, and Lindsey Galloway. "Textbooks Enter the Digital Era." *U.S. News and World Report,* online edition, October 8, 2006.

Kirp, David L. *Shakespeare, Einstein, and the Bottom Line: The Marketing of Higher Education.* Cambridge, Mass.: Harvard University Press, 2003.

Kirwan, William E. "The Research University of the Future." Speech delivered March 22, 2010, before the AAU Government Relations Professionals, www.aau.edu/WorkArea/showcontent.aspx?id=10590.

Kolowich, Steve. "Adios to Spanish 101 Classroom." *Inside Higher Ed,* October 21, 2009.

———. "Dodging Swine Online." *Inside Higher Ed,* September 18, 2009.

———. "Open Courses for Community Colleges." *Inside Higher Ed,* April 28, 2010.

———. "Recession May Drive More Adult Students to Take Online Classes." *Chronicle of Higher Education,* online edition, January 16, 2009.

———. "Seed of Doubt." *Inside Higher Ed,* June 22, 2010.

———. "The Specialists." *Inside Higher Ed,* April 5, 2010.

———. "What Doomed Global Campus?" *Inside Higher Ed,* September 3, 2009.

Kresge Foundation. "Foundation Center: Grant Details," http://maps.foundationcenter.org/grantmakers/grant_prosfile_page.php?nonp=1&nof=1&id=16902083&gmkey=KRES002.

Ladine, Bret. "MIT to Offer Access to Materials Online." *Yale Daily News,* online edition, April 5, 2001.

Lederman, Doug. "In Search of 'Big Ideas.'" *Inside Higher Ed,* February 6, 2006.
———. "Student Loan Bill Scorecard." *Inside Higher Ed,* March 24, 2010.
Lee, Ellen. "Full Cal Courses Are on YouTube." *San Francisco Chronicle,* October 4, 2007, C1.
Lerman, Steven R. "Recommendation of the OCW Faculty Advisory Committee on Sustaining OCW into the Future," September 12, 2005.
Lerman, Steven R., Shigeru Miyagawa, and Anne Margulies. "OpenCourseWare: Building a Culture of Sharing," in *Opening Up Education: The Collective Advancement of Education through Open Technology, Open Content, and Open Knowledge,* ed. M. S. Vijay Kumar and Toru Iiyoshi. Cambridge, Mass.: MIT Press, 2008.
Lessig, Lawrence. *Remix: Making Art and Commerce Thrive in the Hybrid Economy.* New York: Penguin, 2008.
Leung, Linda. "UC Berkeley Offers Course Materials on iTunes." *Network World,* online edition, April 25, 2006.
Levin, Richard C. "The Internationalization of the University." Speech delivered May 6, 2008, Athens, Greece, http://opa.yale.edu/president/message.aspx?id=7.
Levin, Richard C., and Linda Koch Lorimer. "The Internationalization of Yale: 2005–2008,"December 2005,http://world.yale.edu/about/pdf/Internationalization _Yale.pdf.
Levine, Brian. "A Victory for Students and Their Families." Middle Class Task Force blog, http://www.whitehouse.gov/blog/2010/03/30/a-victory-students-and-their-families.
Lewin, Tamar. "Textbook Publisher to Rent to College Students." *New York Times,* online edition, August 13, 2009.
———. "U.S. Universities Rush to Set Up Outposts Abroad." *New York Times,* online edition, February 10, 2008.
Lovett, Marsha. "Support Models for Teaching with OLI." Undated document.
Lovett, Marsha, Oded Meyer, and Candace Thille. "The Open Learning Initiative: Measuring the Effectiveness of the OLI Statistics Course in Accelerating Student Learning." *Journal of Interactive Media in Education,* May 5, 2008, http://jime.open.ac.uk/2008/14.
Mackie, Christopher J. "A Modest Proposal for Utterly Transforming Higher Education Pedagogy and Intellectual Property Generation on the Way to Achieving Sustainable OER—And Why Your Campus Might Want to Try It." Presentation, Open Education Conference 2009, Vancouver, August 13, 2009.
Mahadevan, G. "A Seamless Hi-Tech Learning System." *The Hindu,* English edition, online edition, June 8, 2009.
Maron, Nancy L., K. Kirby Smith, and Matthew Loy. "Sustaining Digital Resources: An On-the-Ground View of Projects Today." Ithaka Case Studies in Sustainability, July 2009, http://www.ithaka.org/ithaka-s-r/strategy/ithaka-case-studies-in-sustainability/report/SCA_Ithaka_SustainingDigitalResources_ Report.pdf.

Massy, William F., and Robert Zemsky. "Using Information Technology to Enhance Academic Productivity." White paper prepared by Educom's National Learning Infrastructure Initiative (NLII), http://net.educause.edu/ir/library/html/nli0004.html.

Mayfield, Kendra. "All the World's an MIT Campus." *Wired,* online edition, October 4, 2002.

McCarthy, Ellen. "U-Md. Professor Archives History of Dot-Com Bombs." *Washington Post,* online edition, October 28, 2004.

McKinsey Global Institute. "The Emerging Global Labor Market: Part II—The Supply of Offshore Talent in Services," June 2005, http://www.mckinsey.com/mgi/publications/emerginggloballabormarket/part2/index.asp.

McMurtrie, Beth. "Foreign Students Pour Back into the U.S." *Chronicle of Higher Education,* online edition, November 21, 2008.

McPherson, Michael S., and Gordon C. Winston. "The Economics of Cost, Price, and Quality in U.S. Higher Education," in *Paying the Piper: Productivity, Incentives, and Financing in U.S. Higher Education.* Ann Arbor: University of Michigan Press, 1993.

Means, Barbara, Yukie Toyama, Robert Murphy, Marianne Bakia, and Karla Jones. "Evaluation of Evidence-Based Practices in Online Learning: A Meta-Analysis and Review of Online Learning Studies." U.S. Department of Education, May 2009, http://ifap.ru/library/book440.pdf.

Minden, Sonia. "Higher Ed Goes Broadband." *The Guardian,* online edition, February 2, 2009.

MIT OpenCourseWare. "About OCW," http://ocw.mit.edu/OcwWeb/web/about/about/index.htm.

———. "About OCW: Our History," http://ocw.mit.edu/OcwWeb/web/about/history/index.htm.

———. "About OCW: Site Statistics," http://ocw.mit.edu/about/site-statistics/.

———. "MIT OpenCourseWare Diversifies Revenue Approaches." Press release, January 28, 2010, http://ocw.mit.edu/about/media-coverage/press-releases/revenue/.

———. "Translated Courses," http://ocw.mit.edu/OcwWeb/web/courses/lang/index.htm.

———. "2005 Program Evaluation Findings Report." June 5, 2006, http://ocw.mit.edu/ans7870/global/05_Prog_Eval_Report_Final.pdf.

———. "2009 Program Evaluation Findings Summary." November 6, 2009, http://ocw.mit.edu/ans7870/global/09_Eval_Summary.pdf.

"MIT OpenCourseWare: A Proposal Submitted to The William and Flora Hewlett Foundation," April 27, 2001. Principal investigators Harold Abelson, Robert A. Brown, and Steven R. Lerman.

"MIT to Make Nearly All Course Materials Available Free on the World Wide Web." Press release, MIT News, April 4, 2001.

MyMathLab, "Frequently Asked Questions," http://www.mymathlab.com/faqs.

Naha, Abdul Latheef. "NPTEL Set for Second Phase." *The Hindu,* English edition, online edition, November 27, 2007.

"Nair Set to Retire: Bemoans Poor Quality of Higher Education." *Press Trust of India/Bangalore,* October 16, 2009. *Business Standard,* http://www.businessstandard.com/india/news/nair-set-to-retire-bemoans-poor-quality-higher-education/76136/on.

National Programme on Technology Enhanced Learning. "Frequently Asked Questions." http://nptel.iitm.ac.in/faq.php.

———. "Project Document: July 2003–June 2006." July 2006, http://nptel.iitk.ac.in/NPTELBooklet.pdf.

Navarrete, Ignacio. Committee on Educational Policy document contributed to "Berkeley Division of the Academic Senate Committee Responses to Remote and Online Instruction at UC," http://academic-senate.berkeley.edu/issues/Senate_Committee_Responses_to_Online_TF_Report.pdf.

Needham, Paul. "Cyber Yale: You and Me and Everyone We Know." *Yale Daily News,* online edition, February 20, 2009.

———. "Digitization: Just a Click Away." *Yale Daily News,* online edition, October 30, 2008.

Neelakantan, Shailaja. "Elite Technology Institutes in India Double Their Tuition." *Chronicle of Higher Education,* online edition, May 16, 2008.

———. "India Plans New Elite Institutes." *Chronicle of Higher Education,* online edition, September 7, 2007.

Neelakatan, Shailaja, and Karin Fischer. "News Analysis: What Recent Moves in India Could Mean for American Higher Education." *Chronicle of Higher Education,* online edition, June 17, 2009.

Ngugi, Catherine. Keynote address, 2009 Open Education Conference, Vancouver, August 12, 2009.

Noble, David F. "Digital Diploma Mills: The Automation of Higher Education." *First Monday* 3, no. 1 (January 5, 1998), http://firstmonday.org/htbin/cgiwrap/bin/ojs/index.php/fm/article/view/569/490.

"Now Anyone Can 'Audit' Popular Yale Courses Via Internet." *Yale Bulletin & Calendar,* online edition, 36, no. 13 (December 14, 2007).

Obama, Barack. "Remarks by the President on the American Graduation Initiative," July 14, 2009, Macomb Community College, Warren, Michigan. Transcript released via Office of the White House Press Secretary, http://www.whitehouse.gov/the_press_office/Remarks-by-the-President-on-the-American-Graduation-Initiative-in-Warren-MI/.

Oblinger, Diana. "Will E-business Shape the Future of Distance Learning?" *Open Learning: The Journal of Open and Distance Learning* 16, no. 1 (February 2001), 9–25.

Office of Educational Technology, U.S. Department of Education. "Transforming American Education: Learning Powered by Technology." National Educational Technology Plan 2010, March 5, 2010, http://www.ed.gov/sites/default/files/NETP-2010-final-report.pdf.

O'Leary, Mary. "Popular Yale Courses on 'Net." *New Haven Register,* online edition, December 23, 2007.

Open Learning Initiative. "Frequently Asked Questions," http://oli.webl.cmu.edu/openlearning/initiative/faqs.

————. "The Initiative: Publications," http://oli.web.cmu.edu/openlearning/initiative/publications.

————. "The Initiative: Team," http://oli.web.cmu.edu/openlearning/initiative/team.

————. "Open and Free Courses," http://oli.web.cmu.edu/openlearning/forstudents/freecourses.

"Oxford, Princeton, Stanford, Yale to Invest $12 Million in Distance Learning Venture." News from Princeton University Office of Communications, September 28, 2000.

Pacia, Raymond. "AllLearn Expands Reach." *Yale Daily News,* online edition, March 25, 2005.

Parry, Marc. "Agenda for Open Online Courses Can Go Forward, Federal Officials Say." Wired Campus blog (*Chronicle of Higher Education*), April 12, 2010, http://chronicle.com/blogPost/Agenda-for-Open-Online-Courses/22496/.

————. "Free Web Site Helps Harvard Students Cut Class." Wired Campus blog (*Chronicle of Higher Education*), December 14, 2009, http://chronicle.com/blogPost/Free-Web-Site-Helps-Harvard/9205/.

————. "In Potential Blow to Open-Source Software, Mellon Foundation Closes Grant Program." Wired Campus blog (*Chronicle of Higher Education*), January 5, 2010, http://chronicle.com/blogPost/In-Potential-Blow-to-Open-S/19519/.

————. "Obama's Great Course Giveaway." *Chronicle of Higher Education,* online edition, August 3, 2009.

————. "Open Courses: Free, but Oh So Costly." *Chronicle of Higher Education,* online edition, October 11, 2009.

————. "Sloan Foundation Ends Major Grant Program for Online Education." *Chronicle of Higher Education,* online edition, April 6, 2009.

————. "They Thought Globally, but Now Colleges Push Online Courses Locally." Wired Campus blog (*Chronicle of Higher Education*), June 29, 2009, http://chronicle.com/blogPost/They-Thought-Globally-but-Now/7253/.

————. "Utah State U's OpenCourseWare Closes Because of Budget Woes." Wired Campus blog (*Chronicle of Higher Education*), September 3, 2009, http://chronicle.com/blogPost/Utah-State-Us-OpenCourseWare/7913/.

Parry, Marc, and Karin Fischer. "How Obama's $12-Billion Plan Could Change 2-Year Colleges." *Chronicle of Higher Education,* online edition, July 17, 2009.

Paul, Noel C. "Beset by New Haven's Ills, Yale Revitalizes City." *Christian Science Monitor,* online edition, September 14, 2004.

Pelikan, Jaroslav. *The Idea of the University: A Reexamination.* New Haven: Yale University Press, 1992.

Phillips, Stephen. "E-Outfits Go the Distance." *Times* Higher Education Supplement, *New York Times,* online edition, February 7, 2003.

Plotkin, Hal. "Free Higher Education: MIT's OpenCourseWare Plan Fires the First Real Shot." SF Gate (*San Francisco Chronicle*), May 10, 2001, http://www.sfgate.com/cgi-bin/article.cgi?file=/gate/archive/2001/05/10/mit.DTL.

Powell, Russell S. "The Productive PR Office." *Chronicle of Higher Education,* online edition, December 11, 2009.

Press Information Bureau, Government of India. "The National Programme on Technology Enhanced Learning (NPTEL)." Press release, September 19, 2006, http://pib.nic.in/release/release.asp?relid=20799&kwd.

"Proposal to the Hewlett Foundation Education Program." Yale University, Diana E. E. Kleiner, principal investigator. June 2006.

"Proposal to the Hewlett Foundation Education Program." Yale University, Diana E. E. Kleiner, principal investigator. April 5, 2007.

Rangarajan, A. D. "NPTEL Streaming Knowledge to All." *The Hindu,* English edition, online edition, March 9, 2009.

Read, Brock. "How to Podcast Campus Lectures." *Chronicle of Higher Education,* online edition, January 26, 2007.

Riismandel, Paul. "How to Manage Video Content in Higher Education." *Streaming Media Magazine,* online edition, February–March 2008.

Rowe, Lawrence A., Diane Harley, Peter Pletcher, and Shannon Lawrence. *BIBS: A Lecture Webcasting System.* Paper CSHE4'01, June 2001, http://bmrc.berkeley.edu/research/publications/2001/160/bibs-report.pdf.

———. "BIBS: A Lecture Webcasting System—Executive Summary." *BIBS Report Executive Summary,* June 2001, http://bmrc.berkeley.edu/research/publications/2001/160/bibs-exec.html.

———. "BIBS: Usage Statistics." *BIBS Report Executive Summary,* July 2002, http://bmrc.berkeley.edu/research/publications/2001/160/bibs-stats.html.

Rupp, George. From "Current Communications: President's Office," February 29, 2000, http://web.archive.org/web/20000817225454/http:/www.columbia.edu/cu/president/current.html.

Schonfeld, Roger C., and Ross Housewright. "2009 Faculty Survey: Key Strategic Insights for Libraries, Publishers and Societies," April 7, 2010, http://ithaka.org/ithaka-s-r/research/faculty-surveys-2000-2009/Faculty%20Study%202009.pdf.

Sengupta, Somini. "Skills Gap Hurts Technology Boom in India." *New York Times,* online edition, October 17, 2006.

Shirky, Clay. "Newspapers and Thinking the Unthinkable." Blog post, March 13, 2009, http://www.shirky.com/weblog/2009/03/newspapers-and-thinking-the-unthinkable/.

Singer, Karen. "Distance-Learning Ventures Propel Top Universities into For-Profit Sector: Harvard, Cornell, and Stanford among Those Lured by $10 Billion Potential." *Matrix: The Magazine for Leaders in Higher Education,* online edition, 1, no. 4 (November 1, 2000).

Smith, Marshall. "Opening Education." *Science* 323 (January 2, 2009), 89–93.

Smith, Marshall S., and Catherine M. Casserly. "The Promise of Open Educational Resources." *Change* 38, no. 5 (September–October 2006), 8–17.

Snyder, Susan. "Number of Free, Noncredit Courses on Web Increasing." *Philadelphia Inquirer,* online edition, January 12, 2010.

Special Correspondent. "Quota Bill Will Not Face Opposition." *The Hindu,* English edition, online edition, September 4, 2006.

Stallman, Richard. "About the GNU Project," http://www.gnu.org/gnu/thegnuproject.html.

Stripling, Jack. "Tarnished Jewel." *Inside Higher Ed,* July 13, 2009.

Stross, Randall. "First It Was Song Downloads. Now It's Organic Chemistry." *New York Times,* online edition, July 27, 2008.

Suber, Peter. "Open Access Overview: Focusing on Open Access to Peer-Reviewed Research Articles and Their Pre-prints." Last revised June 19, 2007, http://www.earlham.edu/~peters/fos/overview.htm.

Taylor, Paul, Richard Fry, Wendy Wang, Daniel Dockterman, and Gabriel Velasco. "College Enrollment Hits All-Time High, Fueled by Community College Surge." Pew Research Center, October 29, 2009, http://pewsocialtrends.org/assets/pdf/college-enrollment.pdf.

Teachout, Zephyr. "A Virtual Revolution Is Brewing for Colleges." *Washington Post,* online edition, September 13, 2009.

"Thanks, But We Don't Need Your Courses: IITs Tell MIT." *Indian Express,* online edition, December 8, 2007.

Thille, Candace. "Building Open Learning as a Community-Based Research Activity," in *Opening Up Education: The Collective Advancement of Education through Open Technology, Open Content, and Open Knowledge,* ed. M. S. Vijay Kumar and Toru Iiyoshi. Cambridge, Mass.: MIT Press, 2008.

"Top 200 World Universities. *Times Higher Education Supplement 2009,* online edition, http://www.timeshighereducation.co.uk/Rankings2009-Top200.html.

Trounson, Rebecca. "UC System Accepts Record 55,242 Calif. Applicants for Fall Term." *Los Angeles Times,* online edition, April 20, 2006.

Trow, Martin. "The Development of Information Technology in American Higher Education." *Daedalus* 126, no. 4 (Fall 1997), 293–314.

Twigg, Carol A. "Improving Learning and Reducing Costs: New Models for Online Learning." *Educause Review* 38, no. 5 (September–October 2003), 28–38.

2008 NACUBO Endowment Study results, http://www.nacubo.org/documents/research/NES2008PublicTable-AllInstitutionsByFY08MarketValue.pdf.

United Nations Children's Fund. "India: Statistics," http://www.unicef.org/infobycountry/india_statistics.html.

University of California, University Committee on Educational Policy. "Online Undergraduate Instruction at a Selective University: An Intensive, Faculty-Led Evaluation of Opportunities, Challenges, Quality, Cost, and Viability." Draft prospectus, version 12, March 30, 2010, http://ccfit.ucdavis.edu/calendar/2009-10/docs/ucep%20project%20description%20final.pdf.

University of California Office of the President. "Access Provisions of the California Master Plan for Higher Education," http://www.ucop.edu/acadinit/mastplan/mpaccess.htm.

———. "The California Master Plan for Higher Education in Perspective," http://www.ucop.edu/acadinit/mastplan/mpperspective.htm.

———. "Major Features of the California Master Plan for Higher Education." http://www.ucop.edu/acadinit/mastplan/mpsummary.htm.

———. "Recommendation for Declaration of Financial Emergency and Approval of Budget Reduction Actions." For Meeting of July 15, 2009, of the committees on finance and compensation, http://www.universityofcalifornia.edu/regents/regmeet/jul09/j2.pdf.

University of Michigan News Service. "U-M Joins Fathom," November 15, 2000, http://www.ns.umich.edu/index.html?Releases/2000/Nov00/r111500a.

Urley, Sarah. "Ivy League Curtain Opened: Yale University Allows Free Access to Select Undergraduate Courses." *ABC News Online,* http://abcnews.go.com/Business/story?id=3997573&page=1.

Vaidhyasubramaniam, S. "Funding Higher Education." *Hindu Business Line,* online edition, September 30, 2009.

Vaidya, Akanksha. "Scientists Present Open Learning Interplay." *The Tartan,* online edition, March 31, 2008.

Van der Werf, Martin. "Yale's Ambitious Renovation Tops Any Undertaken by a University." *Chronicle of Higher Education,* online edition, October 20, 2000.

Vedder, Richard K. *Going Broke by Degree: Why College Costs Too Much.* Washington, D.C.: American Enterprise Institute Press, 2004.

Vencatesan, Jayshree. "Recent Initiatives in Distance Education." *Current Science* 91, no. 7 (October 10, 2006), 891–93.

Vest, Charles M. "Disturbing the Educational Universe: Universities in the Digital Age—Dinosaurs or Prometheans?" Report of the President for the Academic Year 2000–01, http://web.mit.edu/president/communications/rpt00-01.html.

———. Email to Dick Yue and other members of the committee, October 28, 2000.

———. "Why MIT Decided to Give Away All Its Course Materials via the Internet." *Chronicle of Higher Education,* online edition, January 30, 2004.

"Welcome to Notre Dame OpenCourseWare," http://ocw.nd.edu/.

Wessel, David. "Yale Safeguards Its Top Spot." *Wall Street Journal,* online edition, April 24, 2008.

"What They're Watching." *New York Times,* online edition, April 8, 2010.

Wilson, Fred. "My Favorite Business Model." *A VC,* March 2006, http://www.avc.com/a_vc/2006/03/my_favorite_bus.html.

Winston, Gordon C., and David J. Zimmerman. "Peer Effects in Higher Education," in *College Choices: The Economics of Where to Go, When to Go, and How to Pay for It,* ed. Caroline M. Hoxby. Chicago: University of Chicago Press, 2004.

Yaffe, Jonathan. "Online Lectures Get Mixed Reviews." *Daily Californian,* online edition, October 4, 1999.

Yale Center for Media and Instructional Innovation. "Open Access to the Yale Classroom Experience," http://cmi2.yale.edu/projects.php?action=view_project&project =oyc&category=platform.

"Yale University: Yale Doubles Number of Free Online Courses." Press release, *M2 PressWIRE,* October 17, 2008.

Young, Jeffrey R. "College 2.0: More Professors Could Share Lectures Online: But Should They?" *Chronicle of Higher Education,* online edition, March 7, 2010.

Young, Samantha. "University Leader Warns of More Steep Budget Cuts." *Mercury News,* online edition, August 20, 2009.

Zemsky, Robert. *Making Reform Work: The Case for Transforming American Higher Education.* New Brunswick, NJ: Rutgers University Press, 2009.

Zezima, Katie. "Data Show College Endowments Loss Is Worse Drop since the '70s." *New York Times,* online edition, January 26, 2009.

LIST OF INTERVIEWS

Whenever possible, interviews were conducted in person with the author, and often included follow-up communication in the form of brief phone calls or email messages.

Abelson, Hal. October 31, 2008.

Allison, Herbert M. March 11, 2009.

Ambrose, Susan. September 11, 2008; September 11, 2009.

Ananth, M. S. February 14, 2009; April 2, 2009.

Baraniuk, Richard. September 3, 2008.

Bays, Terri. September 17, 2008; September 24, 2008.

Bellinger, Margaret. December 18, 2008.

Bernstein, Peter. April 28, 2009.

Bhattacharya, Bani. April 3, 2009.

Bowen, William G. July 23, 2008.

Brenzel, Jeffrey. April 23, 2009.

Breslauer, George. June 9, 2009.

Brest, Paul. August 20, 2008.

Brown, Robert A. October 27, 2008.

Burrus, C. Sidney. September 4, 2008.

Candee, Catherine. August 21, 2008.

Carson, Steve. October 27, 2008; March 17, 2009; July 30, 2009; December 9, 2009; March 18, 2010.

Carter-Galvan, Sheree. December 18, 2008.

Casserly, Catherine. August 19, 2008; April 20, 2010.

Cervenka, Katie. September 4, 2008.

Cohon, Jared. September 10, 2008.

Cowell, Glynis. April 30, 2010.

Crow, Michael. December 22, 2008.

Dehlin, John. September 24, 2008; March 4, 2009.

Diamond, Marian. June 9, 2009.

d'Oliveira, Cecelia. October 29, 2008.

Etchemendy, John. August 19, 2008.

Fuchs, Ira. December 2, 2008.

Goodman, Paul. March 19, 2009.

Gray, Paul. June 9, 2009.

Greenstein, Daniel. June 8, 2009.

Hancock, Mara. August 19, 2008; June 8, 2009; June 9, 2009; April 16, 2010.

Harley, Diane. August 21, 2008.

Henry, Geneva. September 2, 2008; September 4, 2008.

Hirsch, David. December 17, 2008.

Hockfield, Susan. October 30, 2008.

Hubbard, Benjamin. June 8, 2009; June 9, 2009; March 15, 2010.

James, Kate. October 28, 2008.

Johnson, Don. September 4, 2008.

Kamlet, Mark. September 11, 2008.

Khakhar, Devang V. April 9, 2009.

Kim, Kristin. May 7, 2009.

Kirschner, Ann. July 28, 2008; August 5, 2008; August 10, 2009.

Kleiner, Diana. December 18, 2008; January 22, 2009; February 25, 2009.

Koedinger, Ken. September 11, 2008; September 8, 2009.

Krishnan, Mangala Sunder. February 23, 2009; March 31, 2009; April 1, 2009.

Kumar, M. S. Vijay. October 27, 2008; December 11, 2008.

Lane, Andy. March 3, 2009.

Lawrence, Paul. December 17, 2008.

Lerman, Steven. October 31, 2008; August 3, 2009.

Levy, Eugene. September 5, 2008.

Lindsay, Cindy. September 8, 2008.

Lorimer, Linda. March 6, 2009.

Margulies, Anne. August 17, 2008; October 28, 2008.

Maslach, Christina. August 20, 2008.

Matkin, Gary. September 23, 2008.
Meyer, Oded. September 10, 2008; September 8, 2009; December 24, 2009.
Miyagawa, Shigeru. October 29, 2008.
Mogulof, Dan. June 18, 2009.
Moudgalya, Kannan M. April 8, 2009.
Murphy, Paula. August 21, 2008.
Nagarajan, Usha. April 1, 2009.
Ng, Yvonne. March 18, 2009.
Ostriker, Jeremiah. July 24, 2008.
Phatak, Deepak B. April 8, 2009.
Ravindranath, K. R. March 31, 2009.
Ray, Anup K. April 3, 2009.
Reif, Rafael. October 30, 2008.
Rowe, Lawrence A. June 8, 2009.
Rupp, George. August 7, 2008.
Schiffman, David. December 18, 2008.
Schwartz, Stephanie. December 17, 2008.
Sen, Kushal. April 6, 2009.
Shapiro, Harold. July 24, 2008.
Shevgaonkar, R. K. April 9, 2009.
Smith, Joel. September 10, 2008; August 6, 2009; December 21, 2009.
Smith, Marshall. August 19, 2008.
Swineford, Lucas. January 22, 2009.
Thierstein, Joel. September 2, 2008; September 12, 2008.
Thille, Candace. August 18, 2008; November 17, 2008; August 11, 2009; October 28, 2009.
Vest, Charles M. September 30, 2008.
Vuchic, Victor. August 20, 2008.
Wang, Phoenix. October 9, 2008.
Weeramuni, Lindsey. October 28, 2008; August 12, 2009.
Wiley, David. August 18, 2009.
Wyatt, Tristram (interview with Roger Schonfeld of Ithaka S+R). June 25, 2008.
Ying, Bill. July 11, 2008.

INDEX

Page numbers for entries occurring in figures are suffixed by an *f*; those for entries in notes, by an *n*, with the number of the note following; and those for entries in tables, by a *t*.